A

FICTIONAL

COMMONS

Michael K. Bourdaghs

A

FICTIONAL

COMMONS

NATSUME SŌSEKI & THE PROPERTIES

OF MODERN LITERATURE

DUKE UNIVERSITY PRESS *Durham & London* 2021

Project editor: Annie Lubinsky
Designed by Matthew Tauch
Typeset in Garamond Premier Pro by Westchester Publishing Services

Library of Congress Cataloging-in-Publication Data
Names: Bourdaghs, Michael K., author.
Title: A fictional commons : Natsume Sōseki and the properties of modern
literature / Michael K. Bourdaghs.
Other titles: Natsume Sōseki and the properties of modern literature
Description: Durham : Duke University Press, 2021. | Includes bibliographical
references and index.
Identifiers: LCCN 2020050745 (print) | LCCN 2020050746 (ebook)
ISBN 9781478013693 (hardcover)
ISBN 9781478014621 (paperback)
ISBN 9781478021926 (ebook)
Subjects: LCSH: Natsume, Sōseki, 1867–1916—Criticism and interpretation. |
Japanese fiction—Meiji period, 1868–1912—History and criticism. | Property in
literature. | Right of property—Japan—History.
Classification: LCC PL812.A8 Z566525 2021 (print) | LCC PL812.A8 (ebook) |
DDC 895.63/42—dc23
LC record available at https://lccn.loc.gov/2020050745
LC ebook record available at https://lccn.loc.gov/2020050746

Cover art: Wanda Tuerlinckx, *Soseki Android*. Nishogakusha University.
Tokyo, Japan. Courtesy of the artist.

For

VERSEA BOURDAGHS

(1941–2008)

CONTENTS

NOTE ON USAGE

In nearly all cases, I list Japanese personal names in the Japanese order: family name first, personal name second, for example, Natsume Sōseki. Following conventional practice in Japan, however, I refer to canonical authors by their given names, often a pen name. For example, Sōseki is the pen name that Natsume Kinnosuke adopted for his literary efforts.

ACKNOWLEDGMENTS

Recent decades have brought an alarming bloat to the acknowledgment sections of scholarly books: what used to be a tidy paragraph now often spills across several pages. And like the interminable end credits of recent Hollywood blockbusters, nobody actually reads through them anymore—except to scan to see if their own name is included. At least, that is what I do. I have a real fondness for older films that simply conclude, "The End," so I will keep things short and simple. More than likely, your name will not appear. Please do not interpret that as a sign of ingratitude: I am profoundly thankful to many, many colleagues, friends, and antagonists.

The basic research was carried out with the support of a 2000–2001 Japan Foundation Research Fellowship. I thank Nihei Michiaki and the faculty, students, and library staff of Tōhoku University for hosting me. Additional research was carried out at Waseda University in 2016–17, and I am thankful to Toeda Hirokazu and his colleagues for their support. Sabbatical leave and research funding from UCLA and the University of Chicago also contributed to this project, and I want to thank colleagues and students at both institutions for helping me work through the ideas that led to this book. I have presented material from this book in forty-four different lectures and conferences (I just went back and counted) and received many excellent questions that nudged me to rethink what I was doing. Ken Wissoker and his colleagues at Duke University Press were tremendously supportive, and two anonymous referees for the press helped make this a better book.

Over the course of my work on this project, my children Walter and Sonia went from grade school to graduate school. They and my partner Satoko provided incredible support: physical, intellectual, spiritual. My mother, Versea Bourdaghs, passed away about halfway through the writing. I wish she had lived to see the finished book, because she would see traces throughout of what she taught me about the possibilities of artistic creation and hope. I dedicate the book to her.

Owning Up to Sōseki

If man in the state of nature be so free, as has been said; if he be absolute lord of his own person and possessions, equal to the greatest, and subject to no body, why will he part with his freedom? why will he give up this empire, and subject himself to the dominion and controul of any other power? To which it is obvious to answer, that though in the state of nature he hath such a right, yet the enjoyment of it is very uncertain, and constantly exposed to the invasion of others: for all being kings as much as he, every man his equal, and the greater part no strict observers of equity and justice, the enjoyment of the property he has in this state is very unsafe, very unsecure. This makes him willing to quit a condition, which, however free, is full of fears and continual dangers: and it is not without reason, that he seeks out, and is willing to join in society with others, who are already united, or have a mind to unite, for the mutual preservation of their lives, liberties and estates, which I call by the general name, property.

JOHN LOCKE, *Second Treatise of Civil Government* (1690)

The first man who, having enclosed a piece of ground, to whom it occurred to say *this is mine* and found people sufficiently simple to believe him, was the true founder of civil society. How many crimes, wars, murders, how many miseries and horrors Mankind would have been spared by him who, pulling up the stakes or filling in the ditch, had cried out in kind: Beware of listening to this impostor; You are lost if you forget that the fruits are everyone's and the Earth no one's.

JEAN JACQUES ROUSSEAU, *Discourse on Inequality*
(trans. Victor Gourevich; 1755)

The argument of this book revolves around a wager—a wager in which no specific property is at stake, because the idea of property itself is at stake. Modernity arrived in Japan, as elsewhere, largely in the form of a new regime of ownership. A complex and uneven assemblage that patched together embodied practices of everyday life, disembodied ideologies, scientific knowledge, and legal codes—often instituted after the fact to legitimate the existing distribution of resources—this regime became a key framework for understanding not only society and the world, but one's own selfhood.[1] In Europe, liberal philosophers ranging from Locke to Smith and Hegel defined modernity and modern selfhood in terms of ownership—just as their critics, ranging from Rousseau and the German Romantics to Marx and beyond, identified property and its inherent threat of alienation as modernity's original sin. When Japan confronted modernity in the form of encroaching Western imperialism, it countered by reinventing itself as a modern empire, complete with the property schema that such an empire demanded. And thinkers and artists in Japan who questioned this transformation often did so by criticizing the emergent property regime.

To explore this problematic, I take up the writings of Natsume Sōseki (1867–1916), often celebrated (correctly, to my mind) as Japan's greatest modern novelist. I read his writings as critical and creative responses to the new property system that emerged during his lifetime. Virtually all of Sōseki's fictional narratives revolve directly or indirectly around property disputes: time and again, he spins tales about thieves and burglars, misappropriated estates, stolen affections. He is a master of the inheritance plot, a subgenre that is as prone to render property into "an insoluble puzzle" as it is to reproduce the presumed naturalness of ownership.[2] Moreover, in his ambitious attempt to theorize the category of literature, Sōseki proposed rethinking literature as a domain that inherently troubled conventional notions of ownership. My claim is that Sōseki's writings, both fictional and theoretical, probe the hazy interstices of the new property regime, mining its ambiguities and contradictions for raw materials that could be used to fabricate new kinds of stories, stories that often enact alternative practices of owning and sharing. He liked to spin stories that trouble our ability to distinguish between owner and owned—about animals, for example (chapter 1), or about younger siblings, women, and colonial subjects (chapter 4)—and that imagined what might lie beyond the sphere of private property. Both in practice and in theory, literature provided Sōseki a laboratory for experimenting with something like a new commons: an ongoing collective project that belongs to no one and everyone.

This is in part a historical question. Modernity around much of the globe arrived in the form of what Michael Hardt and Antonio Negri call "the republic of property."[3] In Japan, after the 1868 Meiji Restoration and the launch of the new nation-state's campaign to achieve parity with the Western powers, systems of ownership provided the focal point for practical and theoretical controversies—ranging from state economic policies aimed at accumulating the capital necessary to finance Japan's rise as an industrial and military hegemon to intellectual controversies surrounding the discourses of individualism, success, and family. For the Meiji state, struggling to win revision of the Unequal Treaties (a goal finally attained in 1899, the year before Sōseki headed to London as a government-sponsored overseas student) and attain recognition as an imperial power, the establishment of a modern private property system was a key political task. The promulgation of the Meiji Civil Code in 1898, still today in modified form the basis for Japanese property law, was in many ways the culminating event of the era's Civilization and Enlightenment movement.[4]

The new property system that emerged during Sōseki's lifetime was a complex and hybrid machine. It cobbled together older practices from the Tokugawa period (recoded to fit the needs of state-driven industrial capitalism and imperial expansion) with new legal codes, ideologies, and sensibilities translated from elsewhere.[5] A narrative of its rise might start with the reform of Japan's land ownership system launched as part of the new taxation system introduced in 1873.[6] The unit for tax payment was no longer the collective village, but rather the individual landowner, and tax assessments were no longer calculated as a percentage of anticipated rice yield to be paid in kind, but rather as a percentage of assessed value of the plot of land, paid in cash. Since 1643, it had technically been illegal to sell land in Japan.[7] While the ban was widely violated so that de facto private land ownership certainly existed before 1868, it was only with the new regime that private landed property became a universal reality de jure: one could now legally buy and sell ownership rights in land, rights that were certified by the state. Along the way, various forms of commons and joint ownership were appropriated and transformed into private property. The new taxation system unleashed market forces into the Japanese countryside with unprecedented vigor, resulting in a rural society that was increasingly bifurcated between wealthy landowners and impoverished tenant farmers. It also rewrote the urban landscape, producing new slums, intensified class stratification, and intricate neighborhood patterns whose shapes emerged in response to the complexities of ownership.[8]

Another important development arrived in 1890 with the enactment of the Meiji Constitution and its implementation of a property qualification for suffrage. To vote in the new national parliamentary elections, one had to be male, twenty-five years of age or older—and a property owner who paid at least fifteen yen in annual taxes. Two more important steps came with the abovementioned 1898 Meiji Civil Code and with Japan's 1899 signing of the Bern Treaty for International Copyright Protection: Japan's legal codes defining property were now on par with those of other dominant global powers. In 1897 Japan also adopted the gold standard, making the yen fully convertible on world currency markets, linking its property systems all the more firmly to the emerging global capitalist economy.[9] These new legal forms for tangible and intangible property in turn enabled new modes for circulating capital to generate surplus value, the ghostly excess produced through the magic formula of commodity exchange. The new system ensured that such surplus value was directed into the pockets of proper owners, thereby enabling the capitalist economic system to reproduce itself.

As Japan's empire expanded, the new property regime was extended to its colonies via such measures as the Former Natives Protection Law in Hokkaido and the Okinawa Prefecture Land Reorganization Law (both 1899), which resulted in massive dispossession and "replacing communal with private land ownership."[10] Similar measures were introduced in the colony of Taiwan, and then in the 1910s—that is, at the peak of Sōseki's writing career—in Japan's newest imperial acquisition with the Korean Land Cadastral Survey (discussed at length in chapter 4).[11] In this expansion, the Japanese empire was following a model previously established by the British and other empires, in which property law provided both an ideology and technology for establishing colonial power. As Brenna Bhandar notes, the modern property regime "operates as a set of both techniques and mechanisms encapsulated in legislation, legal judgments, and myriad everyday practices of ownership that have structured colonial capitalist modes of accumulation. It is also a central fixture in philosophical and political narratives of a developmental, teleological vision of modernization that has set the standard for what can be considered civilized."[12] To be civilized meant to have the proper subjective capacity for acquisition, a status that was defined in racial and ethnic terms in the Japanese and other empires.

Our historical narrative of the rise of Japan's modern property regime might conclude in 1925, nine years after Sōseki's death. That year, the

General Election Law abolished the property qualification for adult male suffrage—but only after the Peace Preservation Law enacted that same year made it a crime to advocate the abolition of private property. Questioning the new ownership regime became literally a thought crime.[13]

PROPERTY AS POWER/KNOWLEDGE

This new property regime was as much a question of power as of wealth. As Tateiwa Shin'ya points out, the free-market economy and the exchanges so beloved of liberal and neoliberal economists can only emerge after property rights have been defined by some power—usually, in modern societies such as Meiji Japan, the state.[14] In other words, to participate in this new system of ownership was to accept the authority of the Meiji government to define who owned what. This was hardly unique to Japan: as Dick Pels argues, despite attempts by Marxists, anarchists, and others to distinguish power from property, in modern societies "they are often defined in terms of one another," so that the two concepts "have a curious habit of reappearing in each other's definitions."[15] For example, Hardt and Negri describe as "the really dominant forms of power" today that "power embodied in property and capital."[16] Karatani Kōjin provides one model (discussed at more length in chapter 3) for understanding this blurring. Revising the conventional Marxist theory of world history, Karatani replaces "modes of production" as the primary stages of social development with what he calls "modes of exchange," noting that these do not form successive steps in a linear temporal development, but rather consist of four different modes of exchange that coexist in any given society, albeit with different degrees of clout. In Karatani's framework, the modern property regime required both mode B (an exchange of submission to state power in return for protection) and mode C (capitalist commodity exchange).[17]

Alongside its centrality to legal and economic systems, property also became a dominant scholarly question, generating prolific studies in law, anthropology, sociology, history, philosophy, and other modern disciplines that were emerging together with the new university system. For example, as we will explore in chapter 2, scientists in the rising discipline of psychology frequently turned to models of property to explain the mechanisms of our own psyches. Likewise, philosophical debates over the nature of the self, that supposed hallmark of modernity, frequently took place by way of questions and practices of ownership. To own something—that is, to be

an owning subject in relation to an owned object—requires first an objec-
tification of the self, which immediately raises the tricky problem of who
owns that objectified self. As one legal scholar notes, "Almost any theory
of private property rights can be referred to some notion of personhood"
because such theories "must address the rights accruing to individual persons, and therefore necessarily implicates the nature of the entity to which
they accrue."[18] The modern self was a self-contradictory project, a subject-
becoming-citizen that was simultaneously a citizen-becoming-subject
(meaning, among other things, that the self always emerges in the company
of other selves, as something that is therefore always in some sense shared
rather than owned outright), and theories and practices of property were
one of the hinges around which this unstable entity revolved.[19] According
to the tenets of what C. B. MacPherson called "possessive individualism,"
property ownership became a fundamental figure for explaining selfhood
and a wide swath of human experience.[20] A proper self or subject, it was
increasingly believed, was one qualified and able to act as the owner of
property: in most modern societies, male, heterosexual, and white (or at
least honorarily white).

Property simultaneously became a central concept in Japan and elsewhere in demarcating the stages of history in teleological narratives of
civilization. In Meiji literature, for example, we often encounter the use of
property systems as a yardstick for measuring degree of civilization. Kamei
Hideo discusses the following passage from Kanagaki Robun and Fusō
Kan's *By Shank's Mare through the West* (*Seiyō dōchū hizakurige*, 1870–76),
in which the narrator promises to "speak about the transformation of all
the nations of the world brought about by the progress of civilization": "In
the beginning, there were those peoples who knew not how to cook food,
nor how to weave clothing, nor how to set up shelter and mark boundaries,
who wandered hither and thither hunting animals for food, who had no
such thing as money, who lived in the wilds together with fowl and beast,
who did not know how to conduct agriculture. The people of that time are
called uncivilized, or, in the Western term, 'semi-barbarian.'"[21]

We find a similar ranking of various peoples of the world by means of
the existence or lack thereof of a stable property system in Yano Ryūkei's
Tale of the Floating Castle (*Ukishiro monogatari*, 1890). As Kamei notes,
these works rely on the knowledge produced in such modern textbooks
as *A Brief Geography* (*Yochishi ryaku*, 1870–75), edited by Uchida Masao.
Uchida's text provides the following classification of different peoples:

Semi-barbarians, when compared with the previously discussed group [savages], are somewhat advanced in their knowledge, and in them we see the existence of private property. . . . The first type among them are called nomads. . . . The second type are partially nomadic and partially agricultural, and among its numbers are some that establish villages and live in a fixed place for a year, sometimes even two or three years. . . . The third type engages in agriculture and herds livestock, or, in some cases, in fishing and hunting. . . . As village size grows larger, some emerge that could be called states, and among these are some in which *laws* exist and people submit to the guarantees of their chief.[22]

In chapter 3, we will explore how the discipline of sociology mobilized property systems as an indicator of the civilizational stage of any given society.

In sum, from state economic policies that aimed at the capital accumulation necessary to finance Japan's rise as a world power to the intellectual debates surrounding new concepts of selfhood, the question of property was central to the project of modernizing Japan. In his initial canonization in both Japan and the West, Sōseki was often celebrated as Japan's first truly modern writer, so that he became a symbol of Japan's successful modernization.[23] In more recent decades, Sōseki's role as a critic of modernity, particularly Western modernity, has been championed by critics from Japan and elsewhere.[24] Still other critics have taken to task his complicity with more unsavory aspects of modernity—including imperialism, patriarchy, and heteronormativity. Whichever position one takes, however, my wager here is that for Sōseki, the question of modernity was in many ways one of property.

LITERATURE BEYOND PROPERTY

There is some evidence that late in his life, Sōseki took an interest in left-of-center politics, including a critical stance toward capitalism and its property regime.[25] He had long borne at least some interest in socialist thought. From his time in London (1900–1902), he owned Marx's *Capital* in English translation, but apparently never read it: the pages in his copy remain uncut. In an oft-quoted 1902 letter to his father-in-law, Sōseki wrote:

The failure of civilization in Europe today is clearly based on the extreme gap between the rich and the poor. I am afraid this imbalance has a tendency to starve or freeze to death many promising human resources every year, or leave them without any education. It turns rather to implementing the common ideas of very ordinary rich men. . . . If we tend toward the same conditions in Japan (and I believe we are tending toward them at present), it will be a matter of grave importance for the future development of labor's literacy and intelligence. Although I believe that Karl Marx's theories have faults, even simply as pure rationalizations, it is quite natural that such teachings should appear in a world like the present one.[26]

This is not to say that Sōseki outright rejected the idea of private property. Like most intellectuals of his era, he knew and no doubt at least partially sympathized with arguments for the fundamental morality of property developed by such figures as Locke, Smith, and Hegel.[27] But as one who lived through dramatic changes in property regimes, Sōseki was also aware of the historical contingency of ownership norms and of the reality that we constantly participate in multiple economies, each characterized by its own practices of property and sharing.[28] Sōseki, then, did not necessarily reject market exchange with its presumption of private ownership, but in his literary writings he again and again relativized the increasingly dominant position of that form by probing its lacunae and by situating it in relation to other possible models.

Literature for Sōseki, then, was a realm for thinking not just about, but beyond, property. What did that beyond consist of? Rather than attempt to construct one overarching explanation, I employ a number of different theoretical models—some from Sōseki's day, some more recent—to tease out the multiple alternatives to classic liberalism's notions of property and self-ownership that I think Sōseki's writings gesture toward: primitive communism (such as characterizes much of domestic family life), open-access models such as commons and public trusts (often governed by shared codes of custom and morality), gift exchanges and pure gift nonexchanges, dialogic relationality, and rhizomatic forms of nonexclusionary selfhood. Such a dispersed range of approaches seems appropriate not only to the diversity of Sōseki's writings but also to the messy, uneven reality of modern property regimes.

I also explore how Sōseki's literature probed contradictions inherent to the dominant notion of individual private property presumed by a liberal market economy. Through its legal codes, practices, and ideologies, the modern property regime generated numerous legal fictions: new forms of owning subjects and owned objects, all of which rested on unsteady foundations laced with self-contradictory axioms.[29] In fact, private property as a system is from the start something like a commons. As Carol Rose argues, "a regime of individual property is itself a kind of collective property or metaproperty; a private property regime holds together only on the basis of common beliefs and understandings."[30] Moreover, property claims require persuasion, often pursued through such techniques as narrative, to obtain consent from others. As Hegel noted in his chapter "Property" in *Philosophy of Right*, to claim ownership over something, we have to find some way of designating that ownership in a manner that those around us will recognize.[31] This involves "a kind of assertion or story, told within a culture that shapes the story's content and meaning. That is, the would-be 'possessor' has to send a message that others in the culture understand and that they find persuasive as grounds for the claim asserted."[32] Claims of ownership thus depend on narratives and the rhetorical functions of language.[33] For legal codes, this dependence on the productivity of language and rhetoric is a kind of scandal, a source of panic that has to be concealed via ideology: the existing property regime has to acquire the sense of naturalness and inevitability, and the codes of ownership have to be magically granted the status of pure, transparent referentiality.[34] The flimsy literary origins of property, that is, have to be repressed: ideologically, the system claims to sit on solid ground that has existed for all time. But, as Sōseki understood remarkably well, the repressed scandals underlying property make for excellent stories in the domain of literature, which shamelessly foregrounds the techniques of narrative and rhetoric. They provide another means for literature to imagine what lies beyond modern property systems.

In sum, the modern property regime was riddled with contradictions and ambiguities that were a boon to storytellers. Legal fictions labored to conceal the property system's scandalous lack of grounding, while literary fictions took pleasure in uncovering those scandals. Sōseki was, of course, neither a political scientist nor an economist, neither a socialist nor an anarchist activist; he was a novelist and literary theorist. In other words, his field of practice was literature—a field that already in his day had a considerable history as a realm for countering the forces of capitalist privatization, enclosure, and dispossession. Our modern senses of literature as a part of culture are products of the nineteenth-century reaction against changes that the Industrial Revolution and its political and economic forms were inducing. As Raymond Williams argues, in this process, culture emerged as "the normal antithesis to the market."[35] Literature in the sense of imaginative, artistic forms of writing emerged in the Anglophone world that Sōseki studied as "a major affirmative response, in the name of an essentially general human 'creativity,' to the socially repressive and intellectually mechanical forms of a new social order: that of capitalism and especially industrial capitalism."[36]

The early theorists of literature and aesthetics, in our modern senses of those words, saw them in these terms. In the late eighteenth century, for example, Friedrich Schiller (whose writings Sōseki cited in his *Theory of Literature*) defined "freedom" as a "kind of perceptual superposition," one that served as "a sudden perception of an intolerable present which is at the same time, but implicitly and however dimly articulated, the glimpse of another state in the name of which the first is judged."[37] An emerging alienation in the social realm (under the first wave of the privatization of everything) generated a counterpart in the inner realm, "a spiritual deformation which is the exact equivalent of the economic alienation in the social world outside."[38] The utopian desire to imagine a better world generated an impulse to play, and in particular to literary imagination, in which "beauty . . . is the form freedom takes in the realm of sensory appearance."[39] Literature was to become the realm where we undergo "a practical apprenticeship for the real political and social freedom to come."[40]

Many previous critics have pointed out the limitations of this emancipatory view of literature. It can function ideologically as a mystification that aids in the reproduction of the very social regime it aims to criticize. In Mary Poovey's formulation, the contradictions inherent in early nineteenth-century claims for literary value rendered it unable "to challenge the market model of value that increasingly dominated British society."[41] Such critiques are not easily dismissed, and yet part of my argument here is that we need to take seriously the claims made for the aesthetic in modern bourgeois literature, even as we remain alert to its political limitations. The aesthetic is often criticized as a retreat from the political, as an ideological safety valve that participates in the reproduction of modern capitalism, including its property regimes. As I've noted, many studies of Sōseki, both inside Japan and out, have linked his work to the perceived pathologies of modernity: imperialism, patriarchy, heterosexism, capitalism, nationalism. While acknowledging the relevance and importance of such critical readings of his work, my purpose here is different. If such readings engage (for good reason) in a paranoid hermeneutics of suspicion bent on exposing links between his work and the brutal hierarchies, political and economic, of modern Japan, I will engage in a more reparative hermeneutics, one that seeks to uncover how his works attempt "to provide the self with pleasure and nourishment in an environment that is perceived as not particularly offering them."[42]

Sōseki's fiction and theory of literature were undoubtedly imbricated in the modern regime of private property that he saw rewriting the world around him in late Meiji Japan, but an important element of that imbrication was the way in which his practice and theory attempted to imagine something beyond that regime, a new commons. Realizing such a vision would require political activism, of course—but also something beyond. As Mark Fisher argues, direct political action is crucial, but on its own insufficient: "we also need to act *indirectly*, by generating new narratives, figures, and conceptual frames." This is because the "reordering" of our imagination and thinking, of our "affects, desires, beliefs, and language plainly cannot by achieved by 'politics' alone—it is a matter for culture in the widest sense."[43]

In his theoretical writings, Sōseki tried to explain why literature provided an appropriate domain for such imagining. Fictional narratives and other literary forms are constantly playing with new forms of subjects and objects, a process that is necessarily shared in common between the writer, fictional characters, and the reader. Moreover, literature's inherent mobilization of the productivity of narrative and rhetoric is one route toward imagining and practicing a new possible commons. Whereas modern property systems abhor contradictions and ambiguities, in literature these are welcome as sources of narrative energy: they make for good stories. For example, whereas the modern property regime asserts that the only genre appropriate to the commons is tragedy, the literary commons suggests we imagine other possibilities: comedies of the commons, romances of the commons, epics of the commons.

* * *

And so my wager: that for Sōseki, literature provided a venue for grappling with and imagining beyond modern forms of ownership. A number of his fictional works deal with stories of inheritance, thievery, and the struggle to obtain or preserve material wealth—often as allegories for the impossibility of attaining self-possession. Rivalries between males to assert ownership over females is another vein of narrative raw material to which he returns repeatedly. Ownership is a slippery category in Sōseki's writings: the owning subject often finds himself (or, less frequently, herself) in a relationship of disconcerting dependence on the owned object. Daisuke, the protagonist of *And Then* (*Sore kara*, 1909), issues a scathing critique of the corrosive power of money in his society, even as he grapples with his father over his share in the family wealth—here, as in so many of Sōseki's works, struggles over property define the relationships that structure the family. In the autobiographical novel *Grass on the Wayside* (*Michikusa*, 1915), the protagonist is alarmed to find himself a commodity exchanged back and forth between families, complete with disputes over the distinction between alienable and inalienable rights of possession. On a different note, *The Miner* (*Kōfu*, 1908) uses the allegory of labor in an industrialized mine for a brilliant exploration of the impossibility of self-possession. Its protagonist vows, "I don't own anything but my body. With neither property nor honor to be robbed or cheated of, I'm obviously an unpromising commodity."[44] *Kusamakura* (1906), the most overtly philosophical of Sōseki's novels, explicitly defines artistic and literary practice as arising from a renunciation of any claim over the depicted object: it requires complete detachment, "being free of self-interested motives."[45] For Sōseki, as for many of his contemporaries, aesthetic value can only appear with the negation of use and exchange value, the rights that come with ownership.

This book pursues a three-pronged argument: first, that Natsume Sōseki's writing engaged in an imaginative troubling of the modern property regime that emerged over the course of his lifetime. Second, that through an epistemological critique that questioned the very tools through which modern societies produced knowledge, Sōseki placed literature as an alternative form of knowing in relation to the sciences, natural and social, that were increasingly dominating the world (even as he accepted the tenets of scientific knowledge). Finally, that in both his theory and his practice, Sōseki saw literature as a realm for experiments in modeling what might lie beyond the modern property system. To borrow from Karatani again, literature provided a site for exploring mode of exchange D, the return of a gift economy (mode of exchange A) in a higher dimension.[46] I'll work out each of these lines of argument at length in the chapters that follow. If my wager is successful, I will persuade you that with Sōseki, literature becomes a playful, noninstrumental site for imagining a different economy, a new commons, alternative modes of communal owning—which is to say, sharing.

CHAPTER ONE

Fables of Property

Nameless Cats, Trickster Badgers, Stray Sheep

> I see in myself, in our neighbours, in professors and statesmen noth-
> ing but beasts—bestiality incarnate, with superadded structures so as
> to meet with the twentieth century society.
>
> NATSUME SŌSEKI (1904, English-language text fragment)

> For everything outside the phenomenal world, language can only be
> used allusively, but never even approximately by way of comparison,
> since, corresponding as it does to the phenomenal world, it is con-
> cerned only with property and its relations.
>
> FRANZ KAFKA (aphorism; trans. Ernst Kaiser and Eithne Wilkins)

A stray kitten wanders into a budding novelist's Tokyo home, circa 1904.
To whom does it belong? The Meiji Civil Code, enacted in 1898 and in
amended form still the basic legal code for modern property rights in
Japan, tried to anticipate this sort of situation:

> Article 195.—A person in possession of an animal other than a domestic
> animal (formerly) kept by another person acquires rights exercised over
> the animal if, at the commencement of the possession, he acted in good
> faith and no demand for restoration is made by the (former) keeper within
> one (1) month from the time of its escape.[1]

According to Article 195, if our novelist acts in good faith (whatever
that might mean), and if no one else claiming ownership shows up within
a month, the cat would be his. The cat would have no say in the matter.

But imagine a realm in which the cat would have some say. As Donna Haraway notes, our attempts to own animals often end in reciprocal possession: I may have a cat, but that cat also has me.[2] Especially if that cat is given a say, permitted to tell its side of the story. In that imaginary case, a different practice of ownership might emerge, something beyond the notion of private property. The same might be true for other animals—in, for example, a playful tale narrated by a *tanuki* (often translated as raccoon dog or badger, one of the tricksters of Japanese folklore) or in the meanderings of a stray sheep.

Animals complicate our ideas about ownership. The current shift in American English from speaking of a dog's "owner" to its human "father" or "mother" is the latest wrinkle in a long history of animals troubling the boundaries of our concepts of property. This is, perhaps, why Sōseki kept returning to critters in his fiction. Like his contemporary Franz Kafka, Sōseki delighted in telling stories about animals—and in having animals tell stories—as a playful tactic for imagining a way out from the velvet-lined cages of modernity and its regime of ownership.

In this chapter, I sketch in Sōseki's literary zoology by way of three animal figures: a nameless cat, a trickster tanuki, and a stray sheep. Along the way, I touch on the first step of the argument laid out in the introduction (the historical situation of property law and norms of ownership in turn-of-the-century Japan), but I focus more on the latter two steps: the way different modern disciplines attempted to account for property as a form of knowledge and Sōseki's attempt to theorize and practice literature as a domain for imagining something beyond the new scientific conceptualizations of private property.

THE PROPERTIES OF A NAMELESS CAT

Natsume Sōseki's first major success as a writer came with *I Am a Cat* (*Wagahai wa neko de aru*). The work began as a comic short story published in the January 1905 issue of the literary monthly *Hototogisu*. When the piece became an unexpected hit with readers, the journal's editors prevailed upon Sōseki to write a second installment for their February number. The March issue contained no installment, and sales fell off a cliff. Between April 1905 and August 1906, Sōseki serialized nine more installments, and the work was published in book form in two volumes, in October 1905 and May 1907. Its success established Sōseki as one of Japan's most promising new novelists—a promise he would more than fulfill in the decade that remained before his death.

A substantial body of scholarship looks at *I Am a Cat* in terms of its playful structure, in which the story is not only narrated to us by a cat, but by a cat who appropriates to itself the first-person pronoun *wagahai*, usually reserved for persons of elite status: similar to the royal *we*. Previous criticism reads this cat-narrator as challenging new norms for realist fiction that emerged in Japan around the turn of the century with the rise of the *genbun itchi* (literally, unification of speech and writing) vernacular writing style.[3] *I Am a Cat* gains critical force by relativizing the recently established norm for fictional narration, and it does so by mobilizing devices from earlier modes of storytelling that Sōseki knew well, whether from the playful *gesaku* or *rakugo* genres of the Edo period or from eighteenth-century British literature—for example, Laurence Sterne. The cat is, after all, a remarkable narrator: unable to speak Japanese (at several moments in the work, it laments its inability to communicate crucial information to the humans around it), it nonetheless understands the language in both spoken and written forms. It is also mysteriously able to write in Japanese—unless what we are reading is a translation from cat language (and this in a text that frequently toys with problems of translation and mistranslation). And, as the German translator of the work notes, the cat pulls off a remarkable feat of narrative technology ("ein erzähltechnisches Husarenstück!"): a first-person narrator who narrates its own death.[4]

Building on this previous criticism, I want to reconsider the narrative experiment that is *I Am a Cat* in relation to the new property regime that took hold in Meiji Japan. I'm interested in how the novel gives the cat some say in the matter of ownership, and what that might mean. What alternative notions of possession emerge in the world generated through this feline narrating voice? Viktor Shklovsky, in his classic essay "Art as Device" (1917), examined Tolstoy's use of a horse-narrator in the novella *Kholstomer*, in particular how that gelding voice defamiliarizes the human institution of private property.[5] It's unclear whether Sōseki knew that particular novella, but it seems beyond question that he was pursuing a similar experiment in *I Am a Cat*.[6] Sōseki creates an impossible story about an impossible world, in part as a playful way of imagining currently impossible forms of owning and sharing—and in doing so, the very act of narrative performance starts to blur the boundary between impossible and possible: the imagined becomes virtual. Whereas the most productive readings of *I Am a Cat* to date have focused on the way it mobilizes residual Edo-period forms to challenge the dominant genbun itchi modes of narration, I want to push a little further and think about the possible emergent future worlds its feline narration might be suggesting—in particular, what sorts of ownership such worlds might entail.

John Berger argues that a central component of modern capitalism is a rendering of the gaze between humans and other animals into a one-sided affair, so that we look at animals in zoos and picture books, but "the fact that they can observe us has lost all significance."[7] Keeping that in mind, it seems clear that Sōseki is not only playing with the idea of giving cats a say but also restoring their ability to gaze back at us. And one of the things that comes under scrutiny in that imaginary feline gaze are human practices of ownership. This external gaze generates snickers, what Mark Fisher calls "laughter from the outside" that exposes "the arbitrariness and contingency of any system" that it sees.[8]

Animals have proved an often complex case for modern property regimes. Does anyone own wild animals? Much important case history in property law revolves around the possession of wild animals. In recent years, courts have had to adjudicate questions of whether animals can legally own property or whether they form a new category of "living property."[9] As for domestic animals, is our relation to household pets correctly thought of as ownership? A lovely moment occurs in *Paddington Helps Out* (1960), the third book in Michael Bond's Paddington series. On a family visit to the cinema, Mr. Brown is confounded to see a notice projected on the screen, requesting that the "owner" of a certain young bear come to the manager's office. What can it mean?

> "I don't know, Mary," he said, as he made to get to his feet, "but I'm certainly going to find out."
>
> "Owner indeed!" snorted Mrs. Bird. "As if anyone owned Paddington."
>
> "The boot's on the other paw, if you ask me," began Mr. Brown. "Paddington owns us." As he was speaking a strange expression came over his face.[10]

Strange expressions come over our face when we think about owning animals—or when we think about animals as owners. Do we possess domestic animals in the same way that we possess real property (a house in the country) or inanimate objects (a picture book on our shelves)? And is property ownership something that distinguishes humans from animals—or is it rather something that links them? In other words, are property systems a product of 'civilization' and hence something that distinguishes our species from the bestial, or are they rather a product of natural instinct, akin to practices of territoriality in other animals, and hence something that we share with other species? Akira Lippit reminds us that philosophical attempts to distinguish human from animal through such markers as language or reason have been repeatedly haunted by traces of the bestial other that infected the human interior.[11] The same is true for property norms: they become a strange site where the human-animal distinction is drawn, only to be struck out in the same gesture.

Much of the narrative energy in *I Am a Cat* comes from instances of threats to property: a burglar steals belongings from the Kushami family; students from a neighboring school ignore the Kushami house's property boundaries; and so on. In the opening pages, the reader encounters a number of playful turnabouts. As already noted, the cat appropriates the first-person pronoun *wagahai*, akin to the royal or editorial *we* in English, assuming a lofty position to which our common sense tells us cats don't belong. A precursor to the ape-scholar of Kafka's "Report to an Academy" (1917), the cat-narrator presents himself as a sort of anthropologist, studying the strange habits of the tribe known as "the human" and contrasting its "savage" behavior to that of the more civilized realm of felines.[12] The cat's first human encounter is with a *shosei*, a student-boarder, described as belonging to the most barbaric "tribe" (*ichiban dōaku na shuzoku*) among the humans. This is only the first of countless descriptions throughout the novel of the human world as savage, barbaric, bestial.

A few pages after the introduction of the student-boarder, the narrator cat describes some other primitive practices of this human race:

> And the three-colored tom-cat living next door is especially indignant that human beings do not understand the nature of proprietary rights. Among our kind it is taken for granted that he who first finds something, be it the head of a dried sardine or a gray mullet's navel, acquires thereby the right to eat it. And if this rule be flouted, one may well resort to violence. But human beings do not seem to understand the rights of property. Every time we come on something good to eat, invariably they descend and take it from us. Relying on their naked strength, they coolly rob us of things which are rightly ours to eat.[13]

A similar complaint about human lack of respect for property rights occurs shortly thereafter, when Kuro, the black cat who lives with a neighboring rickshaw puller, accuses his humans of stealing rats that he catches and turning them over to the hygiene police to pocket the reward money. Likewise, in chapter 8, Kushami-sensei appropriates furniture that belonged to a deceased relative because, according to the narrator, he fails to grasp civilized norms of ownership and hence is, like all humans, something of a thief. These failures to understand norms of ownership are, the cat indicates, signs of the barbarous state of human civilization.

As we will explore more fully in chapter 3, the cat here is parodying a commonplace of Meiji-period sociology: that a stable system of private property provided a benchmark for measuring the degree of civilization of any given society. This worldview was widely shared across many modern disciplines, not only in Japan but also in the West. According to it, a society in which one person could simply seize the property of another person (or cat) was inherently uncivilized.

We find this commonsense view of property as measure of civilization in a number of works that Sōseki owned and read. The most immediately relevant title in Sōseki's own library of books (now held at Tōhoku University) is Charles Letourneau's *Property: Its Origin and Development* (1892). Letourneau, an early leader in French anthropology, traces the social evolution of human societies by way of their property systems. The most highly evolved property system is that of contemporary Europe, of course—though Letourneau also argues that "the unrestrained and selfish right of private property" can only lead to "decadence" and "ruin," even for highly civilized societies.[14] Property is for Letourneau a yardstick for assessing degree of civilization and enlightenment, as well as degeneration. It also serves to mark the distance between human and animal. Yet Letourneau begins his study with the chapter "Property amongst Animals," arguing in the first paragraph (in a sentence underlined in Sōseki's own copy) about property, "An instinct it certainly is, an innate and ruling propensity."[15] In Letourneau's sociology, property is both something that links the human to the animal and a yardstick for measuring the gap between them: property is simultaneously what distinguishes and what fails to distinguish the human from the animal.

Sōseki pushes this ambiguity further. In using his cat-narrator to gaze back anthropologically at the human race, Sōseki engages in a playful inversion of the animal/human hierarchy. In the cat's eyes, it is the humans who are barbaric and the cats who truly understand the morality embodied in a civilized property system. This playful turnabout defamiliarizes human property systems, rendering them into something barbaric, beneath the dignity of a cat. Human property is theft, the cat implies, an irrational abomination maintained only through brute violence.

In chapter 4, the cat describes his practice of sneaking around the neighborhood to pilfer information through stolen glimpses and illicit eavesdropping on private conversations. He particularly targets the Kaneda clan, a nouveau riche family who are attempting to conclude an advantageous marriage for their daughter (marriage being, of course, central to property regimes old and new, as we will explore in chapter 4). The family name can be translated as Gold-Field, an amalgamation of two crucial forms of property, and their incessant striving for material and social advantage makes them one of the novel's primary butts of humor.

One might think sneaking into the Kanedas' property to gather evidence makes the cat a kind of thief, but he assures us that is not the case. This is because human property boundaries have no meaning when seen from the perspective of a cat.

> In the first place it is my opinion that the sky was made to shelter all creation, and the earth was made so that all things created able to stand might have something to stand on. Even those human beings who love argument for the arguing's sake could surely not deny this fact. Next we may ask to what extent did human effort contribute to the creation of heaven and earth; and the answer is that it contributed nothing. What right, then, do human beings hold to decide that things not of their own creation nevertheless belong to them? Of course the absence of right need not prevent such creatures from making that decision, but surely there can be no possible justification for them prohibiting others from innocent passage in and out of so-called human property. If it be accepted that Mr. So-and-so may set up stakes, fence off sections of this boundless earth and register that area as his own, what is to prevent such persons from roping off blue sky, from staking claims on heaven, an enclosure of the air? If natural law permitted proprietorial parceling-out of the land and its sale and purchase at so much the square foot, then it would also permit partition of the air we breathe at so much the cubic unit and its three-dimensional sale. If, however, it is not proper to trade in sky, if enclosure of the empyrean is not regarded as just in natural law, then surely it must follow that all land-ownership is unnatural and irrational. That, in fact, is my conviction: therefore I enter wherever I like.[16]

The cat goes on to declare that he goes wherever he pleases, but takes care not to be caught, because no matter how irrational human claims to ownership might be, they are quick to resort to violence to enforce those bogus rights.

This is a stunning passage in many ways. The cat understands John Locke's labor theory of value: just as cats should own the rats they catch because of the labor they have invested in the acquisition, humans should have no right to own land because they have not labored to produce it. The cat touches explicitly on the problem of enclosure—and it is worth reminding ourselves that Sōseki's academic specialization was the literary culture of seventeenth- and eighteenth-century Britain, the age of enclosure and dispossession, when common lands at home and abroad were widely usurped and transformed into private property.[17] There is an insane, unstoppable logic behind enclosure, the cat declares: if people can enclose common land and transform it into private property, what is to stop them from doing the same with air? As Gavin Walker reminds us, enclosure should be understood as referring not simply to the historical event of the private appropriation of common lands in early modern Britain, but rather more generally as the process of border creation that drives capital's expansion. Enclosure is the technique by which capital captures heterogeneous singularities and translates them into specific bounded differences (read: properties) that can then enter into exchange relationships; enclosure is the mechanism through which capital achieves its own reproduction.[18] But Sōseki's cat declares that when confronted with enclosure, the best policy is simply to ignore the boundaries it draws. That is also, it turns out, how you get the best stories.

In chapter 5, the cat narrates a burglary in Kushami-sensei's house. Once again, a violation of property norms moves the narrative forward. The cat witnesses the burglar's entrance, but his efforts to alert the family to the intruder's presence fail—in this case, the cat doesn't got his tongue—and it ends up simply watching as the thief carries out the robbery. The discovery the next morning of the theft by the humans leads to a subsequent conversation about the uselessness of cats: since they aren't territorial, like dogs, they make poor guards. One character even threatens to boil and eat the cat, since it seems otherwise worthless. Its value severely questioned, the cat resolves to prove his worth by catching one of the rats that plague the household. The following night, he stands on guard in the kitchen, but when rats show up to pilfer the family's food supply, the cat proves to be just as ineffective at chasing off rodent marauders as he was at warding off human thieves.[19]

The chapter works by playing off resemblances between the human and animal realms and the failure of property norms to prevent intruders from making away with household goods. The problem of resemblance is raised repeatedly throughout the chapter as a kind of master trope.[20] But what strikes me as particularly interesting is that this tale of stolen goods is related in tandem with an extended metameditation on the very act of storytelling. The chapter opens with the cat discussing the inherently selective nature of any narrative—it must reduce reality through an act of sacrifice:

> To write down every event that takes place during a period of twenty-four hours and then to read that record would, I think, occupy at least another twenty-four hours. Though I am all in favor of realistically descriptive literature, I must confess that to make a literal record of all that happened in a day and a night would be a *tour de force* quite beyond the capacities of a cat. Therefore, however much my master's paradoxical words and eccentric acts may merit being sketched from life at length and in exhaustive detail, I regret that I have neither the talent nor the energy to set them all down for my readers. Regrettable as it is, it simply can't be helped. Even a cat needs rest.[21]

This is just one instance of a key feature of *I Am a Cat*: its metafictional bent, in which the narrator often takes up the significance of the act of writing.[22] This meditation on the inherent incompleteness of any written narrative is mirrored a few pages later in the human realm, when Kushami-sensei and his wife fall into an argument over their inability to produce an exhaustive list for the police of all the property stolen by the burglar.

The cat, thus, begins the story of the burglary with a metafictional discourse on the necessity of any narrative to reduce lived reality to a manageable quantity of words—a kind of enclosure. But what the cat actually does in narrating the tale is quite the opposite. Halfway through its comical, step-by-step account of the burglar's progression through the midnight household, the cat pauses for an extended digression, offering its own cat's-paw philosophy rejecting the omnipotence of God. In other words, instead of contracting actual lived time into a condensed narrative temporality, the cat's performance does the opposite: it freezes the progress of the story by taking one moment and dilating it exponentially to fill many pages with parodic theological exposition. As Andō Fumihito notes, in this passage we have moved far from a *shaseibun* (sketching-from-nature) style narrator, one focused on the act of showing, to a self-reflective narrator focused almost entirely on the act of his own telling.[23] In other words, even as it is relating a story about property, the cat is performing the ability of storytelling to expand and contract time and space to produce alternate modes of experience and pleasure that are shared with the reader. It is perhaps inevitable, then, that the end result of the burglary in question is not a loss, but rather an enhancement of the family property. When the police capture the burglar, they return the family's property (minus a box of stolen yams, which the burglar consumed), and it turns out the thief has mended and cleaned all of the clothing he stole in preparation for selling it. The family's property has grown more valuable through being robbed.[24]

In sum, in the act of fictional worlding that Sōseki performs here, with his cat-narrator unfurling the imaginative properties of words and storytelling techniques, we encounter an alternative universe with its own strange practices of ownership. In doing so, the novel ultimately suggests different modes of being and becoming in the world, modes of selfhood that go beyond the norms of the doctrine of possessive individualism that was characteristic of Meiji Japan.[25] Modern man, the characters in the novel proclaim at some length in the final chapter, is too self-possessed, too wrapped up in the self. Kushami-sensei laments (using metaphors of ownership and theft) that "modern man, even in his deepest slumber, never stops thinking about what will bring him profit or, even more worrying, loss. Consequently, as with the burglar and the detective, his self-absorption grows daily more absolute. Modern man is jittery and sneaky."[26] This will lead to the doom of artistic creation, including literature, the members of the salon conclude: antisocial individualism will produce a world in which no one has any interest in sharing poetry written by (and implicitly for) any other individual. Having eavesdropped on this lament over the pathologies of modern self-consciousness, the cat vows that his species must somehow avoid becoming similarly possessed by a self-regarding individualism.[27] Moreover, the cat's very existence—the ordinarily impossible contradiction of a feline that is unable to speak with the humans in the depicted world, yet somehow can communicate with human readers at the level of narration—is rendered possible through the act of storytelling, an act that opens up a shared space with the reader, who derives pleasure from ignoring that central impossibility, from suspending disbelief in the existence of this impossible world.[28]

As we will see in the chapters that follow, the critique of possessive individualism forms a kind of leitmotif found across Sōseki's writings. One of the theorists Sōseki relied on in formulating his critique was William James. Sōseki knew James's work well—as does the cat. In chapter 2 of *I Am a Cat*, the narrator overhears the human characters discussing James's hypothesis that the unconscious realm might be the world of the dead: that when subconscious impulses bubble up to the surface in the domain of conscious thought, we might be encountering traces of our own belonging to a much broader world, a communal self that includes the dead and even God. Rather than possessing ourselves, such manifestations might be signs of how we are possessed, in multiple senses of that term. As we will see in chapter 2, James argues this point at length in *Varieties of Religious Experience*, a book Sōseki knew well by the time he wrote *Neko*.

William James returned to this problem in his 1909 book, *A Pluralistic Universe*, which Sōseki would also read—albeit not until after publishing *I Am a Cat*. In that later book, James uses a striking metaphor to explain how our consciousness may belong to some greater consciousness, even though we remain unaware of it. "We may be in the universe as dogs and cats are in our libraries, seeing the books and hearing the conversation, but having no inkling of the meaning of it all."[29] Unfortunately for my purposes, this passage is not underlined in Sōseki's copy of the book, but it suggests a way of understanding the world of *I Am a Cat*, where the cat-narrator can read the books and understand the conversations around it. In the imaginary world created through this fictional narrative, we explore the possibility that humans might not own even their own selves: that they instead share in that ownership, not only with divine beings but also with cats.

We also learn in the second line of the novel that the cat-narrator is nameless: "As yet I have no name" (Namae wa mada nai).[30] The word *mada* (as yet) implies an expectation that at some point it will acquire a name, but in fact the cat is fated to remain nameless through the end of the novel. As Komori Yōichi argues, to have a personal name means to occupy a subject position within the dominant patriarchal symbolic order of family lineage that was integral to the Meiji property system.[31] Without a name, the cat floats outside the realm of modern property systems. Andō pushes this further: *wagahai*, he notes, can function as either a first-person singular pronoun (I) or a first-person plural pronoun (we). The cat exploits this ambiguity to open a new realm of experience shared with the reader—the fictional commons of storytelling.[32]

Yet in addition to its reliance on pronouns, the novel also often playfully coins names for characters. The cat itself joins in at times, coming up with nicknames for the humans and cats that share its world: its master becomes, for example, Kushami-sensei, Professor Sneeze.[33] That being the case, why doesn't the cat simply name itself? The cat explains its decision not to acquire a name in relation to the problem of greed: "it's no use crying for the moon" in Ito and Wilson's translation, but more literally, "once you start giving voice to your wants, there is no end to it."[34] Instead of a name, the cat merely possesses a pronoun: *wagahai*. Pronouns, as Tolstoy's horse-narrator points out, play a key role in ideologies of property. Humans, the horse complains, have no right to say "my horse": the very act of speaking the possessive pronoun *my* has the effect of naturalizing a claim to ownership that the horse emphatically rejects.

Pronouns are fundamentally different from proper nouns such as personal names. As Emile Benveniste notes, first-person and second-person pronouns function to create subject positions for the speaker and interlocutor in linguistic utterances: the English "I" has no referent outside the specific utterance in which it is deployed; like other indicators ("here," "now," "this"), it is pegged to the act of a specific utterance and refers to no objective existence beyond that.[35] These indicators then shift to indicate something else in the next utterance: when I speak to you, I call myself "I" and call you "you," but when you respond, the positions are reversed.[36] What allows them to function in this way is their fundamental anonymity, their lack of any content outside the act of speaking: the fact that we all share them. Pronouns function as a kind of linguistic commons: they "are always available," because language "is so organized that it permits each speaker to appropriate to himself [*sic*] an entire language by designating himself as *I*."[37] This is the case even in languages like Japanese that avoid using pronouns, and even for Japanese pronouns like *wagahai*, which bear indications of the speaker's relative social status, gender, intimacy with the interlocutor, and so on.[38] On at least one occasion, for example, the cat's master becomes *wagahai* in the novel.[39]

Benveniste argues that the importance of pronouns can "be measured by the nature of the problem they serve to solve, which is none other than that of intersubjective communication."[40]

> If each speaker, in order to express the feeling he has of his irreducible subjectivity, made use of a distinct identifying signal (in the sense in which each radio transmitting station has its own call letters), there would be as many languages as individuals and communication would become absolutely impossible. Language wards off this danger by instituting a unique but mobile sign, I, which can be assumed by each speaker on the condition that he refers each time only to the instance of his own discourse. This sign is thus linked to the exercise of language and announces the speaker as speaker. It is this property that establishes the basis for individual discourse, in which each speaker takes over all the resources of language for his own behalf.[41]

Pronouns are what make possible linguistic sharing: intersubjective communication, what we commonly call dialogue. They are a common property of language, not of individual speakers.[42]

Pronouns, in sum, are fundamentally different from proper nouns like personal names, which are supposed to belong only to one person. Hence, proper nouns can't be translated—as Kushami-sensei learns, when his students trick him into translating the name Columbus. To put this too schematically, we may be able to claim ownership over proper nouns, but we can't own pronouns: they belong to everyone, and we can only borrow them temporarily from the shared pool of language. So when the cat declines to name itself, it is declining to participate in a certain kind of ownership.

But I think Sōseki's experiment goes further: the cat actually does have a name. It is the first word in the book's title and in the novel's text: *wagahai*. Sōseki achieves a humorous effect by assigning this aristocratic pronoun to a mere cat, and as the novel proceeds, in strange fashion this pronoun comes to belong to the cat, becoming a kind of pet name. The boundary between a pronoun, shared by everyone and belonging to no one, and a proper noun, a name belonging solely to one individual, starts to blur in the imaginary world produced through this act of narration. The nameless cat that wandered into the novelist's house turns out not to belong to anyone, not even to itself, and yet at the very same time, as a pronoun, it becomes something that potentially belongs to us all. At the very least, we are allowed to share in the pleasure its storytelling produces.

That, at any rate, is the kind of thing that happens when you give a cat some say in questions of ownership. What about a tanuki?

A TRICKSTER BADGER AND THE THEORY OF LITERATURE

Sōseki's reimagining of modern ideologies and practices of ownership was in part an epistemological critique—a critical reconsideration of how it is we know what we think we know. Accordingly, his fictional attempts to imagine alternative modes for belonging and sharing often involved questioning (sometimes playfully, sometimes with deadly seriousness) the authority of disciplinary knowledge. Sōseki was both a product of and contributor to the new elite higher education infrastructure instituted by the Meiji state. His major scholarly contribution was his *Theory of Literature* (*Bungakuron*), published in 1907, but based on research carried out during his 1900–1902 sojourn in London as an overseas student dispatched by the Japanese government and further developed through a series of lecture courses he taught at Tokyo Imperial University in 1903–5.[43]

The key issue for Sōseki's theory is the relationship between two distinct realms of knowledge, what he calls literature and science. Meditations on the relationship between these two modes of knowing turn up frequently in his critical essays and fiction. In his 1908 lecture "The Attitude of a Creative Author" ("Sōsakuka no taido"), Sōseki theorized the distinction between scientist and literary writer in terms of "attitude" or "stance" (*taido*). He defines "attitude" as "a way of holding the mind, a way of looking at things" (*kokoro no mochikata, mono no mikata*); such attitudes are, he argues, the product of "education" and "habit."[44] In distinguishing a scientific attitude from its literary counterpart, emotions or affect emerge as the crucial point of difference. In *Theory of Literature*, it is the active role played in literature by the emotional fringes to our conscious focal point that distinguishes the mental experience of literature from that of science. In science, only the cognitive focal point itself is relevant, whereas literature requires the presence of affect. As we will explore more fully in chapter 2, this is the crux of the famous $(F + f)$ formula by which Sōseki defined literature.

Sōseki devotes book 3 of *Theory of Literature* to an extended comparison of literature and science as forms of knowledge. Faced with a given phenomenon, science needs to unpack the "how" behind it, which inevitably includes a temporal dimension: the scientist maps out the timeline of causal factors that led to the appearance of the phenomenon. Literature, on the other hand, is relatively free from the obligation to explain how or to trace through lines of causality. Instead, Sōseki argues, literature cuts a phenomenon out of the complex interweaving of temporal development to focus on a single, simple segment of time.

This difference in approaches is paralleled in different "attitudes." A scientist's attitude is, according to Sōseki, ruthlessly analytical: given a phenomenon, the scientist wants to break it down into its composite elements. Any analysis that a literary writer performs, on the other hand, is secondary to his or her primary purpose: producing wholes that solicit an emotionally vivid impression of the depicted object. Hence, writers are satisfied with the naked eye and do not need a microscope; they have no need to carry out laboratory experiments to dissect their object. Scientists also sometimes deal in wholes, but in such instances we again find a crucial distinction between their attitude and that of literary writers. The scientist grasps a whole via abstract concepts and as a means to explain the phenomenon's form and mechanical structure. Ultimately, the goal is classification: a stripping away of inessential singularities from the phenomenon in order to locate it on a grid of abstract categories. Hence, numbers and mathematical formulas are the preferred language of science, according to Sōseki.

For literature, on the other hand, it is crucial is to convey a picture of the whole. Rather than attempting to locate the object's position within an abstract system, the literary writer attempts to convey an impression of its essence as a singular thing, including the emotional resonances it elicits in us. In place of abstract numbers, literature uses rhetorical tropes and symbols to convey what is difficult to express explicitly.

> The literary writer gives fragrance to that which is without fragrance, form to that which is formless. In contrast, the scientist strips away the form from that which has form, the flavor from that which has flavor. In this regard, the literary writer and the scientist carry out their translations of things in completely opposite directions, one going left, the other right, each carrying out their allotted duties indifferent to the other. Accordingly, literary writers use the technique of symbolism in order to express sensations and emotions, while scientists record things using their own particular set of signs without any regard for sensation or emotion.[45]

Ultimately, Sōseki concludes, there are different modes of truth in science and literature. Literary truth is achieved when the depicted object directly summons up its feeling as if it were necessarily true—when what we read feels exactly like the depicted object, even if this means violating reality. Hence, to reach literary truth a writer uses techniques that would be anathema to a scientist. This also means, Sōseki notes, that unlike scientific truth, literary truth shifts with time. What one generation perceives as literary truth may not be accepted as such by a subsequent generation.

As Joseph Murphy demonstrates, there are good historical reasons that help explain why an intellectual trained in Meiji Japan would not only feel compelled to explore the boundary between literature and science, but also enjoy literacy in the languages of both.[46] Crucially, though, Sōseki did not attempt to collapse the domains of literature and science, but rather used a kind of transversal strategy to both distinguish and connect the two. Sōseki's rethinking of property likewise has to be thought transversally, in the way his work insists on the boundary between literature and science even as it at the same time repeatedly crosses over that boundary. These crossings often open up questions of ownership, particularly of self-possession.

We encounter such crossings in one of Sōseki's earliest stories, "Hearing Things" ("Koto no sorane," 1905). It is the tale of a young scholar who falls prey to phantoms that lead him astray, shaking the foundations of his own knowledge. "Hearing Things" was published in June 1905 in *Shichinin*, a fairly obscure literary journal. The story has received relatively little critical attention, both inside and outside Japan.[47] I find this relative neglect hard to understand: it is a wonderful piece, playful and intelligent. It also foreshadows many themes that would reappear in Sōseki's later, better-known novels. Moreover, the tale is particularly useful in understanding how Sōseki saw the role of literature in relation to science—how literary truth contrasted with scientific truth.[48] Given that property was a key object of scientific analysis in a number of academic disciplines, the story also helps us understand the alternative forms of ownership that Sōseki was imagining through literature. And once again, we encounter in the story the figure of an animal narrator—in this case, a trickster tanuki. That is to say, "Hearing Things" is, at least in part, a fable.

The main narrator of this story, however, is human—all too human. Told in the first person by its protagonist, "Hearing Things" narrates a day and night in the life of Yasuo, a recent graduate of the faculty of law at the university who is engaged to marry Tsuyuko. The story opens with Yasuo visiting Tsuda, an old school chum, at the boarding house where they used to be housemates. Tsuda studies under the faculty of literature and specializes in psychology. The two engage in chitchat until Yasuo notes a book on Tsuda's desk, scribbled over in handwritten notes. He asks about it.

Tsuda answers that it is a book about ghosts. The narrator expresses surprise and even envy that Tsuda has the leisure to expend time reading about something so impractical as ghosts and compares this to his own harried life as a salaried worker who faces the strain of a long daily commute. Under these stressful conditions, he says, "I feel, in fact, as though I were in the process of becoming a ghost myself."

Tsuda changes the subject:

"But how's your new home? Do you feel properly masterly now that you own a house?" Tsuda, as might be expected from a man who studies ghosts, asks questions that pierce to the psychological heart of the situation.

"I don't feel much of a master. . . . Of course, if the house were completely in order, I might be able to enjoy that special feeling of being a master; but while one boils water in a brass kettle and washes one's face in a tin basin, there's little scope even for looking like the master of a house." . . .

"Even with such embarrassments, a master is a master. Surely, whenever you think 'this is my house,' you can but feel somehow pleased. For, by and large, it's a true principle that owning and attachment go hand in hand." Tsuda explained away my state of mind in his usual psychological manner. A scholar is one who explains everything, even when not asked for an explanation.[49]

The story is poking fun at the discipline of psychology and the forms of knowledge it produces. In particular, psychology as a modern science is set in contrast to Japanese folk traditions and what the narrator calls "superstition." The story will pursue this comparison up through the end, raising along the way numerous issues related to the discipline of psychology: the subconscious processes of mental association, the influence of external suggestion on internal consciousness, the process by which phenomena of perception such as the ringing of a bell unfold in our cognition, and so on.[50]

The passage quoted above never identifies a specific source for Tsuda's ideas about the feelings of mastery and ownership. But a likely candidate is William James's *Principles of Psychology* (hereafter abbreviated as *Principles*), since its publication in 1890 one of the primary university textbooks used around the world in the field. As we will see in chapter 2, *Principles* had been introduced into Japan in the 1890s by figures whom Sōseki knew well. He purchased his own copy while in London and returned to it frequently as he wrote *Theory of Literature*.

In the chapter "The Consciousness of Self" in *Principles*, James explicates what he calls the "Empirical Self," invoking the pronouns of ownership that so vexed Tolstoy's horse-narrator:

> The Empirical Self of each of us is all that he is tempted to call by the name of *me*. But it is clear that between what a man calls *me* and what he simply calls *mine* the line is difficult to draw. We feel and act about certain things that are ours very much as we feel and act about ourselves. . . . And our bodies themselves, are they simply ours, or are they *us*? . . . *In its widest possible sense*, however, *a man's Self is the sum total of all that he CAN call his*, not only his body and his psychic powers, but his clothes and his house, his wife and children, his ancestors and friends, his reputation and works, his lands and horses, and yachts and bank-account. All these things give him the same emotions.[51]

James argues that an "instinctive impulse" causes us to accumulate property, and that we develop an emotional bond of intimacy with the things we own, so that they become integral to our sense of self.[52] This sense of ownership occurs at the level of affect as a preconscious sensation. James repeatedly describes the sense of "warmth" and "intimacy" we feel toward things that we own. That embodied feeling is the mark of our ownership, and it in turn helps us generate the sense we have of a steady, proprietary relationship with our own selves.

Accordingly, when Tsuda asks the narrator about the feeling of ownership that Yasuo should have as the master of his own house, he is, as the narrator notes, summoning up knowledge from the discipline of psychology, such as William James. As Walter Benn Michaels has argued, James at this point in his career provides us with a striking instance of "possessive individualism."[53] As we will explore more fully in chapter 2, James's *Principles* provides a paradigmatic instance of possessive individualism—even as his later works, such as *Varieties of Religious Experience* (1902), move away from that position. In reading the early James, we encounter notions of property ownership at every turn: they provide his favorite metaphor for explaining human consciousness.

Returning to "Hearing Things," Tsuda's remarks about the feeling of being master of a house rehash James's ideas about how our selves include the things we own. But the story makes fun of this idea: Yasuo, it turns out, doesn't feel much like a master. We eventually learn that he fails even to obtain mastery over the woman he has hired as a housekeeper: she keeps driving him crazy with both the details of her housekeeping expenses and her superstitions. Sōseki is asking us to imagine a man who is far from being master: Yasuo falls short of properly owning things or even his own self in the ways that James asserts that he should. Tellingly, this also involves an overturning of gender hierarchies: instead of acting as patriarchal master possessing the women of his household, Yasuo will end up being laughed at by both the housekeeper and his fiancée—and he doesn't seem to mind.

Following their discussion of Yasuo's new house and the sense of mastery it should bring, the two friends continue their chat. Tsuda asks after Yasuo's fiancée, Tsuyuko. Yasuo tells Tsuda that Tsuyuko has been sick with influenza lately, but that it is nothing serious. Tsuda immediately changes tone, speaking in a low, haunting voice that the narrator describes as physically penetrating, like a needle piercing into the brain. "You must take great care," he warns Yasuo.[54]

He proceeds to recount a mysterious occurrence. A female relative of his died unexpectedly of pneumonia. At the time, her soldier husband was away from Japan, fighting in the Russo-Japanese War (in Sōseki's works, the empire is a constant source of pressure on life in metropolitan Japan).

Before he left, she promised she would visit him if she died while he was away. At the very moment of her death, the husband happened to pull out a small pocket mirror and was mystified to discover her image reflected in it, gazing wordlessly back at him. Hearing this anecdote, Yasuo feels spooked, and he notes that this case study belongs to territory far beyond the grasp of a graduate from the faculty of law: he acknowledges that he is beyond the boundaries of his own disciplinary knowledge.

Tsuda goes on to tell Yasuo that his book on ghosts contains similar case studies:

> "I've got a book here which records an exact similar story," came his [Tsuda's] calm reply and he reached for that book on his desk. "The very latest research seems to suggest that the possibility of the objective reality of such phenomenon is likely to be proven." When I [Yasuo] reflected that, unbeknownst to Bachelors of Law, the psychologists have resurrected specters, I felt no longer able to sneer with confidence at spookiness. One cannot offer opinions on matters on which one is entirely ignorant. Ignorance is a form of incompetence. I think that in respect of ghosts, a Bachelor of Laws must take the word of a Bachelor of Arts.
>
> "Even though separated by great distances, when the brain-cells of two persons are in simultaneous sympathy, a certain chemical change occurs. . . ."[55]

Tsuda is studying the science (or pseudo-science) of parapsychology—another one of William James's specialties, as we will see shortly.

After this, Yasuo walks home in the dark, and the landscape around him comes to seem haunted: he is fully spooked, especially when he passes two men carrying the coffin of a child. Yasuo finally reaches home in a state of sheer panic. Rather than possessing himself, he is clearly possessed by fear and the external suggestion of his fiancée's possible death.

And it only gets worse at home. There, Yasuo finds the troublesome housekeeper in a state of panic because of the terrible howling of dogs in the neighborhood. The two of them manage to spook each other into believing that the howling is a ghostly omen, signaling a turn for the worse in Tsuyuko's condition. Yasuo vows he will visit his fiancée first thing in the morning. He lies in bed, his consciousness overwhelmed with sounds he hears in the dark, certain that they are all ghostly premonitions of death. Sōseki depicts the waves of his conscious thought and sense perception in fine detail in a kind of anticipation of the "pure and intense sonorous material" invoked in Kafka's 1922 short story, "Investigations of a Dog."[56] Tsuda describes his mental perceptions:

> Normally the barking of a dog is a straight-lined sound, as though a long straight line of blocks of clean-cut wood were clapped successively together. But the girning I now hear is no such simple thing. The width of the voice has continual variations: it has curves, it has roundness to it. It begins from a thin bleak end of candlelight and gradually broadens into plumpness: then, dwindling down to a wick that exhausts its fuel, gradually it disappears. And there's no telling whence these dog-sounds are coming. One moment they come from miles away, riding faintly on the blowing wind. Then, as the sound comes nearer, it leaks through the eaves and forces itself close even into pillow-covered ears. The sound oo-oo-oo, a chain of rounded punctuations, loops twice, perhaps three times, around the house: then the rhythm changes to wa-wa-wa and, finally, gusted off by a jerk of the wind, its tail-end changes to a distant n-n-n as it peters out in the far-off worlds of darkness.[57]

This close attention to the texture of sound perception again invokes the discipline of psychology. Matsumoto Matatarō, Sōseki's former classmate and in 1905 a faculty colleague at the First Higher School, had eight years earlier published the results of his laboratory experiments at Yale University on the spatial cognition of sound perception.[58] Terada Torahiko, one of the young writers whom Sōseki mentored (and supposedly the model for the character Kangetsu in I Am a Cat, who undergoes his own momentary crisis of self-possession, perhaps at the hands of a tanuki), would earn his doctorate from Tokyo Imperial University in 1908 with a dissertation on the acoustical science of the shakuhachi flute.[59] In "Hearing Things," we see Sōseki crossing the line between literature and science, appropriating scientific discourse on sound perception into the domain of literature to produce a comic effect.

Yasuo's introspective analysis of the minutiae of sound perception is interrupted when a policeman knocks on his door. He and the housekeeper learn from the patrolman that the dogs are howling because burglars are about in the neighborhood: in other words, there is a threat to property ownership. But even this rational explanation for the creepy sonic phenomenon fails to calm Yasuo.

At this point in the story, Yasuo is a man who has lost any mastery over himself. He no longer possesses his consciousness; rather, his consciousness has been possessed by external stimuli and by mental associations that others have injected into his stream of perception. A domain of Yasuo's mental life that lies beyond his control has hijacked his stream of consciousness. Rather than the authoritative subject facing the object world—the master of the house who finds his sense of self reinforced by all of the belongings around him—he increasingly assumes the position of a medium, passively transmitting the thoughts of others, neither quite I nor you.

Oddly enough, we are back to William James here. In *The Varieties of Religious Experience*, James writes:

> I cannot but think that the most import step forward that has occurred in psychology since I have been a student of that science is the discovery, first made in 1886 [the date is underlined in Sōseki's copy], that, in certain subjects at least, there is not only the consciousness of the ordinary field, with its usual centre and margin, but an addition thereto in the shape of a set of memories, thoughts, and feelings which are extra-marginal and outside of primary consciousness altogether, but yet must be classed as conscious facts of some sort, able to reveal their presence by unmistakable signs. I call this the most important step forward because, unlike the other advances which psychology has made, this discovery has revealed to us an entirely unsuspected peculiarity in the constitution of human nature.... In particular this discovery of a consciousness existing beyond the field, or subliminally as Mr. Myers terms it, casts light on many phenomena of religious biography.[60]

James lists the many psychologists he thinks deserve credit for this discovery of the unconscious, and in his copy of the book Sōseki dutifully underlines the names, including that of Sigmund Freud.

But as the quote suggests, James thinks primary credit for discovery of the unconscious should go to Frederic Myers. In "Frederic Myers's Service to Psychology" (1901), James would expand on his view of Myers's importance to the science of psychology: he was the first to explicitly map out the region of the unconscious.

> Myers definitely attacks this problem, which, after him, it will be impossible to ignore.... These observations have been extended in Germany, America, and elsewhere; and although Binet and Janet worked independently of Myers, and did work far more objective, he nevertheless will stand as the original announcer of a theory which, in my opinion, makes an epoch, not only in medical, but in psychological science, because it brings in an entirely new conception of our mental possibilities.... I am disposed to think it a probability, that Frederic Myers will always be remembered in psychology as the pioneer who staked out a vast tract of mental wilderness and planted the flag of genuine science upon it.[61]

James later published a review of Myers's *Human Personality and Its Survival of Bodily Death* (1903) in which he declared that we should now call the study of the unconscious "Myers's problem."[62]

In identifying the discovery of the unconscious as a crucial turning point in the discipline of psychology, James was on the right track. But in identifying Myers as the central figure in this development, James bet on the wrong horse: Freud, of course, would come to be remembered as the father of this development. Why did Freud emerge as the heroic discoverer of the unconscious in the history of the discipline, while Myers languishes in relative obscurity? The title to Myers's book mentioned above already suggests the answer: Myers thought the unconscious realm, or what he called the Subliminal Self, consisted of the afterlife: it was where our personalities go after death. Myers carried out serious laboratory work seeking to demonstrate that the unconscious realm consisted of ghosts, whose activities lay behind those moments when subconscious pressures burst into and disrupt our consciousness. William James, a founding member of the American Society for Psychical Research, was one of the heirs to this form of scientific knowledge—as Sōseki himself was aware.[63] This knowledge led to an understanding of consciousness as something hybrid and multiple, multilayered—a view that frustrates possessive individualism's desires to draw clean lines of ownership.[64]

Hence, in "Hearing Things" Sōseki links together psychology, consciousness, the sense of ownership and the sense of being possessed, and connects all of these to the scientific study of ghosts. The story's narrative continues: after a sleepless night, Yasuo at the crack of dawn sprints across Tokyo to Tsuyuko's home. His future mother-in-law and fiancée are understandably startled when he bursts in on them before breakfast, a wild look on his face, his clothes splattered in mud. And it turns out that Tsuyuko is just fine.

Yasuo is embarrassed but also relieved. Leaving Tsuyuko's home, he heads for a barbershop. There, he hears more ghost stories, but now the tone turns humorous. The barber and his patrons joke about how unlikely it is for ghosts to persist in this age of electric lights and enlightenment. They conclude that when people see ghosts today, it is all a matter of nerves (*shinkei*): it's all psychological.

One of the patrons starts reading aloud from a book: *Transcript of Lectures on Material Psychology* by May B. True (*Ukiyo shinri kōgiroku* by Uyamuya Dōjin). It's a comical fable narrated by a tanuki who, with bawdy humor, describes how he once bewitched a youth named Sakuzō, transforming himself into the illusion of a tree. Sakuzō tried to hang himself with his loincloth from one of the branches, and at the key moment the tanuki turned itself back into a tanuki, laughing at Sakuzō, who ran away in terror. Here again, the story anticipates Kafka's "Investigations of a Dog," in which the canine narrator oscillates between dog wisdom and scientific knowledge, vowing, "All science, the totality of all questions and all answers, lies with us dogs."[65] The tanuki sums up the incident with Sakuzō by positing a kind of tanuki knowledge that is superior to human science:

> A superficial observer would, no doubt, aver that I had bewitched Sakuzō; but that, I would submit, is more than a little unreasonable. Sakuzō had been hanging about the village just yearning to be bewitched. I cast a spell upon him for no other reason than my kindly readiness to meet Sakuzō's own desire to have a spell cast on him. Our badgerly way of doing things is simply to employ those "hypnotic devices," currently recommended by the best contemporary medical practitioners. From time immemorable we in the School of badgers have, with those devices, cheated no end of virtuous and honorable gentlemen in no end of different places. We note that certain of the citizenry have been designating as "the hypnotic method" or some other such inflated title a technique lately borrowed from Western badgers; and that they worship those who practice this technique as "Doctors." This regrettable state of affairs is entirely attributable to the current infatuation with anything from the West. And I, for one, though secretly, deplore it. When over the centuries Japan's own wonderful devices have been handed down intact from father to son, why should such a fuss be made over shoddy imitations imported from the West?[66]

As one of the barber's clients remarks after hearing this passage, "That is a very argumentative tanuki."[67] Hearing the story, Yasuo concludes that he himself the previous night was bewitched by a tanuki, or perhaps by his own desire to be bewitched.

In the fictional world that Sōseki imagines in "Hearing Things," Yasuo is comically forced to consider the possibility that other ways of knowing exist alongside the scientific. He repeatedly encounters specters that reveal the limits of our ability to comprehend the world, ghostly excesses that haunt our attempts to account for ourselves.[68] In confronting this kind of ghost, we encounter what Jacques Derrida calls a "non-object" and the "being-there of an absent or departed one" that "no longer belongs to knowledge."[69] These uncanny specters pose a playful, imaginary challenge not just to science, but also to possessive individualism and modern regimes of property. Who can own a ghost, after all? Do we inherit ghosts, or do they inherit us?[70] When we try to possess ghosts, we are likely to end up possessed by them.

Can ghosts, tanuki, and other imaginary specters be known scientifically? On the one hand, Sōseki's story suggests the answer is no: they exist only in the domains of literature and superstition. Accordingly, as the tanuki insists, when we think we know them, we are simply bewitching ourselves. But "Hearing Things" ends on yet another playful twist: the boundary between science and literature is redrawn, only to be crossed once more. After he returns home and his foibles are exposed, his fiancée and housekeeper enjoy a good laugh. Yasuo is almost deliriously happy: he thinks he has acquired an even firmer purchase on the affections of his intended. Moreover, he declares in the final lines of the story—the moral of this fable—that his ghostly misadventures have been recaptured by the domain of scientific knowledge:

> Perhaps I just imagine it, but since that day Tsuyuko seems to love me much more than before. When I saw Tsuda later, I told him in full detail of the happenings of that night. He remarked that it would make excellent material for the book which he was then in the process of writing, and he sought my permission to make use of it. The experience of Mr. K. which you can find on page seventy-two of *An Essay On Ghosts* by Tsuda Masakata B.A., is, as you will realize, mine.[71]

In other words, the haunting of Yasuo provides the material for two distinct narratives: one the humorous literary story with the embedded animal fable that the reader has just completed reading, and the second a scientific narrative in a scholarly tome published by Tsuda. The story playfully generates an interruption in the processes of scientific knowing, leaving its narrator suspended between two realms, literature and science, like a translator caught between languages, unable to decide whether to turn left or right.

In "Hearing Things," Sōseki mobilizes his theory of literature to experiment with possibilities for other ways of knowing the world, including property regimes, and again an animal narrator plays a key role. In the story, we see the complexity of Sōseki's literary theory, the way it drew a boundary between science and literature both to divide and reconnect them. In these crossings, animal narrators—even those branded with an owner's mark—take delight in wandering astray, drifting across the boundary between theory and practice. In the final section of this chapter, I turn from Sōseki's literary theory to his literary practice to explore the question of what literature could do.

After his early success with short stories and novellas, Sōseki from 1907 on redirected his literary production toward full-length novels.[72] He originally serialized these in the *Asahi* newspaper (whose literary page Sōseki now edited) and subsequently published them in book form. Critics customarily group his major novels into threesomes: the first trilogy, consisting of *Sanshirō* (1908), *And Then* (*Sore kara*, 1909), and *The Gate* (*Mon*, 1910); and the second trilogy, consisting of *To the Spring Equinox and Beyond* (*Higan sugi made*, 1912), *The Wayfarer* (*Kōjin*, 1913), and *Kokoro* (1914). It is a remarkable body of work, especially given Sōseki's relatively short career: he wrote fiction only during the last twelve years of his life.

Moreover, he produced many other brilliant stories, novellas, and novels that elude capture into this triangulating schema. But critics (myself included) keep trying, perhaps because triangles seem so central to Sōseki's literary practice. It is hardly an original gesture in reading his work to point out the relevance of René Girard's theory of imitative, triangular desire.[73] Under this form, the role of the third-party mediator—the rival whose model triggers the subject's desire for the object—poses a threat to any claim that subject might make to self-possession. Karatani Kōjin notes, for example, that in *Kokoro* the character Sensei's desire for the daughter of his landlord flares up only after his friend K falls in love with her, igniting an ambivalent love/hate relationship between the two men. The novel reveals how our "consciousness and desire, which appear to us as immediate (or unmediated), are already mediated by the other," so that our own inner self only reaches us at a delay, as the product of our relations with others rather than as our own private possession.[74] Others have drawn connections between the triangles depicted in *Kokoro* and the emergence in Meiji Japan of modern homosocial forms of desire.[75] The triangular logic in *Kokoro* is so powerful that a major debate erupted in the 1980s when a new generation of Japanese critics began filling in missing angles and sides, carrying the novel's abruptly suspended storyline forward to what they believed were its implicit trigonometric resolutions.[76]

We can find many obvious instances of triangular desire in other works by Sōseki. *The Gate, The Wayfarer, Kusamakura, To the Spring Equinox and Beyond*, and *And Then* all revolve around romantic triangles, and I am barely scratching the surface. Sōseki in his fiction repeatedly returns to the problem of how our intimate desires are intersubjective, how that desire is actually desire for the desire of the other—that of the third-party mediator. Moreover, Sōseki's characters caught up in these triangles often get trapped under the crushing demands for infinite sacrifice that such an Oedipal structure invokes: both K and Sensei in *Kokoro* commit suicide, Daisuke in *And Then* suffers an apparent nervous breakdown, and Sōsuke in *The Gate* finds himself refused even the solace of religious salvation. That is to say, the triangles here seemingly refer back to the Oedipal complex, the sex/gender system that Gayle Rubin finds at the center of gendered property regimes, under which certain persons (males) hold property rights over others (women).[77] As Deleuze and Guattari argue, the Oedipal traffic in women captures (read: encloses) unruly desire into the forms of subjectivity required by capitalism, generating the "possessive or proprietary ego" that characterizes modern societies and their possessive individualism.[78]

But in Sōseki's literary practice, triangles never quite lead to clean lines of ownership, whether of women or the self. Thinking back to the basic distinction between science and literature that underlies his theory of literature, for Sōseki (F) is the realm of science, a realm where objects stand still and can be owned by subjects, without requiring the presence of a third party. By contrast, $(F+f)$ is the realm of literature, where objects are fluid and can only be experienced via a relationship that is shared in common across at least three subject positions: author, character, reader. Literature opens a realm for practicing alternative possibilities, different economies of owning and sharing, different modes of subjectivity-in-common that gesture beyond self-possession.

To explore more fully the alternative worlds Sōseki imagined in his literary practice, in this final section, I want to focus on a work that does not so easily reduce to triangular logic. *Sanshirō*, the first novel of the first trilogy, was serialized in the *Asahi* in 1908 and published in book form the following year. I have to begin by confessing that the first character in the eponymous hero's name (*san*: 三) means "three." The second character in that name (*shi*: 四), though, complicates matters, because it means "four," and in fact this hints at the nature of this work, or unwork. Nihei Michiaki states the problem succinctly: "Here we have three men and one woman: Nonomiya, Sanshirō, and 'the handsome young man who came and took [Mineko] away,' and, on the other hand, Mineko."[79] We might also throw in the painter Haraguchi, Sanshirō's classmate Yōjirō, Professor Hirota, and Nonomiya's sister Yoshiko. In other words, too many sides for a proper triangle, echoing the hint embedded in the hero's given name, which might be translated "third or fourth son."[80]

This avoidance of tidy triangles does not mean that *Sanshirō* sidesteps the problems of desire. In the first chapter, Sanshirō rides a train that carries him from rural Kyushu to Tokyo, where he will enroll in the university. He engages in conversation a fellow passenger, a man Sanshirō will later learn is none other than Hirota, a professor at the university. After discussing the appetite for peaches of the famous poet Masaoka Shiki (in real life, a close friend of Sōseki's), Hirota declares:

> You know, our hands reach out by themselves for the things we like. There's no way to stop them. A pig doesn't have hands, so his snout reaches out instead. I've heard that if you tie a pig down and put food in front of him, the tip of his snout will grow until it reaches the food. Desire is a frightening thing. . . . It's lucky for us we're not pigs. . . . Think what would happen if our noses kept stretching toward all the things we wanted. By now they'd be so long we couldn't board a train.[81]

Unbeknownst to Hirota, his remark serves as an ironic commentary on what happened to Sanshirō the previous night. An older married woman, one whose dark skin reminds him of his rural hometown and whose husband is away working in semicolonial Dairen, has seemingly tried to seduce the youth. Sanshirō clearly felt a charge of interest: she repeatedly captured his gaze. But he was ultimately unable, or unwilling, to act on her apparent availability. Her parting words the following morning echo painfully in Sanshirō's ears: "Anata wa yoppodo mune no nai kata desu ne," or, in Jay Rubin's translation, "You're quite a coward, aren't you?"[82] Depending on how we translate *mune* here, though, she could also be accusing Sanshirō of lacking heart, passion, or even breasts. One is tempted to translate her dismissal as, "You really don't have any balls, do you?"[83]

This bothers Sanshirō. Not just because the woman seems to be laughing at him but also because he is sure he does possess *mune*. That is to say, he wants things: women, learning, the city, modernity, everything. "He was going to Tokyo. He would enter the University. He would meet famous scholars, associate with students of taste and breeding, do research in the library, write books. Society would acclaim him, his mother would be overjoyed."[84] Sanshirō gets onto that train because he believes that what he desires lies at the other end of the line. But does he ever reach his destination? Or does the work instead exemplify the "poetics of nonarrival" that Judith Butler espies in Kafka?[85]

In fact, what Sanshirō mostly does in Tokyo is go astray, as he follows the dictates of his "light, airy restlessness."[86] Another driving force seems to be an aversion to triangles: it is in large part to escape the triangle formed between himself, his mother, and the odious Miwata Omitsu back home, a triangle seemingly determined to trap Sanshirō into marriage, that he sets into motion along a line of escape. In Tokyo, too, he sometimes finds himself caught up unwillingly in the machinations of triangular desire. For instance, while watching a university track meet, Sanshirō at first thinks the runners are foolish to participate. Then, however, he notices that among the spectators "the ladies were watching with great enthusiasm, and Mineko and Yoshiko more so than any. Sanshirō suddenly wanted to start galloping."[87] When Mineko congratulates Nonomiya for winning the race, Sanshirō cannot help but stare in jealousy, but rather than move in and lay claim to ownership, once again his response is to set into motion and flee the scene.

Sanshirō feels attracted to Mineko, but he never makes his move—in part because he is unable to figure out who his true rival might be. He mainly suspects Nonomiya, but in the end Mineko chooses to marry a man Sanshirō has never even met—again, the object escapes from both the subject and the mediator (whomever he may be). The object of desire turns out, after all, to retain the status of being other—another subject, in this case one whose autonomous possession of money that she can loan to Sanshirō, a gray area under Meiji legal codes, already suggests the confusion she will bring to Sanshirō's worldview.[88] Mineko's possession of money hints that she will refuse the position of owned object to be exchanged between men: she is determined to own herself rather than be trafficked by others. The key term used throughout the novel to describe Sanshirō and Mineko is "stray sheep." I return to this phrase again below, but for now let me point out that it indicates that Sanshirō does not know his place in the trigonometry of romantic love: he constantly wanders astray from the triangles of desire.

At one point in the novel, Sanshirō comes close to defining the three angles of a triangle that might provide direction to his desire. The life he leads in Tokyo, he decides, can be classified into three "worlds."[89] The first is the tranquil and drowsy past, the world prior to the 1880s, the world of Sanshirō's rural hometown and his mother. The second is that of the university and scholars—the world of Nonomiya and Hirota, peaceful and unworldly.

> Sanshirō's third world was as radiant and fluid as spring, a world of electric lights, of silver spoons, of cheers and laughter, of glasses bubbling over with champagne. And crowning everything were beautiful women. Sanshirō had spoken to one of them, he had seen another twice. This world was for him

the most profound. This world was just in front of him, but it was unapproachable, like a shaft of lightning in the farthest heavens. Sanshirō gazed at it from afar and found it baffling. He seemed to possess the qualifications to be a master [*shujinkō*: literally, protagonist] of some part of this world; without him, a void would open up in it. This world should have wanted to fill that void and develop to perfection, but for some reason it closed itself to him and blocked the route by which he might attain free access.[90]

All the elements are in place for triangular desire: Sanshirō (first world) should outrival Nonomiya (second world) to win Mineko (third world). Instead of rivalry, though, Sanshirō decides the best thing would be to combine the three into a new, heterogeneous assemblage: "Then he mixed the three together and from the mixture obtained a conclusion. The best thing would be to bring his mother from the country, marry a beautiful woman, and devote himself to learning." The narrator chides Sanshirō for reaching such "a mediocre conclusion," and even Sanshirō seems dissatisfied and begins to "translate" its terms. Rather than sticking to one beautiful woman, he dreams about coming "into contact with as many beautiful women as possible in order to enlarge the scope of the influence derived from those translations and to perfect his own individuality."[91]

In sum, *Sanshirō* is the comic fable of a man, a "stray sheep" who cannot find a mediator to provide direction to his movements and to define his place in systems of ownership. To borrow Girard's language, he has passions but not desires. *Sanshirō* is sometimes called a bildungsroman, a novel of sentimental education. And yet, much like the eponymous protagonist of Sōseki's earlier *Botchan* (1906), a novel whose plot is set into motion through an act of familial inheritance and in which the hero again borrows money from a female character, Sanshirō does not mature, does not grow up into a socialized, self-possessed ego. Faced with a lecture comparing "Kant's transcendental idealism versus Berkeley's transcendental realism," he can only cover his notebooks with the words *stray sheep*.[92] In the anti-Oedipal formation that emerges (here, as in so much of Sōseki's fiction, fathers are conspicuously absent), Sanshirō remains a "stray sheep" to the very end.[93] Rather than an ego driven by desire to fill a perceived lack in himself or to establish firm ownership over himself and the objects (including women) around him, Sanshirō is more a desiring machine, deterritorializing and reterritorializing the boundaries of his three worlds to cobble together new circuits and mappings by which to follow his passions—and thereby derail his desire.

At one point, Sanshirō reluctantly decides to visit Mineko to borrow twenty yen from her. Mostly, Sanshirō just wants to see her again, as his head fills "with images of Mineko—her face, her hands, her neckline, the obi and kimono she wore."[94] All the while, he tries to imagine Mineko's attitude toward himself: until she reveals this, he will not know how he should act or think. As he waits in Mineko's parlor for his audience with her, he finds himself staring at his own reflection in a long mirror. Finally, Mineko appears before him—not in person but via reflection. "Sanshirō moved half-seeing eyes to the mirror, and there stood Mineko. . . . Mineko was reflected clearly from the chest upward, holding aside the curtain that hung beyond the door. In the mirror, she looked at Sanshirō. Sanshirō looked at Mineko in the mirror. She smiled."[95]

Sanshirō's whole being comes to him by way of external reflection here. He cannot figure out who he is, or what he feels, unless Mineko first reveals her attitude toward him: "She sat looking straight at him, saying nothing, a smile about her eyes and lips, and the sight of her thus filled Sanshirō with a sweet agony. He could not endure being looked at this way, he began to feel, almost from the moment she sat down."[96] Despite her remarkably familiar tone, Sanshirō cannot figure out where he stands with Mineko. The other here is mysterious, unfathomable, and the self cannot become a unified ego until it can figure out precisely how it is reflected in the desire of that other—a position that could become fixed only through the presence of a mediator. In many ways, *Sanshirō* is an experiment in imagining what an alternative mode of selfhood might look like—a self that strays beyond the triangles of Oedipal desire and self-possession.

This alternative form of selfhood is produced in the novel through the very practice of writing and particularly the practice of writing as translation— what Naoki Sakai calls the *"oscilliation or indeterminacy of personality in translation."*[97] Sōseki mobilizes the heterogeneity opened up through the practice of literary writing to suggest that Sanshirō may not after all have arrived at his presumed destination, that he may never quite own himself.

Sōseki's education and early career preceded the emergence of the standardized modern form of Japanese as a national language. That is to say, like Kafka, he was raised to write in a "blur of languages, and not at all a system of languages."[98] As a glance at the marginalia in the books from his own library and at his notes taken during his research for *Theory of Literature* indicate, Sōseki was equally comfortable in jotting memos to himself in the scripts we identify as Chinese, English, and Japanese. *Theory of Literature* presumes a similar heterogeneity on the part of its reader:

the main body of the argument is written in a form of classical Japanese, but the work is studded with untranslated quotations from English literature and even some from classical Chinese. A single page in the work might include Sōseki's own scientific analysis written in formal Japanese, extended English quotations from poems by Spenser and Byron, and lines from an anonymous classical Chinese poem.[99] The text is a blur of inscription styles, one that—as Sakai suggests—makes it not so much a marker of historical particularity, a trait that distinguishes Meiji Japan from other cultures or eras, but rather a potential site for approaching broader questions about the heterogeneity of language in general and about what is produced through the practice of writing.

Early in his career, Sōseki was also an English teacher, a translator, and a scholar of classical Chinese. As I will explore again in the conclusion to this book, he expressed deep skepticism about conventional modes of translation. But in his novels he repeatedly evokes a more experimental and philosophical mode of translation, and in *Sanshirō* translation becomes a central trope organizing the work.[100] Sanshirō the stray sheep follows his restless wanderings and continually bumps into the problem of translation. Translation in typical representations promises to cross a boundary between two supposedly distinct and homogeneous national languages, to bring them into communication, but Sōseki's novel demonstrates that translation in its actual practice is much more complex—that languages don't belong simply to nations and that words and scripts tend to go astray, like a cat ignoring the boundaries of enclosure, or stray sheep meandering across a commons.

At a dinner party, for example, Sanshirō repeatedly hears foreign words. One of the guests speaks a line of French: "Il a le diable corps" is transcribed in roman letters, with a *katakana* pronunciation gloss provided in superscript, followed immediately by a parenthetical translation into Japanese, presumably for the novel reader's benefit. Yōjirō, on the other hand, repeatedly uses the phrase "*de te fabula*," presented to the reader of the novel in the katakana script often used to transcribe words from foreign languages, with no translation provided. After the dinner, Sanshirō privately asks Yōjirō, "What is *de te fabula*?" The response he gets to his query: "It's Greek."[101]

Sanshirō here is placed in a situation that Sakai has analyzed in detail. For example, a Japanese reader presented with an article that he or she is told is written in Swahili likely cannot read Swahili.

The readers who need translation do not know the language to translate from it; it follows that, in principle, they should not be able to know how

a) 「迷<ruby>ひ<rt>ま</rt></ruby><ruby>子<rt>ひ</rt></ruby>」 → b) 「迷<ruby>へる<rt>ストレイ</rt></ruby><ruby>子<rt>シープ</rt></ruby>」 → c) 「<ruby>stray sheep<rt>ストレイ シープ</rt></ruby>」 →

FIGURE 1.1 Stray sheep and straying scripts.

to identify that language which they do not know. If I were to give them a piece of translation from the original in Hattari and tell them it is from Swahili, therefore, they would never be able to tell if I were lying. . . . This is simply because they do not know how to doubt it, just as we do not doubt that many unknown languages . . . exist in this world.[102]

The representation of translation via what Sakai calls "the schema of configuration" disguises our inability even to recognize a language in the absence of an a priori Regulative Idea, an imaginary being that has a poietic function: I lose ability to see that "my ignorance of a language must necessarily be my ignorance of the fact that I do not know it."[103] "De te fabula," after all, is not Greek, but Latin. Moreover, we might translate it into English as meaning "This fable concerns you": in other words, it means something like "This is not foreign to you."[104] Perhaps Sōseki means to poke fun at Yōjirō's pretentiousness, or perhaps Yōjirō is playing a joke at the expense of Sanshirō's ignorance. Then again, perhaps this is all simply riffing off the English expression, "It's Greek to me." In any case, this slippage is symptomatic of the way translation, writing, and heteroglossia are practiced throughout the novel. As Sanshirō later repeats the phrase "de te fabula" to himself, still ignorant of its meaning, he decides that it "was a phrase that called for dancing."[105]

Let me return here to the problem of stray sheep in the novel and see if I can map out some of their lines of wandering, especially in terms of the practice of literary writing and its relation to ownership.[106] A stray sheep is, of course, a piece of living property that has wandered away from its owner. In this novel, however, stray sheep wander in primarily as a problem of translation and writing. After a sequence in which they encounter a lost child, Mineko and Sanshirō drift away from their friends, and Sanshirō becomes anxious that the others may think that they have become lost. Mineko asks Sanshirō, "Do you know how to translate *maigo* into English?" Sanshirō cannot answer, and so Mineko supplies the answer: "'Stray sheep.' Do you understand?" This query again leaves Sanshirō speechless: "He thought he understood the meaning of 'stray sheep,' but then again perhaps he did not." In terms of script, we move here from maigo (lost child), written with Chinese characters and a *hiragana* superscript pronunciation gloss,

d) 「羊（ひつじ）」 → e) 「迷羊（ストレイシープ）」 → f) 「迷羊（ストレイシープ）、迷羊（ストレイシープ）」

FIGURE 1.1 (cont'd)

indicating a Japanese word (see figure 1.1a), to *suterē shīpu*, the same Chinese characters albeit conjugated with Japanese hiragana differently, and a katakana superscript pronunciation gloss tells us to pronounce this hybrid Japanese/Chinese phrase as the English words *stray sheep* (figure 1.1b).[107]

The next sighting of a stray sheep in the novel arrives in Sanshirō's notes from the philosophy class, already mentioned above. Here, both when the narrator describes the words jotted down in the notebook and when Yōjirō is quoted reading the notes aloud, we get English written in roman letters, with a katakana superscript pronunciation gloss, indicating that we should pronounce the English as English (figure 1.1c)[108] The subsequent appearance comes in a hand-painted postcard that Sanshirō receives, he supposes, from Mineko:

> The sender had drawn a picture on one side of the card. It showed a little stream with shaggy grass on its banks and two sheep lying at the edge of the grass. Across the stream stood a large man with a walking stick. He had a ferocious-looking face modeled closely on the devil in Western paintings. Lest there be any doubt, he had been carefully labeled "Devil" in a phonetic rendering of the English word. The card's only return address, written in tiny script, was "Lost Child." Sanshirō knew who that was, and it thrilled him that she had put two stray sheep in the picture, suggesting that he was the other one. Mineko had included him from the beginning, it seemed. Now at last he understood what she had meant by "Stray sheep."[109]

This postcard, with its suggestion of a triangular relationship, pleases Sanshirō because Mineko seems to be expressing desire for him—but it again renders him speechless, as he finds himself unable to send the expected response to her message. In terms of drifting script and languages, the passage here is attempting to translate a visual image of sheep into written language (echoing the subplot of an attempt by male characters to capture Mineko in an oil painting). In the description of the watercolor on the postcard, the figures are called *hitsuji* written with the standard Chinese character meaning sheep, plus a hiragana pronunciation gloss giving the standard Japanese name for the animal (figure 1.1d). Several of the words in this passage use Chinese characters given katakana pronunciation glosses (stick, devil), and in the end the phrase that Sanshirō believes he has finally grasped is rendered again as *stray sheep*, English in roman letters with a katakana pronunciation gloss (figure 1.1c).

As the novel nears its climax, after Sanshirō learns Mineko will marry another man, he stands outside a church on Sunday morning. He is waiting for Mineko to emerge, and we get a sentence fragment that seems to represent Sanshirō's thoughts, though the attribution of speaker could also be the narrator: "Stray sheep. Stray sheep. The cloud had taken the form of a sheep."[110] Here, Sōseki apparently invents a neologism, a phrase that looks like but is not a Chinese word, using characters that bear a meaning like "stray sheep" and again the katakana gloss assigning an English pronunciation (figure 1.1e). The line Mineko utters to herself after emerging, "For I acknowledge my transgressions, and my sin is ever before me," comes from Psalm 51, a song of triangular desire, in which David repents for having stolen Bathsheba from her husband Uriah.[111] In the biblical story (2 Samuel 12), the prophet Nathan uses a parable about stolen sheep to confront David with his wrongdoing: when he wanted to provide hospitality to a traveler, a rich man owning many sheep chose to slaughter and serve the sole ewe owned by a poor man. When David erupts with anger at the injustice described in the story, Nathan points out that this is precisely what David, who already has many wives, has done to Uriah, stealing the man's wife and killing him.

In other words, in Mineko's utterance outside the church, the stray sheep derive from the Word of God, with all the issues of writing and tangled questions of possession that this entails. Finally, in the last words of the novel, Sanshirō confronts a painting of Mineko and is asked what the title of the portrait should be. Again, Sanshirō is struck dumb: "Sanshirō did not answer him, but to himself he muttered over and over, 'Stray sheep. Stray sheep.'"[112] Here again we find an attempt to translate from visual image to written script, and we learn that Sanshirō apparently speaks to himself (there are no quotation marks setting off the phrase in the original Japanese) in Chinese neologisms accompanied by a Japanese script that instructs him how to pronounce the Chinese as if it were English (figure 1.1f). Stray sheep, indeed.

In this blur of languages and scripts that characterized Sōseki's practice of literature, can we find patterns of usage? Should we be attentive to how what "can be said in one language cannot be said in another" and how "the totality of what can and can't be said varies necessarily with each language and with the connections between these languages"?[113] Stray sheep are a symbol of property that has wandered away from its owner, and a metaphor for a certain kind of wildness. In the drifting scripts that Sōseki unleashes here, stray sheep also become an enactment of the excess produced by literary writing, the way the script of writing exceeds proper boundaries of stable meaning and national language. An ethics of heteroglossia, translation, and passion characterizes Sōseki's work, generating a practice of literature that seeks a relation to the other that is not defined by the schema of configuration. In other words, in *Sanshirō* the practice of translation does not presume the existence of two (or three or four . . .) distinct, homogeneous identities, each characterized by self-possession.

Fredric Jameson, even as he addresses the potential pitfalls of reading Sōseki by way of translation, discusses the "modern irony" that characterizes Sōseki's fiction, "one of inner comfort and familiarity with which, on the inside, each is deeply comfortable; the self as the old clothes we wear around the home—which, however, looks different and unfamiliar, somehow shocking, from the outside."[114] It is the shock that breaks through the illusion of familiarity, a shock available only to someone "outside." This irony "can essentially be described as a brusque movement in which the inside becomes aware . . . that it has an outside in the first place."[115] There is a sense of an unknowable outside that haunts the interiors here, a kind of unintelligible noise of language that derails any desire for stable identification or self-possession. The relation to this external other is enacted through script and through "a pure and intense sonorous material that is always connected to *its own abolition*—a deterritorialized musical sound, a cry that escapes signification, composition, song, words—a sonority that ruptures in order to break away from a chain that is still all too signifying."[116] De te fabula, a phrase that calls for dancing.

There is a noise in *Sanshirō*, a scribbling that gestures toward an exterior reader, a reader who is other and who approaches the text through the attitude of a translator. Such a reader finds in these texts not identity or self-possession but rather, as Karatani suggests, "diversity," or to use Sanshirō's vocabulary, stray sheep.[117] The figurative animal here is not just an instance of metaphor, but of what Akira Lippit calls "an originary metaphor" in which "the animal is already a metaphor, the metaphor an animal. . . . The animal brings to language something that is not a part of language and remains within language as a foreign presence. That is, because the animal is said to lack the capacity for language, its function in language can only appear as an other expression, as a metaphor that originates elsewhere, is transferred from elsewhere."[118] Confronted by its figure, the reader should, like Sanshirō, produce his or her translation not by choosing between one of the three worlds (or languages), but rather by ignoring the boundaries that try to enclose them—by becoming, that is, a stray sheep.

It seems that the attitude through which Sōseki approaches literary practice might best be compared to that of the translator, as defined by Sakai: a "subject in transit." This interrupted subject jams up the schema of cofiguration, a conceptual apparatus that functions to reproduce the mimetic desire for homogeneous identification. In its place, we should consider the attitude of Sōseki the translator as that of one who stands in the gap between "the difference of attitudes and stances," a site of "essential linguistic hybridity inherent in the position of the translator."[119] In this interruptive practice, the translator's desire for identification is displaced by his or her practice. Translators are unable to identify with either the "I" or the "you" in the enunciation, so that the translation becomes "an instance of *continuity in discontinuity* and a poietic social practice that institutes a relation at the site of incommensurability."[120] Sōseki's practice distinguishes science and literature precisely so that he, as translator, can sidestep the desire to identify with either one, becoming in the process a kind of stray sheep, guided only by his passions.

Sōseki's literary practice becomes a laboratory for exploring "affective gestures that refuse alignment along the secure axes of filiation to seek expression outside, if not against, possessive communities of belonging."[121] These gestures open up a commons to be shared with the reader, with no one able to claim exclusive ownership: we are instead invited to lose ourselves in the story. This shared space is characterized by feeling, sentiment, affect: what Sōseki summed up as f in the $(F+f)$ equation that defines literature. Affect, like language, is something inherently shared in common.[122] Literature, the domain defined by the presence of affect, is a relationality that seeks to transcend even boundaries between species, so that animals could not only feel, but express those feelings via literary narratives and thereby "begin the work of postulating an alternative reality."[123] Sōseki's literary practice is less about self-possessing subjects and more about being possessed and losing oneself, a "performance of strange alliance, unlikely kinships, and impossible identification."[124] Stray sheep, bewitching tanuki, talking cats.

* * *

Karatani Kōjin posits that a distinguishing feature of Sōseki's literary practice is the remarkable diversity of genres in which he wrote.[125] A key to reading a work by Sōseki is thus to identify the genre in play. *I Am a Cat*, according to Karatani, is an instance of the encyclopedic genre of anatomy (Karatani cites Northrop Frye's *Anatomy of Criticism*), while "Hearing Things," by contrast, is a romance, and *Sanshirō* adheres to the genre of *shasei*: sketching, derived from the poetics of haiku and haikai. But I would like to argue here that these three works can also be read as fables—specifically modernist fables.

Fables, of course, often take animals as their heroes and narrators. They had a long history in Japan before Sōseki: Aesop's fables had circulated widely in Japanese translations since the 1600s. In their classical form, fables are characterized by extreme laconism and brevity and also by a strong sense of closure and pastness. As Susan Stewart argues, "the fable has always already been dead. . . . It is a tableau form, oriented toward stasis and an eternally transcendent meaning, a meaning by which every element of the plot is encompassed and accounted for. It combines thereby the systematicity of allegory with the totalizing power of symbol; our experience is one of a closure that turns back into an even stronger closure as we read the moral back into the narrative."[126]

Sōseki's modernist fables depart from these norms, however. Sōseki's fabulous narrators playfully dilate narrative time to partake in the pleasures of prolixity, and his works, including the three considered here, are famous for avoiding any sense of narrative closure: nothing is dead in them, not even the dead. The classic fable is monologic; Sōseki's modernist fables are dialogic, even when they take the form of a monologue. Hence, the narrator's death at the end of *I Am a Cat* has not prevented numerous other writers from continuing its story in unauthorized sequels: the story never ends, as other narrators rush in to pick up the thread.[127] Whereas the classical fable often tends toward "the legitimation of territory and property, both private and national," Sōseki's fables work differently, to imagine possible alternatives.[128] After all, "Fable is as fable does."[129]

Sōseki's modernist fables do differently: they look forward rather than backward. The employment of an animal narrator inevitably opens Sōseki to the possible charge of anthropomorphism—that in pretending to move beyond the human to the animal, he merely replicates the human in another guise. But as Joseph Anderton argues, this suspicious reading of animal narrators misses another important possibility.[130] The criticism that human writing in an animal voice inevitably misrepresents the animal too often presumes that human language is capable of adequately representing human experience. Modernist writings like those of Kafka—or, as I am arguing, Sōseki—call precisely this into question. In other words, "the disjunctions that mark the relationship between human and nonhuman animals to an extent also mark the relationship between self and writing," so that we are forced to realize that "writing the self can involve writing the other in the same way that writing the other can involve writing the self."[131] Sōseki's cat, tanuki, and stray sheep become modernist fables not just because as stray or wild animals they escape human regimes of ownership, but also because their very practices of storytelling suggest our inability to own ourselves as human. They write fables of our complex relationship of nonrelationship to human property.

CHAPTER TWO

House under a Shadow

Disowning the Psychology of Possessive Individualism in The Gate

> Private proprietorship cannot be practically abolished until human nature is changed.
>
> WILLIAM JAMES, *Talks to Teachers on Psychology* (1899)

> Human beings are not the "owners" of desires and drives—they don't "have" them. Rather, human beings are the playing out of these impulses, instruments through which trauma is registered.
>
> MARK FISHER, "What Are the Politics of Boredom?" (2005)

The shadow of madness falls across the writings of Natsume Sōseki.[1] In the celebrated preface to *Theory of Literature* (*Bungakuron*, 1907), he recounts his experiences as a government scholar dispatched to London to study English, experiences that led him to undertake an ambitious rethinking of the concept of literature that would result in *Theory of Literature* itself. During his stay abroad, Sōseki notes, he fell victim to depression and was widely rumored among the local Japanese community to have gone mad. Even after he returned to Tokyo, he writes, people still thought him insane—including his own relatives. And yet, "it was thanks to my neurasthenia and to my madness that I was able to compose *Cat*, produce *Drifting in Space*, and publish *Quail Cage*. Thinking about this now, I believe I owe an enormous debt of gratitude to my neurasthenia and madness."[2] Here, madness makes fiction possible: it brings the gift of literature, for which he feels "an enormous debt of gratitude."

In Sōseki's first newspaper novel, *The Poppy* (*Gubijinsō*, 1907), another neurasthenic figure appears. Angered by his stepmother's machinations to marry off her daughter, Kingo vows to abandon his stake in the family's property. He will simply renounce all rights to inheritance from his deceased father. Two friends discuss this apparently crazy behavior:

> "But it's so stupid, right? To just throw away property [*zaisan*] that is naturally his to inherit."
> "But if he doesn't want it, what else can he do?"
> "The reason he doesn't want it is because of his neurasthenia."
> "It isn't his neurasthenia."
> "But if that's not pathological behavior, what is?"
> "There's nothing pathological about it.... That's the type of person Kingo is. If everyone calls it pathological, then everyone is wrong."
> "But it's certainly not healthy!"[3]

Here, the characters treat the act of renouncing property, of giving up what one owns without remuneration, as a symptom of mental illness. But is the madness that causes one to withdraw from property ownership related to the madness that delivers the gift of writing?

The answer I argue for here is yes. For Sōseki, literature—in particular, literature conceived as a kind of madness, as a kind of loss of self—is directly related to questions of ownership. Madness is a form of (spiritual) possession that troubles the possibility of (economic) possession, including self-ownership, and literature is the realm for experimenting with seemingly crazy alternatives. To write literature is to indulge in madness—madness defined, in part, as a withdrawal, voluntarily or involuntarily, from the subject position of owner. This literary madness involves Sōseki in both an appropriation and an overturning of psychology, the new scientific discipline that claimed madness as its special object of knowledge. Responding to the modern property regime of Meiji Japan and to the ways of knowing generated in the modern discipline of psychology, Sōseki explores literature as a realm for playful—sometimes comic—experimentation with alternative modes of sharing our experiences in the world.

To explore these issues, I will take up *The Gate* (*Mon*). Sōseki originally serialized the novel in the *Asahi* newspaper from March through June 1910. The timing is crucial: the work appeared when Japan was on the verge of annexing Korea as part of its expanding empire. In fact, the 1909 assassination of senior statesman Itō Hirobumi in Manchuria by a Korean nationalist crops up in the novel as a shadowy, mystifying topic of conversation.[4] Oyone, the protagonist's wife, confronts her husband, Sōsuke, and his younger brother, Koroku, with a question they cannot answer: "But how did he . . . well, get himself killed?" Sōsuke misunderstands (or pretends to misunderstand) the question and responds that Itō was shot. Oyone persists: "But why did he go to Manchuria?" The two men avoid answering the question directly; Koroku simply avers, "At any rate, Manchuria, Harbin—these places seem to be pretty rough-and-tumble. To me, they just spell danger, somehow."[5] Yet shortly thereafter, when the younger sibling feels let down by his older brother, who pleads "a case of nerves" (*shinkei suijaku*: literally, neurasthenia), Koroku himself threatens to run off to Manchuria or Korea.[6]

Empire is only one of the multiple sources of shadows that darken this novel. *The Gate* also delves into shadows cast by the emerging capitalist economy of white-collar labor and urban anonymity. Sōsuke is a faceless bureaucrat, commuting by streetcar six days a week as he struggles to make ends meet in a new modern economy that seems utterly beyond his capacity to negotiate. Still other shadows derive from more personal matters: *The Gate*'s narrative centers on the story of Sōsuke and Oyone, a married couple whose relationship originates in a past act of betrayal that now, six years later, returns to haunt them—a shadow that is the real cause for Sōsuke's failure to support his younger brother adequately.

Many previous critics, beginning with Maeda Ai, have approached the novel in terms of its setting, the house at the bottom of the cliff (*gake*).[7] This landscape already suggests hierarchies of ownership: the prosperous house atop the cliff is owned and occupied by Sakai, the landlord who leases out the modest dwelling below to Sōsuke and Oyone. The two terrains separated by the cliff will be linked repeatedly through questions of property: a burglar, for example, who inadvertently drops loot stolen from Sakai (along with his own feces) down the cliff into the garden of Sōsuke's house—thereby providing Sōsuke an opportunity to open social relations with his landlord by returning the stolen goods to him. This restoration of absconded property opens up an exchange of gifts between the two households, which in turn establishes relations of friendship between them—and, eventually, a solution to the problem of what to do about younger brother Koroku.

In other words, much of the novel's plot revolves around negotiating the vertical hierarchies symbolized by the cliff. But instead of focusing on the cliff (gake), I center my reading of the novel on its shadows (kage 影). In the opening chapter, for example, after a short discussion with Oyone about the poor state of his nerves, Sōsuke putters around their rented house:

> He opened these [shōji sliding doors] and stepped onto the eastern veranda. Here a high cliff, which seemed to press down upon the eaves of the house, rose from beside the veranda, so that even the morning sun, which should have come streaming in, could not easily disperse the shadows (影). (Mathy translation)[8]

> He opened these as well. Yet even here on the eastern veranda, where one might expect the sun's rays (影) to strike in the morning, at least, they scarcely penetrated at all because of a cliff-like embankment that loomed over this side of the house, sloping down so steeply that it all but brushed the eaves. (Sibley translation)[9]

The original Japanese is ambiguous about this kage: "attate shikarubeki hazu no hi mo yōi ni kage o otasanai." What Mathy translates as "shadows" Sibley translates as "the sun's rays." Both are correct: depending on how the reader imagines this scene, this kage could signify either a dark spot without light, or a bright spot glowing with light.

The cliff is not the only source of shadows darkening Sōsuke's and Oyone's world. In chapter 4, shortly after a description of how Sōsuke's family property seemingly evaporated (much of it literally went up in smoke), we encounter the following description of everyday life in the marriage of Sōsuke and Oyone: "They shared at all times a kind of stoic forbearance or resignation to fate. Almost no ray (影) of hope for the future ever reached them. They spoke little of the past, and at times it even seemed as if they had mutually agreed to avoid the subject."[10]

Here, Mathy's English equivalent for kage is "ray": the shadow becomes a kind of light, rather than darkness. Then, in chapter 17, we encounter the following passage: "The sin of Sosuke and Oyone cast its shadow over their entire lives and engulfed them, so that they felt very much like ghosts adrift in the world of men. They had a vague realization that deep in their hearts, too deep for eye to penetrate, was concealed a dreadful canker. Yet as they faced each other day after day, they pretended to be unaware of this."[11]

Translator Mathy has done something interesting here: he's moved *kage* from the Japanese to a different part of the sentence. Sibley's translation of the passage is more literal: "The union between Sōsuke and Oyone had dyed their existence a somber hue and reduced their presence, they felt, to mere wraiths that barely cast a shadow on the world."[12] But once again, we are faced with an ambiguity: is *kage* here a shadow or is it an image—or both? (We should note, too, that the "dreadful canker" in Mathy's translation is *kekkakusei* [tuberculosis] and that it was during Sōseki's lifetime that diagnosis of this disease shifted to a search for shadows in images of the patient's lungs generated by the new technology of the X-ray scan).[13]

The kage that darken (or illuminate) *The Gate* are frequently haunted by this sort of ambiguity. This ambiguity in turn provides an opening for connecting the novel to the modern science of psychology. In terms of psychology, what is a shadow? As we will see below, one of the notions that Sōseki appropriates from psychology is the definition of a normal, healthy psyche as a continuous, uninterrupted flow—as a stream of consciousness. By contrast, shadows in this novel tend to disrupt and stop up that flow, leading to pathological outbreaks, such as neurasthenia or hysteria. Moreover, such shadows provoke anxiety not only in individual psyches but also in systems of property. When shadows emerge in this novel, people go mad and lines of ownership blur. The effect can be troubling, but it also has its comic side.

The *Kenyusha New Collegiate Japanese-English Dictionary* cites five English equivalents for *kage*: a shadow, light, a reflection, an image, a trace. Other Japanese-English dictionaries list a few more possible equivalents: silhouette, phantom, figure, sign. All of these various, sometimes contradictory, meanings are at work in the kage that fall across the pages of *The Gate*. Unpacking Sōseki's appropriation of psychology means, in many ways, to unpack the novel's complex psychology of shadows—a process that in turn carries us into the hazy fringes of the modern property regime.

THE NEW PSYCHOLOGY

In Sōseki's Japan, it was a matter of common sense that literature was supposed to depict the "psychology" of human characters. Tsubouchi Shōyō's pioneering essay of modern literary criticism, *The Essence of the Novel* (*Shōsetsu shinzui*, 1885–86), had already established the link between literature and psychology (*shinri*). Tsubouchi relied primarily on the work of

Alexander Bain (1818–1903), who in attempting to establish psychology as a scientific discipline in the 1850s and '60s had stressed the importance of locating physiological causes for mental phenomena.[14]

Sōseki himself first studied psychology in the early 1890s under Japan's first professor of the discipline, Motora Yūjirō (1858–1912), at Tokyo Imperial University. There, he was exposed to the work of such figures as Bain and others.[15] Karatani Kōjin has argued that 1890s Japan saw the emergence of a new modern literature in tandem with the discovery of a new kind of interior subjectivity, a Cartesian inner self fundamentally alienated from the external landscape.[16] But at the dawn of the twentieth century, when Sōseki launched into his extensive survey of psychology in preparation for writing *Theory of Literature*, a new generation of psychologists was emerging, one that was trying to distinguish itself from the earlier generation represented by Bain, in part by rejecting the earlier generation's model of an inner self. One problem: introspective observation of the inner self wasn't sufficiently scientific.[17] As Edward Scripture (1864–1945) declared in his 1897 book, *The New Psychology* (a work that Sōseki cites in *Theory of Literature*), introspection in the form of "unaided observation is an inadequate method." Scripture goes on to assert that "we must find a new method" and proposes three possible tools: "statistics, experiment, or measurement."[18] These debates were reported in print in Japan by Motora as early as 1888, with Motora siding with the experimentalists against the introspectionists.[19]

It was primarily this New Psychology that Sōseki read in London.[20] Moreover, the New Psychology was emerging as an important force in Japanese academic life when Sōseki returned to Tokyo in 1903. That year, Sōseki's former teacher Motora would establish Japan's first experimental psychology laboratory at Tokyo Imperial University—the same year in which Sōseki joined the faculty and began delivering the lectures that would ultimately result in *Theory of Literature*. Among Motora's chief disciples was Matsumoto Matatarō (1865–1943), a former classmate and friend of Sōseki's—and in 1903 a faculty colleague of Sōseki's at the Higher Normal School. Matsumoto had studied with both Scripture at Yale and Wilhelm Wundt (1832–1920) at Leipzig.[21]

Sōseki's opening gambit in *Theory of Literature* was to define literature by distinguishing it from science: literature was what science was not. But at the same time Sōseki was trying to define the essence of literature through this distinction, psychology was trying to distinguish itself from literature—trying to establish its own identity as a natural science, a modern discipline that relied on exact measurement and on replicable laboratory experiments that yielded precise quantitative and statistical results. This was part of a general disentanglement of science from literature that characterized the rise of the modern university system with its division into discrete specializations, a trend in which "science's relationship to literature was, first, one of emancipation. The disciplines constituted themselves through the delimitation of a field of knowledge that was carved out from the generalized knowledge of men of letters, and in this sense by becoming sciences they freed themselves from literature."[22]

For psychology, in particular, this meant breaking with its own past as a quasi-literary discipline. The British psychologist Francis Galton (1822–1911) is one of the scientists responsible for this shift—he pioneered the use of statistical methods to map the distribution of various measurable abilities within a population, as well as the degree of correlation between different abilities. His student Cyril Burt (1883–1971) described his mentor's accomplishments in the following manner: "When he [Galton] took it up, individual psychology was just a speculative topic for the fancies of the poet, the novelist, the biographer, and the quack and charlatan on the seaside pier. By the time he left it and handed it on to others, it had been transformed into a reputable branch of natural science—perhaps for mankind the most important branch there is."[23]

Conventional histories of psychology trace its origins back to thinkers—typically philosophers such as Descartes, Locke, and Kant—who tried to think about how we think. Most early professors of psychology, such as William James at Harvard or Wundt at Leipzig, actually held seats in departments of philosophy. *Shinrigaku*, the standard Japanese term for psychology, first appeared in the mid-1870s as a translation for "mental philosophy"; it would take a couple of decades before the term stabilized into its current usage.[24] Self-reflection on the interior—introspection—as a formal investigatory technique was a product of the early nineteenth-century efforts by Bain and others to separate psychology as a science from the domain of philosophy.[25] But by Sōseki's day, introspection was regarded by many as unscientific, as a symptom of the all-too-literary origins that the discipline needed to overcome in order to become a real science.[26]

Sōseki was familiar with the controversies over introspection. In one of the books he read, *Principles of Physiological Psychology*, Wilhelm Wundt declares, "We take issue, upon this matter, with every treatment of psychology that is based on simple self-observation or on philosophical presuppositions."[27] Wundt was an important pioneer in the rise of the new scientific psychology, establishing in 1879 the first modern experimental laboratory in the field at Leipzig (where he trained a number of Japanese students, including Matsumoto). While Wundt did not reject introspection, he insisted that it be pursued only under rigorously controlled laboratory conditions and that its data was relevant only to a limited domain of the range of problems covered by the discipline of psychology. Nonetheless, it was in many ways Wundt's continued reliance on the notion of an inner self as derived from philosophy that ultimately led to what one historian calls his "repudiation" by the field.[28]

Some psychologists would continue to argue for the relevance of introspection. Figures such as Edward B. Titchener (1867–1927), a student of Wundt and English translator of the latter's *Principles of Physiological Psychology*, advocated "systematic experimental introspection" as a scientifically valid method, but by the time of World War I the discipline had largely rejected this position.[29] Sōseki himself read the work of psychologists who advocated for the continuing validity of introspection, and from his marginal comments we get a sense of where he stood in these debates. G. F. Stout (1860–1944), for example, in his *Analytic Psychology* (1886) insisted on the importance of introspection for the discipline, even as it transformed itself into a laboratory science. Stout maintains that psychology has become a "positive science of mental process" and recounts how the discipline has become more rigorous in scientific testing of its hypotheses since its origins as a branch of philosophy.[30] As we read on, however, we realize that Stout is in fact performing a sort of rearguard action for the old psychology. While not denying the potential importance of physiological laboratory studies of the brain and nervous system, Stout insists on the priority of introspection: without starting from introspection of the contents of consciousness, he argues, we would not know what to look for physiologically as its physical counterpart.

In Sōseki's marginal comments on such passages, we find a skeptical reader. Stout argues that "the distinctive aim of the psychologist is to investigate mental events themselves, not their mechanical accompaniments or antecedents."[31] Written in the margins next to this in Sōseki's copy, we find the comment (in English): "This is your aim, not all the psychologists." Next to a passage in which Stout insists on our inability to connect with any certainty mental and physiological processes, we find another handwritten rebuttal: "Too bold!"[32] Finally, next to a passage in which Stout attempts to defend the possibility of introspective analysis by distinguishing the relatively stable object of consciousness from the fleeting presentations of it that might appear to consciousness at any given moment, we find the following dismissive comment: "I am very sorry Mr. Stout."[33] In other words, given the choice between the old psychology that sought continued relevance for introspection and the New Psychology's rejection of introspection as unscientific, Sōseki seems to have preferred the latter.

The rejection of introspection was related to another tenet widely shared in the New Psychology. The old psychology had relied on a dualistic worldview, in which human psychological experience is divided into two distinct realms, the inner life and the exterior world, mind and body. The New Psychology, however, working under "historical conditions that reduced language and spirit to epiphenomena of a neuroelectrical data flow," rejected this, adopting in its place a monistic view of the psychological subject.[34] Again, Wundt's *Principles of Physiological Psychology* is representative: "We must, however, remember that the life of an organism is really one; complex, it is true, but still unitary. We can, therefore, no more separate the processes of bodily life from conscious processes than we can mark off an outer experience, mediated by sense perception, and oppose it, as something wholly separate and apart, to what we call 'inner' experience, the events of our own consciousness."[35]

In *Outlines of Psychology*, another work that Sōseki owned and read, Wundt attacked the notion that psychology provided a "science of inner experience." "There is, then," Wundt argues, "no such thing as an 'inner sense' which can be regarded as an organ of introspection, and as distinct from the outer senses, or organs of objective perception."[36] Wundt rejects any division between inner and outer sense, and argues that both are inseparably linked with external objects that we perceive. Rejecting the dualistic Cartesian model of interiority that characterized earlier versions of psychology, the New Psychology asserted that there was only one unified plane of psychological experience: interior and exterior, mind and body, were linked in a single unified circuit of electrical impulses conveyed from the outside world through the nervous system to the brain, which in turn responded to these impulses with further electrical charges that were conveyed back along the nervous system and out into the object world as motor responses. As Sōseki would remark in his 1907 lecture, "Philosophical Foundations of the Literary Arts" ("Bungei no tetsugakuteki kiso"):

> Without the self there are no objects, and likewise without objects there can be no self. "Objects" and "self" necessarily appear in tandem. We use two different words to express them only to make things easier to understand

and as a matter of fundamental principles. Since the two cannot, in fact, be distinguished from one another, we don't really need a separate word to express their mutually indistinguishable status. Accordingly, the only thing that clearly exists is consciousness. And we ordinarily refer to this continuous stream of consciousness by the name "life."[37]

This is the line of psychology that will lead in the twentieth century to such work as the behaviorism of John B. Watson and B. F. Skinner.

A third aspect of New Psychology that appealed to Sōseki was its insistence that consciousness was not a thing, but rather a continuously unfolding process.[38] In this view, our psychological experience is an uninterrupted flow, a circuit in which stimuli are fed into the nervous system and brain, provoking mental responses in the subject, which in turn lead to embodied actions that alter the external world. The passage from the 1907 "Philosophical Foundations" lecture quoted above continues, "When I refer to a continuous stream here, it includes the sense that consciousness is in flux," after which Sōseki enumerates the specific qualities of this fluidity.[39] Later in the lecture, he notes, "we seem unwilling to interrupt this continuity. In other words, we don't want to die. We wish nothing more than for this continuity to continue. I can't explain why we wish for that. Nobody can explain that." In the end, he argues, we can only assume that "consciousness tends toward more continuousness."[40] A healthy mind is one that remains in constant motion; interruptions in this continuity, by contrast, lead to psychoses or neuroses. This stress on fluidity is the flip side of the monistic model: mind and body, inner and outer world are one precisely because of the constant trafficking that links them together in a single flow.

WILLIAM JAMES AND THE STREAM OF CONSCIOUSNESS

This notion of a stream of consciousness is especially associated with the work of William James (1842–1910). In James, moreover, the fluidity of consciousness is inherently connected to questions of property: the constant movement of consciousness is what makes self-ownership possible in the first place. James's thought had a deep impact on Sōseki, as many previous scholars have demonstrated.[41] Sōseki first encountered James's thought in the early 1890s, while still a university student. The journal *Tetsugaku zasshi*, which Sōseki helped edit from 1891 to 1893, printed articles introducing James and his *Principles of Psychology* (1890, hereafter abbreviated as *Principles*). Motora Yūjirō, Sōseki's professor at Tokyo Imperial University, likewise published articles in the early 1890s on James's *Principles* and almost certainly discussed the work in lectures that Sōseki attended. As we will see in chapter 3, Motora received his PhD at Johns Hopkins University in 1888, studying under G. Stanley Hall—a student of William James's.[42]

But it was Sōseki's stay in London that fully ignited his interest in James. When Sōseki arrived late in 1900, James was the talk of the town, following his influential British lecture tours of 1899 and 1900. James's fame in England grew further in 1901–2 when he visited Edinburgh to deliver the Gifford Lectures on Natural Religion, subsequently published as *The Varieties of Religious Experience* (1902; hereafter abbreviated as *Varieties*). While in England, Sōseki purchased copies of both *Principles* and *Varieties*, and the underlining and marginal comments written in his copies of both show that he read them with care.[43] His notes indicate that after returning to Japan he reread these works around 1907—the year *Theory of Literature* appeared.[44] Later, while recuperating from a near-fatal illness after completing *The Gate*, he would read James's *A Pluralistic Universe* (1909; hereafter abbreviated as *Pluralistic*). Sōseki's autobiographical reminiscence of this period in his life, "Omoide no koto" (Things remembered, 1910–11), describes the strong impact that work had on him—in particular, its introduction of Henri Bergson's thought.

> From my standpoint as a literary writer [*bungakusha*], I read with great interest how the Professor [James], relying on nothing else, takes as his basis concrete reality and then by way of analogies crosses into the domain of philosophy. I don't necessarily dislike dialectics. Nor do I arbitrarily reject intellectualism. But I was especially pleased to find a kind of tacit understanding, an intimate proximity between the views I embrace in terms of literature and the ideas the Professor [James] expresses with regard to philosophy.[45]

Previous scholarship has located traces of James's ideas in virtually all of Sōseki's fiction. There are direct references to James in both *I Am a Cat* (*Wagahai wa Neko de aru*, 1905–6) and *And Then*, and in particular the works "Ten Nights of Dreams" ("Yume jūya," 1908), *The Miner* (*Kōfu*, 1908), and *To the Spring Equinox and Beyond* (*Higan sugi made*, 1912) have been connected to James.[46]

For our purposes, the association with James is particularly fruitful because of the role property plays in his thought. The link between early twentieth-century psychology—with its languages of investment, lack and surplus, and desire—and capitalist market economies has been frequently noted. As early as 1926, Lewis Mumford had criticized James for his "persistent use of financial metaphors," which Mumford saw as a sign of "acquiescence" with the Gilded Age capitalism that had undermined American culture since the Civil War.[47] In particular, James's *Principles* provides one of the clearest turn-of-the-century statements of subjectivity as ownership, of "possessive individualism." As Walter Benn Michaels argues, the model of selfhood that James presents in it is fundamentally implicated in a market economy, with its presumptions of private property as an essential and even natural entity.[48]

In *Principles*, James defines consciousness and the self through a number of metaphors, most famously that of a flowing stream or current. But if consciousness is perpetual flux, how is its continuity maintained? If its one constant is change, how do I know I am the same "me" today as I was yesterday, or the day before?[49] To answer this question, James resorts to yet another metaphor. There are two kinds of "me," and one of these owns the other. Self-identity across time is achieved through a system of property. "For common-sense insists that the unity of all the selves is not a mere appearance of similarity or continuity, ascertained after the fact. She is sure that it involves a real belonging to a real Owner, to a pure spiritual entity of some kind."[50] Using the metaphor of a herdsman who owns cattle to explain this self-as-owner, James argues that it is "the real, present onlooking, remembering, 'judging thought' or identifying 'section' of the stream. This is what collects—'owns' some of the past facts which it surveys, and disowns the rest,—and so makes a unity that is actualized." Calling this version of the self "the Thought" to distinguish it from the past selves that it owns, he continues:

> How would it be if the Thought, the present judging Thought, instead of being in any way substantially or transcendentally identical with the former owner of the past self, merely inherited his "title," and thus stood as his legal representative now? It would then, if its birth coincided exactly with the death of another owner, *find* the past self already its own as soon as it found it at all, and the past self would thus never be wild, but always owned, by a title that never lapsed.[51]

Hence, consciousness consists of a constant flow of title transfers, a kind of inheritance plot in which the Thought acquires property and then instantly becomes itself (along with all of its possessions) the property of a subsequent Thought. "Each Thought is thus born an owner and dies owned, transmitting whatever it realized as its Self to its own later proprietor." Or again, "Who owns the last self owns the self before the last, for what possesses the possessor possesses the possessed."[52]

As for the Thought itself, it remains unknowable and ungraspable. It can only own, and can be owned only retroactively, after it has stopped being the Thought. James here is attempting to patch over an objection to introspection as a method raised by Comte and others: that introspection as a method split consciousness into two, the thinker and the observer of the thinker, and in doing so altered the very object it was supposed to observe. James's proposed solution is to shift from introspection to retrospection: one observes the objects of consciousness at a slight delay, after they have stopped being consciousness itself and become rather its properties.[53] This involves a process of reduction through selective memory: "If we remembered everything, we should on most occasions be as ill off as if we remembered nothing. It would take as long for us to recall a space of time as it took the original time to elapse, and we should never get ahead with our thinking."[54] This reduction is what transforms past selves into objects that can be possessed via retrospection.

How does the present-moment self recognize its property, its past selves? Ownership for James is guaranteed not by contract or other arbitrary social convention, but rather is something natural, embodied. One recognizes one's property through a kind of bodily sensation. "A uniform feeling of 'warmth,' of bodily existence," an "animal warmth" that is "the brand from which they can never more escape" pervades all of our past selves.[55] As James extends this metaphor of cattle branding to describe how the present-moment self can sort through various pasts and identify those to which it holds title, he again stresses that ownership is not simply conventional or arbitrary: "No beast would be so branded unless he belonged to the owner of the herd. They are not his because they are branded; they are branded because they are his."[56] Property is essential to the early James; the notion of overthrowing ownership systems is not simply unthinkable, it would be madness.

Moreover, for James, actual material property provides a fundamental component of our sense of self. "*In its widest possible sense*, however, *a man's Self is the sum total of all that he* CAN *call his*, not only his body and his psychic powers, but his clothes and his house, his wife and children, his ancestors and friends, his reputation and works, his lands and horses, and yacht and bank-account."[57] As with the memories of past selves that the present-moment self owns, one recognizes one's material property through an involuntary embodied response. James cites the German psychologist Adolf Horwicz approvingly to the effect that "our own possessions in most cases please us better [not because they are ours], but simply because we know them better, 'realize' them more intimately, feel them more deeply."[58] Horwicz goes on to assert that "we *live closer* to our own things and so feel them more thoroughly and deeply" (the first part of this passage is underlined in Sōseki's copy).[59] As with our spiritual and social selves, the objects that constitute our material selves come "with a glow and a warmth; for the thought of them infallibly brings some degree of organic emotion in the shape of quickened heart-beats, oppressed breathing, or some other alteration . . . in the general bodily tone."[60] Likewise, loss of property leads to depression, to "a sense of the shrinkage of our personality."[61]

We see in such passages what C. B. Macpherson has termed "possessive individualism."[62] In the liberal tradition of psychology, characterized by Bain and the early James and allied with the worldview of such figures as Locke and J. S. Mill, we find a tendency to posit the social right to property ownership as the most fundamental of human rights, as the foundation of all human freedom and morality. Under the doctrine of possessive individualism, moreover, a relationship of ownership becomes the primary means for explaining the individual self. This doctrine became a crucial ideological counterpart to modern property systems in Japan and elsewhere, as well as to the disciplinary regimes that mold modern citizen-subjects. Moreover, temporal continuity in self-identification—the ability, that is, to continuously appropriate and integrate into the present-moment self the past moments of that self—became integral to the definition of the proper individual subject, one whose level of civilization was indicated by its ability to appropriate property, both in its own labor and in the objects of the world.[63] To lack this capacity was to risk being labeled an improper subject, an imperfect sovereign—one incapable of ownership, a savage or a madman.[64]

THEORY OF LITERATURE AND PSYCHOLOGY

How did Sōseki adopt and revise the ideas he borrowed from James and other figures from the discipline of psychology? In *Theory of Literature*, Sōseki takes the notion of consciousness as a flow or wave and uses it to derive the famous $(F+f)$ formula that grounds his definition of literature: "One can perhaps approach the form of literary substance with the expres-

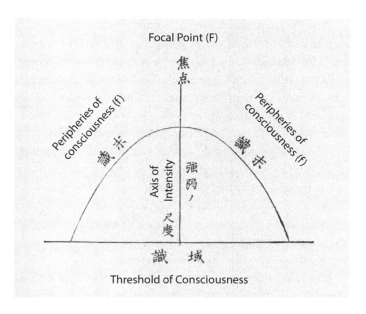

Focal Point (F)

焦
点

Peripheries of consciousness (f)

Peripheries of consciousness (f)

識末

識末

Axis of Intensity

強
弱
ノ

尺
度

識　域

Threshold of Consciousness

FIGURE 2.1 The waveform of consciousness in literary substance in *Theory of Literature*.

sion (F + f). F here indicates impressions or ideas at the focal point of attention, while f signifies the emotions that attend them. In this case, the formula stated above signifies impressions and ideas in two aspects, that is to say, as a compound of cognitive factor F ('large F'), and the emotional factor f ('small f')."[65] He illustrates this by way of a diagram (figure 2.1; I have inserted *F* and *f* into Sōseki's original figure for clarity's sake). As Sōseki explains,

> The moment-by-moment activity of consciousness takes the shape of a waveform, and if represented by a graph would look like the figure below. . . . As you can see, the summit of the waveform, that is to say, the focal point is the clearest portion of consciousness, and before and after this point one finds the so-called peripheries or threshold of consciousness. What we call our conscious experience typically takes the form of a continuous series of these psychological waveforms.[66]

Sōseki cites Lloyd Morgan's *An Introduction to Comparative Psychology* (1894) as his source, but we can find similar language in works by James.[67]

Sōseki goes on to argue that scientific content or substance consists only of *F*, but that in order for something to qualify as literature, it also has to include the emotional factor, f. In other words, when Sōseki looks into the mirror of science in order to define literature, it is the presence of f, the emotional fringe or affect, that secures the identity of literature and distinguishes it from science. For Sōseki, both F and f, cognitive and emotional factors, mark the truth and actuality of human psychology. But only literature can accurately comprise both—and this is what renders it valuable in the face of science, which can only provide access to F.

The focal point F is situated at the peak of consciousness, the most clearly defined image at the center of cognition. By contrast, f hovers at the fringes, the site of amorphous emotional responses that color the focal image. We can think of F as marking denotation, whereas f marks connotation—or again, F as marking signification and f as marking the rhetorical functions of poetic language.[68] The latter is also the site of subconscious associations that link one thought to another.[69]

Crucially, too, there is a temporal component to $(F+f)$. Figure 2.1 represents a single instant of consciousness, artificially cut out from the continuous flow that is consciousness's essence.[70] The waveform here should be imagined together with another arc, and then another, and another, as successive fs rise from the margins to temporarily occupy the peak F position, only then to recede and be replaced in the next moment by yet another f-become-F: the continuously flowing stream of consciousness. Sōseki provides a concrete example of how this might work:

> Let's say we have a person standing before St. Paul's Cathedral. Suppose that as he gazes upon that splendid architecture, his eyes move gradually from the pillars at the bottom section to the balustrade at the upper portion and finally reach the high point at the tip of the cupola. At first, while gazing at the pillars, that portion of the structure is the only part perceived clearly and distinctly, while the rest only enters the field of vision indistinctly. However, in the instant the eyes move from the pillars to the balustrade, the perception of the pillars begins to attenuate, and simultaneously the perception of the balustrade gains in clarity and distinctness. The same phenomenon is observed in the movement from the balustrade to the cupola. When one recites a familiar poem or listens to a familiar piece of music, it is the same. That is to say, when one isolates for observation a moment of consciousness from the continuity of a particular conscious state, one can see that the preceding psychological state begins to attenuate, while the portion to follow, by contrast, is gradually raised in distinctness through anticipation. This is not only something we

can feel in our daily experience; it has been precisely verified by scientific experiment.[71]

Translated into the $(F + f)$ formula, F marks the focal point of consciousness in the present moment. Assuming a left-to-right flow, the f to the right marks the position to which the F of the previous moment has descended after retreating from the crest of the wave; the f to the left marks the still-amorphous cognition that in a subsequent moment will ride the flow of consciousness to the peak of the wave and become the next F. Translated into William James's language, F marks the position of the Thought, the owner in the present moment of all previous fs (and all of their possessions). In the next moment, when this F retreats to the fringes of consciousness and becomes f, this Thought will shift from owner to owned. The implication is that if this smooth flow should break down, mental illness would erupt. Simultaneously, the ownership system of possessive individualism would be thrown into flux: the hierarchical distinction between owner and property would collapse into chaos. The result would be anarchy, madness, and—as I argue below—literature.

BLOCKED STREAMS OF CONSCIOUSNESS

After this long detour, we can now return to *The Gate* and its depiction of consciousness. Komori Yōichi points to *The Miner* (*Kōfu*, 1908) as a striking instance in Sōseki's fiction of the model of consciousness found in his *Theory of Literature*, while Joseph Murphy argues similarly for "The Tower of London" ("Rondon tō," 1905), with its "consistent attention to the ebb and flow of the narrator's consciousness" forming an "experimental embodiment" of the ideas explicated in *Theory of Literature*.[72] A similar case can be made for *The Gate*. We find many passages in the novel where, akin to the St. Paul's Cathedral passage above, Sōseki represents in meticulous detail the flow of consciousness: how external sense stimuli flow in through the nervous system, producing a constantly moving focal point of consciousness, plus its fringes—the receding previous focal point, the emerging subsequent focal point, and the embodied motor responses that this flow generates and which in turn reshape the external world.

For example, an extended passage in chapter 2 depicts a stroll through Tokyo that Sōsuke takes out of a desire for stimulation. Sōsuke in his weekday commutes to his office "was in the habit of simply passing through these places in a daze and had not recently experienced even a moment's awareness that he lived in a thriving metropolis."[73] Accordingly, he decides one Sunday afternoon to allow the sensations of the urban landscape to sweep over him.[74] He boards a streetcar, studies the other passengers, and takes in the advertising posters overhead: "On his weekday rides these went completely unnoticed by Sōsuke, but now he causally glanced up at the first poster, for a moving company, and read the caption: WE MAKE MOVING EASY." He moves on to absorb other advertising placards: "Sōsuke took a good ten minutes perusing all the posters three times over. Not that he had any desire to buy the items or attend the events advertised; rather, he derived considerable satisfaction simply from having found time for the advertisements to impress themselves on his consciousness, and beyond that, the mental leisure to read through each of them with complete comprehension."[75]

He gets off the streetcar and stares at a display of foreign books in a shop window: "For a while he just stood in front of the window gazing at the brilliant gilt letters embossed on red or blue or striped or otherwise patterned book covers. He could, of course, understand the titles, but they aroused in him not the slightest curiosity about what was contained inside."[76] He continues his stroll down the street, taking in the sights and sounds of a watchmaker, an umbrella shop, a haberdashery. He buys a *daruma*-shaped balloon from a street vendor sitting "in the shadows around the corner."[77]

In Sibley's translation, this sequence continues for five pages. In terms of plot development, absolutely nothing happens. Clearly, Sōseki's primary goal here is to delineate something about this character Sōsuke and his consciousness—to trace the wanings and waxings of the protagonist's perceptions as he meanders through the cityscape, exploring how external stimuli feed into his perception, producing responses and reactions that then feedback through his body into the environment around him. The reverie ends when Sōsuke encounters yet another shadow: he looks up to the evening skies, sees a "dark shadow [*kurai kage*] . . . stretching across the damp pavement" and realizes that it is time to return home.[78]

A similar passage occurs in chapter 5 when Sōsuke visits a dentist's office. He takes in the decor of the waiting room, gazing "at the white wall reflected from where he was sitting in a full-length mirror," then picks up magazines at random. One magazine is titled, ironically, *Success*: Sōsuke notes how little his own life has in common with success. But two lines of a Chinese poem leap up off the page into his stream of consciousness. "After he put the magazine aside, the poem alone continued to reverberate in his mind."[79] He then enters the dentist's office proper, and again we follow the stream of stimuli coursing through his nervous system: "he felt a delightful sensation of ease settle over his shoulders, down his back, and around his waist. He simply lay back and gazed at the gas pipe that hung from the ceiling." This experimentation with quasi-stream-of-consciousness narration takes a comic turn when the dentist treats Sōsuke's toothache: "The man proceeded to drill a hole in the tooth's root with a whirring machine; next, he passed a long, wirelike devise through the hole; finally, after sniffing at the wire's tip, he drew out a thin strand of some substance. 'I've removed this much of the nerve,' he said, showing it to Sōsuke."[80] All through the novel, we are told that the problem with Sōsuke is his nerves: his nervous tension, his neurasthenia. Here the dentist holds the threadlike nerve tissue up to display it to Sōsuke, confronting him with the physical material of the body responsible for conveying the flow of stimuli. This strand of nerve tissue in turn becomes a visual stimulus that is conveyed along his (faulty) nervous system to his brain.

In such sequences, Sōseki experiments with capturing in prose the fluid nature of consciousness. If the flow should stop, so too would consciousness: movement is fundamental to its nature.[81] This is true not only of individual consciousness but also of collective social consciousness, Sōseki would argue. For example, in *Theory of Literature* he describes the nature of the shared literary taste of an era—a collective *F* that by its nature must remain in constant motion.

> Just as it is clear that this characteristic [a shared literary taste] will exist, it is also undeniable that it will change. The cause of change is as easily discerned in discrete parts of the individual consciousness as it is in the totality of an individual consciousness and in the consciousness of the entire group. To put it simply and subjectively we might offer the obvious explanation that consciousness changes because people grow tired of one thing and move on to others [ken'en]. In his *Pain, Pleasure, and Aesthetics* [Henry Rutgers] Marshal argues that the difference between pleasure and pain has to do with time. He argues that there is no qualitative difference between the two but that one will change to the other with the passage of a certain amount of time. On this view pleasure and pain are not objectively different. Rather, it is in the nature of our constitution [soshiki] that the duration of a pleasurable feeling past a certain point will transform it into pain.[82]

If any specific *F* stays fixed at the pinnacle of consciousness, failing to move on, it will gradually cause discomfort. In other words, a stream of consciousness that becomes blocked and unable to flow smoothly will generate anxiety, stress, and fatigue.

We see this sort of description in the novel *The Gate* as well. When social relations or everyday life stream forward in a lively current, like the flow of wind that provides a reigning trope in the novel, we sense healthy vitality.[83] But when they get blocked up, the result is anxiety and stress. We are told that the young Sōsuke (that is, before he met Oyone) was an energetic, vivacious person. He "had many friends, to tell the truth, almost everyone without exception who came within range of his laughing eyes became his friends."[84] His mental state matched this robust vitality with a continuous, forward-moving flow. He wandered Kyoto, "immersed in these new sensations" with "the warm blood of youth still coursing through his veins" so that his "racing pulse only caused his whole body to tingle with nervous energy."[85]

> Sōsuke's eyes in those days were always in search of something new. Once nature had displayed to him the colour of her four seasons, he felt no need to revive the images of the past year by going to view once again the flowers of spring or the maple leaves of autumn. Wishing, above all, to live life to the full, he found only the living present or the future, which was coming to birth, of any consequence. The fading past was a phantom [幻影] of such little value that it might as well have been a dream. . . . He was still too alive to be able to spend much time on the half-slumbering past.[86]

Note that *kage* (shadow) shows up again in this passage, as the second character in the word Mathy translates as "phantom" (*gen'ei*).

After the scandal of betraying their friend Yasui, Sōsuke's 'stealing' Oyone in order to marry her, the couple find themselves ostracized by the world. The structure of their consciousness changes dramatically, both individually and socially. They are cut off from the continual flow of changing focus points that characterizes a healthy consciousness.

> It was natural that their lives could not escape monotony. They . . . denied themselves the opportunity to experience directly the variety that life in normal society offers. While living in the city, it was as if they had turned their backs on the privileges accorded to cultured city people. Occasionally they were keenly aware of the lack of variety in their daily lives. They never experienced the slightest feeling of boredom with one another or desired for more than they possessed, and yet each had a clear realization that the rhythm of their lives was too jejune and lacking in stimulation. That they

had spent these long years in daily repetition of the same routine, however, was not because they had from the first lost all interest in the outside world, but rather because this world had placed them in isolation, then turned its cold back upon them.[87]

Sōsuke's problem in a nutshell: after his scandalous marriage to Oyone, the flow from f to F has gotten stuck, both in his individual consciousness and in his social relations. His consciousness no longer streams smoothly from one F to the next. Instead, the shadow of the past persists in the present-moment focal point of consciousness, refusing to move on and cede its position. He has, that is, the kind of psychological disorder that Eugène Minkowski would identify a decade later, a patient for whom "every day was an exasperating monotony of the same words, the same complaints, until one felt that this being had lost all sense of necessary continuity" and in whom "propulsion toward the future . . . seemed to be totally lacking."[88] The opening pages of the novel foreshadow this pathology when Sōsuke finds himself unable to recall the Chinese character for *ima*: "now." The result is stress, monotony, and—specifically—neurasthenia.

The novel draws a sharp contrast between Sōsuke and Oyone's monotonous routine and the lively world of their landlord, Sakai. After establishing relations with Sakai via the burglary incident, Sōsuke begins to frequent his landlord's house. As a result of contact with the vivacious household atop the cliff, Sōsuke's own stream of consciousness seems to resume its flow, regaining the ability to put the past behind him.

> Ordinarily he [Sōsuke] disliked visiting people. . . . For one thing, he had no time for social visits. Sakai was the exception. Occasionally, even when he had no particular business to see him about, he would go to Sakai's and spend some time chatting to him. And yet, Sakai himself was one of the most sociable people he was ever likely to meet. . . . Sitting with this confirmed optimist, Sōsuke could forget the past. He even wondered if he himself might not have become a man like Sakai had he been allowed to develop normally.[89]

Under the influence of Sakai, Sōsuke's stream of consciousness temporarily resumes flowing and he is able momentarily to move on: the shadow of his past sin finally retreats from the position of focal point F.

Paradoxically, it is also through Sakai that the shadow of the past comes flooding back in to overwhelm Sōsuke's mind. Sōsuke learns from Sakai that Yasui, the friend he betrayed to steal away Oyone, is now a colleague of Sakai's brother, that the two of them are currently "adventurers" on the Asian continent—and that they are both due for a visit to Sakai's house. Once more, shadows possess Sōsuke: the penumbras of empire and of Sōsuke and Oyone's shameful past return to the focal point of his consciousness, freezing in place there and refusing to fade away into pastness.

In a novel consisting of twenty-three chapters, it is not until chapter fourteen that the reader finally encounters a flashback that narrates the fatal sin of Sōsuke and Oyone: their origins as a couple in the betrayal of Yasui. The narrator relates the story of Sōsuke's days as a student in Kyoto, of his close friend Yasui, and of the mysterious woman Yasui takes up living with. The first glimpse Sōsuke catches of Oyone comes while he visits Yasui's house. The scene is depicted as a movement from sunlight into darkness, with Oyone herself presented as a literal shadow.

> The day was hot with the lingering heat of summer, and Sōsuke still carried an umbrella with him to university. Placing the umbrella against the front lattice, he peered inside the house and caught a fleeting glimpse of a woman dressed in a large-patterned yukata. From the lattice it was possible to see, though but dimly, quite far into the house. Sōsuke stood and watched until the yukata-clad figure [後影] vanished at the back. . . . This silent, shadowy figure [影のように静かな女] was Oyone.[90]

Shortly thereafter the two finally meet. Yasui leaves them alone as he runs an errand. At this point, they have their first conversation.

> Whenever this extremely short conversation came to mind, word for word, Sōsuke realized again how ordinary, even insipid, it had been; and he marveled that words of so little colour could have dyed both of their futures a deep red. The red, with the passing of the days, had lost its brilliance. The flame which had scorched them had, through a natural process, changed colour and turned black, and their life together had become submerged in darkness. When Sōsuke looked back over the past and retraced the course that their relationship had taken, he realized deep within him how this first simple exchange of words had cast a shadow over their lives [自分らの歴史を濃く彩った]. . . . Sōsuke remembered in great detail those few minutes when he and Oyone were left standing together at the gate. He remembered that their shadows [影] were bent so that the upper halves fell upon the mud wall. He remembered that since Oyone held a parasol in her hand, it was the formless shadow [影] of the parasol—and not the shadow of her head—that was cast upon the wall. . . . He remembered that Oyone, para-

sol still raised, had gone to stand in the shade of the willow tree, though there was not much coolness to be found there. He remembered taking a step backwards and noting the contrast between the purple parasol with a white stripe at the fringe and the willow leaves, which still retained much of their colour.

Every detail was still engraved upon his memory, although there had been nothing remarkable in the encounter. . . . The impressions of that day remained long afterwards in his mind. Even when he had returned home, taken a bath, and sat down before his lamp, the sight of Yasui and Oyone was impressed upon his eyes, as if it were a painting hanging there before him.[91]

From this moment, time has stopped: before meeting Oyone, Sōsuke was interested only in the unfolding stimuli of the present, never pausing in the past, but now the flow of images across his consciousness has gotten stuck. When the shadow of Oyone rises to the position of F, it jams the machinery of his consciousness. A cinematic unfolding of time has congealed into a still-life painting: "Every detail was still engraved upon his memory."

In this passage, *kage* signifies both a dark fringe, the absence of light around a focal image, and the brightly lit focal image itself. In other words, the shadow that is Oyone in Sōsuke's perception simultaneously occupies the positions of both F and f. The succession of waves of consciousness has stopped because the same mental impression occupies both the focal point and the peripheries of his perception. Sōsuke, who was once only interested in chasing after the present, is now unable to move beyond what is repeatedly described as the dark, shadowy past that chains him to Oyone. Its image remains stuck in both the focal point and the fringes of his consciousness, blurring the distinction between those two positions.

This is one reason we find the word *kage* used so often in *The Gate*, especially in passages describing streams of consciousness. William James in *Principles* discusses the relationship between the intense focal point of consciousness and its less intense fringes in terms of a contrast between light and darkness; the fringes around the focal point of consciousness that determine our emotional relation to it are, James writes, its "penumbra," a "shadowy scheme."[92] But in Sōseki's Japanese, *kage* can signify both the shadowy, affective periphery of our perceptual field and the shining focal image at the center of that field. In terms of the waveform of consciousness, *kage* can indicate either F or f: the focal point of consciousness in the present moment, or the emotional fringes that linger around it as the past traces and future anticipations coloring it. The semantic confusion that the word *kage* introduces, undermining the distinction between *F* and *f*, ends up disrupting the smooth flow of consciousness that psychological health demands.

A mirror is one of the places we encounter a kage. Frequently in Sōseki's fiction, mirrors are used as a surface for accessing a sort of alternate universe, often that of a character's subconscious mind.[93] In chapter 13 of *The Gate*, in preparation for New Year's, Sōsuke visits a barbershop. There, he ponders his stagnant life as he waits his turn for a haircut: can a new year really come to him and Oyone?

> As he sat by the heating stove smoking a cigarette and waiting his turn, Sōsuke felt himself ineluctably swept forward by a force beyond his control and, along with the faceless tide of humanity, being propelled toward the New Year. Although in fact he had no fresh expectations for the year that lay ahead, he was unwittingly goaded by the surrounding population into a certain excitement. . . . It even popped into his head that, were it possible, he would choose to linger amid the shadows [陰気] of the nearly spent year. His turn at a chair having come at last, he caught sight of his reflection [影] in the cold mirror, whereupon he asked himself: Who is this person [影] staring at me?[94]

The question he asks himself might more literally be translated, "What in the world is this shadow/image?"

Oyone is also closely identified with mirrors, one of the objects that define the everyday domestic space of her life in the city.[95] The mirror becomes associated with Oyone and Sōsuke's shadowy past: the betrayal of Yasui and the miscarriages and stillbirths that follow in its wake as a sort of divine punishment. The memory of her failed pregnancies haunts Oyone. The third and most recent one resulted in a stillbirth, which she later realizes was due to failings of the midwife.

> Although she [Oyone] had not committed the deed with her own hands, she concluded that she might as well have laid in wait on the shadowy path connecting the darkness with the light in order to wring the breath from the very one to whom she herself had given life. Having reached this conclusion, Oyone could not help viewing herself as a criminal guilty of the most horrendous of acts. Thereafter, unbeknownst to anyone, she had been subjected to hitherto unimagined torments of conscience. And there was not a soul in all the world with whom she could suffer some portion of these torments. She did not divulge her feelings even to her husband.[96]

On several occasions, Sōsuke sees Oyone's reflection (kage) in the mirror and is shocked by how pale she looks. Repeatedly, when the topic of the past comes up, Oyone retreats to her six-mat room to stare at her figure in the mirror. The specific word *kage* is not always used, but the same confused imagery of darkness/light, image/shadow, present/past dominates these sequences. For example, the following passage describes Oyone's recuperation after the abovementioned stillbirth.

> Finally the three weeks were at an end, and nature had restored her to physical health. She neatly folded and put away the bedding, and her eyes reflected in the mirror, stared back at her with a new life. . . . The succession of pleasant days that mark the boundary between spring and summer in Japan had some effect in picking up her spirits. But this stopped at merely exposing to the brilliant light the darkness that had been festering deep within her. She began to feel a kind of objective curiosity with regard to her dark past.[97]

As with Sōsuke, Oyone's stream of consciousness is blocked by a shadow that refuses to move on: F and f have become confused, stemming the healthy flow and generating a painful anxiety that nearly overwhelms her. This blockage produces in her case not neurasthenia, but its feminine counterpart: hysteria.

PATHOLOGIES OF PROPERTY

These disruptions in stream of consciousness produce a corresponding breakdown in the system of ownership. When the flow of consciousness is blocked, as with Sōsuke or Oyone, bonds of ownership over the self begin to crumble. To paraphrase James's language, it becomes impossible to distinguish the Thought from its property, the self-as-owner from the self-as-owned. In exploring this condition, *The Gate* provides a paradigmatic instance of the way Sōseki probed the gaps and contradictions of the new modern property system to locate the raw material for new kinds of stories.

In that sense, *The Gate* is in part the story of a man who fails to own even himself. This inability to possess the self then spreads out to undermine other forms of ownership. When Sōsuke was a young man, back when his "mind was exquisitely socialized," he was "the son of a man of considerable means" (*sōtō ni shisan no aru*; literally, "a man of considerable property").[98] Once his father dies, however, the property that oldest son Sōsuke should inherit transforms into an insoluble riddle. Already disgraced, Sōsuke leaves the family estate—both its landed property and the valuable paintings and antiques his father collected—in the hands of his uncle to liquidate. He procrastinates in asking his uncle to settle up accounts until it is too late: his uncle dies suddenly. When Sōsuke finally visits his widowed aunt to find out what happened to the family property, he learns that it has mostly vanished. Some was spent covering younger brother Koroku's educational expenses, but the majority was invested in a building that burned to the ground without insurance. The paintings and antiques likewise disappeared without a trace into the hands of a crooked dealer. "Sōsuke listened to his aunt's explanation in a daze and was hard-pressed to offer even a token response—further proof, it struck him, of his nervous disorder having robbed him of the capacity he once had to think on his feet and come to quick, clear conclusions."[99]

Sōsuke finally manages to acquire the sole remaining piece of family property: a folding screen by the painter Hōitsu (1761–1828). As per Hor-wicz's take on the psychology of ownership cited by James, Sōsuke knows the screen belongs to him through the affective response it elicits, summoning up memories from childhood: it seems an integral part of his self. By contrast, Oyone's body utterly fails to sense the warmth of ownership: "She made it plain with her body language that she had no idea why any-one would make a fuss over such an object."[100] In the end, even appropriating this single heirloom turns out to be too much for Sōsuke: the screen is far too big for his modest rented house. Oyone proposes they sell the painting to bolster their distressed household finances. But how much is a piece of art worth? She visits a neighborhood merchant who initially offers her six yen. She hesitates, only to have the dealer then offer seven yen. She hesitates again and decides to consult Sōsuke. The price strikes him as too low—but he is also convinced that any property belonging to him will immediately lose value: "As great a work as it may be, it won't matter, since the fact that it's mine means it won't sell for much."[101] The dealer ups his offer to fifteen yen and then finally to thirty-five yen, at which point Oyone and Sōsuke accept.

The mysteries of property and value only compound after this. Just as Sōsuke first found himself socially connected to his landlord Sakai via the robbery incident and the exchanges of gifts that followed, now Sōsuke finds himself unexpectedly connected to his landlord through the mysteries of commodity exchange. He learns that Sakai has acquired a folding screen by none other than Hōitsu. Sōsuke pays a visit in hopes of seeing the screen, to confirm whether it is the one he has just sold—even as he feels reluctant to pursue the matter. "After all, once a thing becomes the property of someone else, establishing whether or not it had originally belonged to one was of absolutely no consequence, practically speaking." When he does see the screen, it turns out to be of course the one he had inherited— only now, since it no longer belongs to Sōsuke, the artwork suddenly appears quite valuable. Being situated within Sakai's prosperous home "made the screen look ten times more precious than when still in his possession." Moreover, it turns out that Sakai has paid the dealer eighty yen, more than double what the dealer paid Sōsuke. But—as with the burglary sequence— this encounter with the mysteries of the property system serves only to build Sōsuke's bonds with Sakai: "After this, Sōsuke and Sakai fell into a kind of friendship."[102]

Under the 1898 Meiji Civil Code, the property of an extended family was controlled by its legal family head (*katoku*), a position that typically passed down from father to first son. But after his transgression with Oyone, Sōsuke has abandoned all possibility of inheriting this position and the control over property that comes with it. As we will explore in chapter 4, under the Civil Code, other family members (wives, younger siblings, retired parents) were in a sense the property of the family head. They could not, for example, marry without the consent of the family head. But having 'stolen' Oyone from Yasui, Sōsuke falls into a condition of uncertainty as to whether his wife really belongs to him. Likewise, the repeated sequence of miscarriages and stillbirths that befall Oyone drive home the point that Sōsuke also fails to produce an heir who will inherit his own position and property. As Ishihara Chiaki notes, Sōsuke (like Sensei in *Kokoro*) represents a doubly failed family head: he not only fails to produce an heir to continue the family line, he also manages to lose the family's property.[103]

In *The Gate* Sōseki creates a narrative that revolves around a man who is unable to function as a proper subject in the modern regime of ownership. As we have seen, this narrative constructed in the interstices of the property system unfolds not only at the level of family estate but also at the level of the protagonist's consciousness, so haunted by shadows. A man whose stream of consciousness lacks a sovereign the Thought to act as master of all it surveys is a man who, finally, can be sure of owning nothing, including his own self.

The novel's final seven chapters unexpectedly change direction. A long-standing disagreement exists among critics as to whether the concluding chapters represent a sudden unmotivated irruption into the plot, or whether they grow organically out of the first half of the novel.[104] Sōsuke is again jolted into crisis: he learns from Sakai that Yasui, the man he and Oyone betrayed, is traveling with Sakai's brother in Manchuria and that the two are now in Tokyo and plan to visit Sakai. The shadow of empire has merged with the darkest shadow from Sōsuke's past, and it is about to reappear in his life, atop the cliff that overlooks his home.

Whatever equilibrium Sōsuke had managed to achieve through time collapses. "The wound that had finally started to heal over the past few years began, suddenly, to throb to the point of burning," we are told.[105] The image of his past betrayal of Yasui returns as a source of mental obsession, driving out all other thoughts. Sōsuke lies awake in bed at night, his hypersensitive nerves keeping him from sleep.

In desperation, he seeks a way out from this pathological condition—and that is when the work introduces a new theme, religion. As Sōsuke plunges deeper into mental crisis, he is more and more attracted to the possibility of religious salvation. Might a spiritual awakening displace the obsessive thought that has jammed up the flow of his consciousness? He recalls a college classmate who achieved peace of mind through the practice of zazen and wonders if this might work for him. He takes time off from work to devote himself to meditation at a temple in Kamakura, hoping to find relief and perhaps even satori: enlightenment. As he explains to Oyone, "My nerves [nō: literally, brain] are really out of sorts. . . . I've asked for a week or so off from work so I can go somewhere and take it easy."[106] His retreat to the temple will also, of course, take him away from his rented house and the possibility that he might encounter Yasui when the latter visits Sakai. (Sōsuke apparently never tells Oyone about the impending reappearance of Yasui).

Darkness, silence, and stillness characterize Sōsuke's mental perceptions of the temple grounds. The monk who serves as his direct mentor provides "some basic guidelines for zazen, followed by a general description of what it was like to rack one's brain morning, noon, and night over a koan posed by the Master, all of which was deeply unsettling for Sōsuke," whose "mind was still more agitated than it had been in the city, perhaps because of the very tranquility of his surroundings."[107] He meets the Master, who gives him a standard koan on which to meditate: his original face prior to his parents' birth—his identity, we might say, prior to any situation within the family or property system. Sōsuke "concluded that, at any rate, the idea was to try to grasp the essence of what, finally, this thing called the self [*jibun*] is."[108]

Desperate for relief from his anxiety, Sōsuke begins to sit in meditation. But zazen fails to deliver him from the curse of consciousness.

> All manner of things drifted through his head. Some of them were clearly visible in his mind's eye, others, amorphous, passed by like so many clouds. It was impossible to determine whence they had arisen or where they were headed. Some would fade away only to be replaced by others. This process repeated itself endlessly. The traffic coursing through the space inside his head was boundless, incalculable, inexhaustible; no command from Sōsuke could possibly put a stop to it, or even momentarily arrest it. The harder he tried to shut it off, the more copiously it poured forth.

He panics and opens his eyes, then tries again. "Only Sōsuke's body remained still. His conscious being was forever on the move: an excruciating, unremitting, almost unbearable motion."[109]

In other words, whereas before the problem was that his consciousness was stuck in obsession, now it refuses to stop moving. His attempt to transcend himself ends in failure. The next morning, he steps out onto the veranda and spots the image/shadow (kage) of a cactus. Sōsuke tries meditation again, but the zazen seems only to aggravate his neurasthenia. "He was in anguish and fatigue as he watched the sun begin to decline" and "the shadows [kage] that fell across his *shōji* began to grow dimmer and to disappear."[110] Filled with self-doubt at his failure to achieve anything like satori, he has another encounter with the Master. He tries to bluff his way through the interview, only to be scolded. He tries again for a few more days, but draws no closer to solving the problem. The monk tells him "what he must do was to focus his attention ever more closely until his concentration was rigidly fixed and he himself became like a rod of iron." But it won't work: "His words paralyzed Sōsuke even further. Suddenly, he began to think again about the return of Yasui."[111]

Sōsuke finally gives up. He realizes that his attempt to escape his problems by fleeing to an isolated temple has failed; he remains stuck:

> He had come here expecting the gate to be opened for him. But when he knocked, the gatekeeper, wherever he stood behind the high portals, had not so much as showed his face. Only a disembodied voice could be heard: "It does no good to knock. Open the gate for yourself."

But how, he wondered, could he unbar the gate from the outside. . . . He was standing in the very same place he had stood before even beginning to ponder the problem. As before, he found himself stranded, without resources or recourse, in front of the closed portals. . . . He looked back. He saw that he lacked the courage to retrace his steps. He looked ahead. The way was forever blocked by firmly closed portals. He was someone destined neither to pass through the gate nor to be satisfied with never having passed through it. He was one of those unfortunate souls fated to stand in the gate's shadow, frozen in his tracks until the day was done.[112]

Stuck at the gate, Sōsuke is unable to master his consciousness, unable to take possession of it in order to transcend it. He is instead possessed by the consciousness of his past error, doomed to remain frozen in place.

Sōsuke returns home, still obsessed. "His thoughts no longer flowed in their normal, spontaneous fashion. There was, however, one subject to which his thoughts would quickly revert, that of the Sakai household," and in particular Yasui's imminent visit.[113] But, miraculously, the crisis has passed: when he finally plucks up the courage to visit Sakai, Sōsuke learns that his landlord's brother and Yasui have already returned to Manchuria. Sōsuke has avoided the immediate emergency. "But he was left with an ill-defined presentiment that from now on he would have to experience anxious times like this over and over, to some degree or another. It was destiny's role to enforce this repetition; it was Sōsuke's lot to dodge the consequences."[114]

In the end, "this couple who were averse to all change found themselves back in calm waters."[115] A plan for Koroku's future is finally agreed upon (Sakai will take him in and sponsor his education), and Sōsuke even gets a small raise at work. The novel's closing passage:

Oyone, looking out from the glass window of the shōji at the bright scene that lay before her, remarked with cheerful face,
"It's a good thing, isn't it. Spring is finally here."
Sōsuke stepped on to the veranda and began to clip his fingernails, which had grown to quite a length.
"But it will soon be winter again," he said, as with downcast eyes he continued to cut his nails.[116]

Oyone here claims that time is moving forward again, but Sōsuke insists it is still stuck in a rut. The man who as a youth could not bear the monotonous repetition of the seasons now sees in the future only an endless cycle of bleak repetition. Once again, a kage shows up, bearing all of the word's ambiguity: focal point or fringe, image or shadow, darkness or light. The word that Mathy translates above as "scene" is *hikage* (日影): either sunlight or shadow. In Oyone's eyes it is something bright (*uraraka*), but Sōsuke sees in it only darkness.

THE PSYCHOLOGY OF RELIGION AND
THE ABANDONMENT OF SELF-OWNERSHIP

This switch from a focus on mechanisms of perceptual consciousness in the first part of the novel to a search for religious grace in its closing chapters mirrors in curious fashion the careers of all of the psychologists discussed above. As Tokyo Imperial University's Kuwada Yoshizō (1882–1967) would inform Japanese readers in 1913,

> Hitherto the focus of psychologists has been turned toward individual psychology, and while they relied too fully on the unreliable methodology of introspection, by the final years of the last century they came to apply new experimental methods and thereby underwent a thorough renewal. After obtaining in this way a relatively reliable foundation for individual psychology, more recently we have seen a remarkable resurgence in research directed toward the previously neglected realm of social psychology (in the broad sense). Ethnic psychology [*minzoku shinrigaku*], together with social psychology (in the narrow sense) and psychology of ethnicity belong to this new tendency.[117]

For example, Kuwada notes, Wilhelm Wundt after the turn of the century turned his attention away from measuring individual sense perception and instead toward cultural psychology, including questions of religious faith and practice.[118] Likewise, Motora Yujirō, always a man of broad scholarly interests, began to write increasingly on matters of religion from around the time Sōseki took up fiction.[119]

As Kuwada Yoshizō noted in another 1913 article, William James also participated in this turn in psychology toward the study of religion, particularly with his *Varieties of Religious Experience*.[120] The religious turn signaled by *Varieties* was accompanied by a pronounced shift in James's stance toward property. As we have seen, *Principles*, published a decade earlier, furnished a striking example of the doctrine of possessive individualism, using ownership as the primary trope for explaining the mechanisms of selfhood. But a very different James emerges in *Varieties*. This allows Cornel West, who focuses on the later James, to assert that James "rejects the possessive individualism of America at the turn of the century."[121] Others have argued that the radical empiricism of the later James should be understood as a kind of anarchism.[122]

Scholars in both Japan and the West have noted this about-face in James's position.[123] Deborah Coon argues that the shift began in the late 1890s as part of James's critical reaction to American imperialism, in particular the Spanish-American War.[124] Francesca Bordogna sees the transformation in James as related to his desire to theorize a new form of sociality "rooted in intimacy and solidarity" that could resist the dominant hierarchies industrial and finance capitalism were imposing on American culture.[125]

How can we understand the abortive attempt to achieve satori at the end of *The Gate* in relation to this religious turn and the accompanying shift in stance toward property that characterize the late James? Sōsuke is above all a weak-willed protagonist. In the mind of the early James in *Principles*, this would render him pathological—a risk to the social order, including its property systems. As we have seen, for the early James, property ownership was natural and given. Property, in particular, helped account for the importance that habit enjoyed in his thought. The early James stressed the ethical nature of habit on the grounds (among others) that it "saves the children of fortune from the envious uprisings of the poor" and that it "keeps different social strata from mixing."[126] For the early James, both individual will and sanity are largely matters of habit. Memory, which guides the selective agency of consciousness as it processes sensations encountered in the present, is nothing more than the "law of habit," the "organized neural paths" in the brain itself, pathways developed over past repetitions that tend to cause a given stimulus to invoke a certain past association.[127]

Hence, the early James's economy of self-ownership revolves around habit. The development of habitual pathways in the brain, the acquisition of a second nature, is valuable for its efficiency: habit will "economize the expense of nervous and muscular energy" needed to produce a given result in response to some external stimulus.[128] Moreover, habit as an ethical practice allows us "to *make our nervous system our ally instead of our enemy. It is to fund and capitalize our acquisitions, and live at ease upon the interest of the fund. For this we must make automatic and habitual, as early as possible, as many useful actions as we can*, and guard against the growing into ways that are likely to be disadvantageous to us, as we should guard against the plague."[129] Will is crucial to this, because it is our pathway to acquiring good habits. It is not sufficient simply to know or feel what is right; if one does not take "advantage of every concrete opportunity to *act*, one's character may remain entirely unaffected for the better." Paraphrasing J. S. Mill, James writes that character "is a completely fashioned will," while will is the product of habit: it "is an aggregate of tendencies to act in a firm and prompt and definite way upon all the principal emergencies of life."[130]

Ultimately, one must will oneself to will; will consists of the habit of willing. "As a final practical maxim, relative to these habits of the will, we may, then, offer something like this: *Keep the faculty of effort alive in you by a little gratuitous exercise every day*. That is, be systematically ascetic or heroic in little unnecessary points, do every day or two something for no other reason than that you would rather not do it." Moreover, the accumulation of good habits, that is, of the will to will, is itself a kind of property: steady accumulation of good habits will build "itself up within him as a possession that will never pass away."[131] Self-possession, then, is a matter of habit; one acquires one's will through repeated acts of willing.[132]

A very different stance emerges a decade later in *Varieties*. There, we see a shift in focus away from habit and instead toward unpredictable facets of consciousness, those that arise unexpectedly and hence cannot be attributed to the force of habit nor claimed as properties of the will. These include the domain of the unconscious. As we saw in chapter 1, in *Varieties*, James describes the discovery of the unconscious as "the most important step forward that has occurred in psychology since I have been a student of that science."[133] James cites "the wonderful explorations by Binet, Janet, Breuer, Freud, Mason, Prince [the names are all underlined in Sōseki's copy], and others, of the subliminal consciousness of patients with hysteria" that have "revealed to us whole systems of underground life, in the shape of memories of a painful sort which lead a parasitic existence, buried outside of the primary fields of consciousness, and making irruptions thereinto."[134]

The meaning of automatic behavior has also subtly shifted in the decade since *Principles* appeared. Now, instead of registering the accumulated wealth of acts of will stockpiled in the form of habit, automatisms, especially in the form of automatic writing or speech, represent not the will but rather uncontrollable irruptions of the subconscious into the field of consciousness. James considers this at least potentially a psychic or supernatural phenomenon: "If there be higher powers able to impress us, they may get access to us only through the subliminal door."[135] As discussed in chapter 1, James credits the key discoveries in the field to the psychologist Gustav Theodor Fechner and to the psychic researcher Frederic Myers, who sought in the subconscious the possibility for contact with the souls of the dead—an aspect of James's thought that Sōseki noted more than once.[136]

In his later works, then, James no longer celebrates habit as "the enormous fly-wheel of society, its most precious conservative agent," nor as the source of will, the most important possession of the self.[137] Instead, James in studying religious experiences dismisses "your ordinary religious believer, who follows the conventional observances of his country" because his "religion has been made for him by others, communicated to him by tradition, determined to fixed forms by imitation, and retained by habit."[138] James's interest now lies in unusual experiences, unexpected and unpredictable, "experiences we can only find in individuals for whom religion exists not as a dull habit"—extraordinary moments of sudden religious awakening.[139]

The experience of instantaneous religious conversion is precisely the rejection of possessive individualism: it involves a radical renunciation of ownership over the self. Spiritual conversion arises in a moment when the self "is completely bankrupt and without resource," and hence the moment of conversion "must be a free gift or nothing."[140] It amounts to an act of self-surrender, of abandoning the will. James describes it in language that foreshadows *The Gate* and the failed conversion that leaves Sōsuke standing before the gate: "So long as the egoistic worry of the sick soul guards the door, the expansive confidence of the soul of faith gains no presence. But let the former faint away, even but for a moment, and the latter can profit by the opportunity, and having once acquired possession, may retain it."[141] Or, to cite one of James's case studies, an unidentified Oxford graduate (in his copy, Sōseki dutifully jots down "Oxford graduate" in the margin next to this passage) puts it, "I gave up to God all ownership in my own life."[142] While this experience in a sense still belongs to the individual—as James puts it, each narrative of conversion is "an original and unborrowed experience"—nonetheless that experience consists of a surrendering of self to some greater force, a handing over of possession of consciousness to some greater consciousness, allowing oneself thereby to be possessed.[143]

James notes that religious conversion is also often accompanied by a renunciation of private property. Religious converts take vows of poverty, because "lives based on having are less free than lives based either on doing or on being and in the interest of action people subject to spiritual excitement throw away possessions as so many clogs."[144] Moreover, he notes,

"the Utopian dreams of social justice in which many contemporary social-
ists and anarchists indulge are, in spite of their impracticability and non-
adaptation to present environmental conditions, analogous to the saint's
belief in an existent kingdom of heaven."[145] This brings James to the brink
of affirming radical political change: "Think of the strength which personal
indifference to poverty would give us if we were devoted to unpopular
causes. We need no longer hold our tongues or fear to vote the revolutionary or reformatory ticket."[146]

In sharp contrast to the arguments James made in *Principles*, in *Varieties*
one's will is now potentially alienable. The later James explores "another
kind of happiness and power, based on giving up our own will and letting
something higher work for us."[147] Rather than assuming an economy of
scarcity, in which acts of will are to be hoarded up as a private endowment,
religious experiences work through a model of abundance.

> The sole condition of our having anything, no matter what, is that we
> should have so much of it, that we are fortunate if we do not grow sick of
> the sight and sound of it altogether. Everything is smothered in the litter
> that is fated to accompany it. Without too much you cannot have enough,
> of anything. . . . The gold-dust comes to birth with the quartz-sand all
> around it, and this is as much a condition of religion as of any other excel-
> lent possession.[148]

LITERARY PROPERTIES OF COMEDY

To the later James, then, our conscious experiences may represent our
sharing in a greater consciousness; they may not belong solely to us. Our
"private experiences" can "become parts of the great system" yet remain
"fully distinguished from one another," just as our various sense perceptions (sight, smell, touch, etc.) remain distinct from one another yet unite
to form a single phenomenal experience.[149] If experience is something we
can own, it is an odd kind of property, both alienable and inalienable—
something like Marcel Mauss's gift, as I argue in chapter 3. When we con-
ceptualize experience, "'mine' excludes 'yours'" and yet "in the real concrete sensible flux of life experiences compenetrate each other so that it is
not easy to know just what is excluded and what not."[150]

Which brings us back to literature, an ideal realm for experimenting
with the late James's surrender of the self "to that conjunctural form of

relation in which the other consistently eludes possession, offering no guarantee of reciprocity."[151] For James, such moments in which we sense our connection to a greater consciousness and accordingly feel a relaxed sense of ownership over our own selves are moments of religious experience that have close ties to madness. As James notes, we often find similar experiences in the realm of literature.[152] Madness and genius, including literary genius, are birds of a feather. In Sōseki's words, "it was thanks to my neurasthenia and to my madness that I was able to compose" the literary works that bear his name.

The Gate is literature in this sense. As we have seen, the narrative in *The Gate* reaches its (anti)climax when Sōsuke decides to pursue his own variety of religious experience. To overcome neurasthenia (and to avoid Yasui's pending visit), he resolves to break out of his habitual daily routine and the obsessive domination of his consciousness by the shadow of his past by going on retreat to a temple. There, he engages in extended meditation, but enlightenment eludes Sōsuke: nothing happens. He finds himself denied the sort of religious awakening that James described. If in his daily life in the city he fails to own himself, in the temple retreat he fails to give himself away.

Sōsuke can neither own nor disown himself: he remains stuck. He had hoped the gate of religious awakening would swing open before him, but in the end is left "standing in the very same place he had stood before," so that he "was someone destined neither to pass through the gate nor to be satisfied with never having passed through it." The future holds only repetition: the arrival of spring delivers only the promise of winter's return. He foresees increasing expenditures of psychic energy that will get him nowhere, that will fail to break through the blockage in his stream of consciousness. The "repeating loop of capitalist accumulation" will continue to turn, with Sōsuke returning to the office each morning to sell the only thing he seems able to possess, his labor power.[153] He likewise remains unable to achieve a new sociality, a new mode of relating to the people and world around him.

Sōsuke's tragedy is to remain stuck in this pathological impasse, unable either to own or not to own. But how tragic is this? It seems possible to view Sōsuke's plight as fundamentally comic rather than tragic. *The Poppy* concludes with a character discussing the relation of comedy and tragedy, and Sōseki's notebooks provide evidence that he pondered this question at some length.[154] Sōseki acquired a copy of Bergson's *Laughter* (after first encountering the French philosopher through William James's *Pluralis-*

tic Universe) and was familiar with the argument that laughter is a social mechanism of ostracization that is deployed to chastise any rigidity blocking up the flow of the social machinery (or, for that matter, of the flow of consciousness). There is, Bergson writes, "a certain rigidity of body, mind and character that society would still like to get rid of in order to obtain from its members the greatest possible degree of elasticity and sociability. This rigidity is the comic, and laughter is its corrective."[155] Sōsuke's blocked consciousness makes him, in this sense, a fundamentally comic figure.

We are accustomed to considering *The Gate*, the concluding volume of Sōseki's so-called first trilogy (following *Sanshirō* and *And Then*), as foreshadowing the darker novels of the so-called second trilogy. But perhaps we should look instead for continuities with his earlier comic fiction— *Botchan* and *I Am a Cat*, among others. Or perhaps with the mode that Lauren Berlant calls "humorless comedy," a "*comedy of the survivor who has to keep surviving*" and in which "one experiences the ordinary as at once too much, not enough, and an infinite middle."[156] Sōsuke and Oyone meet with repeated misfortunes, but nobody dies, everyone somehow survives—and life stumbles forward.

Perhaps we should link *The Gate* to another contemporary realm of glowing shadows. Note that on Sōsuke's Sunday afternoon ramble through the city of Tokyo in search of stimulation, he encounters an advertising poster for a motion picture. In cinema, the brilliant illumination made possible by electricity was reshaping the aesthetic power of images against darkness.[157] In 1910, cinema in Japan and elsewhere was introducing a new form of laughter, the slapstick comedy. Take, for example, *An Interesting Story* (1905, dir. James Williamson), a one-reeler depicting a man so absorbed in the pleasures of reading that he loses contact with the world around him and inadvertently puts himself and everyone around him at risk. He trips over a maid washing the floor, walks into a man on the street, and finally ends up being smashed flat by a steamroller—only to be reinflated by two passing bicyclists with tire pumps. Somehow, he escapes injury, and as spectators we take satisfaction in the presumption that his life will simply continue on into the future as an unending repetition of near misses and misadventures.[158]

One of the oddities of slapstick comedy is that we take pleasure in pain suffered by others—just as in the case of tragedies. This problem fascinated Sōseki, so much that he devoted an entire section of *Theory of Literature* to explicating what he considered the special case of tragedy.[159] In reading *The Gate* we take pleasure in Sōsuke's tribulations, but almost certainly would not wish to trade places with him, stuck as he is in a cycle of unending repetition, unable to either own or disown himself. How is it that we derive pleasure from reading about experiences that would cause only pain if we were to experience them in person? The answer, according to Sōseki's theory, is that while Sōsuke may not have gotten anywhere, through the experience of reading Sōsuke's story, the author and reader have gotten somewhere: they have moved forward through their shared experience of the literary substance $(F+f)$ generated by the novel.

In book 2 of *Theory of Literature*, Sōseki explores two aspects of literary substance that are relevant here. First, he notes that the affect f solicited by direct experience is of a different nature from the f solicited by indirect experience—the difference, for example, between being caught in a vicious cycle oneself and reading about someone else being caught in a vicious cycle. Owing to this difference, we can obtain pleasure in reading about experiences that we would dislike if we experienced them in our own lives. This is why, for example, we enjoy tragedies. If we were to experience Sōsuke's various frustrations directly, we might find them painful—but when we experience them via the mediation of literature, the f they solicit in us can be quite pleasurable.

The second aspect Sōseki describes is the "bewitching" (*genwaku*) that occurs when a reader falls under the spell of a skilled author's technique. There are three levels of f in the experience of literature: the f generated in the author's consciousness toward his or her materials (Sōseki does not distinguish author from narrator); the f generated in the consciousness of characters depicted in the work; and finally the f generated in the experience of the reader encountering the work. Bewitchment happens when readers begin to appropriate into their own conscious experience the f that the author embeds in the work, even to the point of accepting things we would ordinarily reject if we encountered them in real life.

In the 1907 lecture "Philosophical Foundations of the Literary Arts," Sōseki explores this idea further, describing the most intense form of literary experience as being that characterized by *kangenteki kanka*: a term I have translated (somewhat forcibly) as "perfect accordance" or "receptive affinity."

The phrase "receptive affinity" may seem strange and hard to understand. Let me try to explain it more clearly. An artist uses as expedient means various words or colors to express the ideal that he has cultivated. Accordingly, the expressed ideal is nothing more than the exact depiction of a certain model of consciousness, a certain mode of continuity of consciousness. Therefore, to say a work produces pleasure is to say that one is in harmony with the continuity of consciousness expressed by the artist. We cannot experience this sort of pleasure if our own continuity of consciousness does not correspond with that of the artist. "Receptive affinity" is the phenomenon that occurs when this correspondence reaches its highest possible degree.[160]

A few sentences earlier, Sōseki compares the attainment of this state to Buddhist enlightenment—the very state Sōsuke is unable to reach. We achieve this fate when the $(F+f)$ waveform we experience in reading the literary text synchronizes perfectly with the $(F+f)$ waveform of the author. When that happens, we lose ourselves in the text in something like the way James's religious converts lose themselves in the experience of religious awakening: we temporarily surrender ownership in ourselves to another consciousness. This is an experience of radical sharing, one that belongs to neither reader nor author, but that is produced through their mutual encounter via the substance of literature. In literature, we get to experience, at least momentarily, what it might feel like not to own ourselves. Whereas early slapstick comedies like *An Interesting Story* or Buster Keaton's *Sherlock, Jr.* (1924) poke fun at the bookworm for his unmanly absorption in a book, Sōseki celebrates literature precisely for the way it allows us to experience a temporary withdrawal from the real world economies of self-ownership.[161]

If the pleasure of creating art is "the pleasure of a certain abandon" and a "surrendering to grace," then in engaging with the madness that gives rise to literature, Sōseki gives himself away, even as he narrates the tale of a man stuck between owning and not-owning.[162] This is the problem James was working on at the time his death, as he returned to the problem of consciousness and "pure experience" and whether, for example, two minds could share the same experience: "It is, indeed, 'mine' only as it is felt as mine, and 'yours' only as it is felt as yours. But it is felt as neither by itself, but only when 'owned' by our two several remembering experiences, just as one undivided estate is owned by several heirs."[163] Ultimately, James was trying to theorize a "notion of the open self" that "was tailored to allow not only for redemptive experiences with a divine Self, but also for the sharing of experiences, sympathetic understanding, and ultimately for cooperation and solidarity."[164] The domain of literature for Sōseki is not characterized by an economy of private ownership, but rather aims for an experience of sharing (I take up the question of copyright in the conclusion to this book). This is one of the psychological lessons we share in as we read about Sōsuke's failed conversion and his failings as an owner—the comic story that Sōseki generated from out of the cracks and aporia of the new modern property system. As we will see in chapter 3, it is a lesson that Sōseki would also pursue by way of the discipline of sociology.

CHAPTER THREE

Property and Sociological Knowledge

Sōseki and the Gift of Narrative

My dear friend, I send you a little work of which no one can say, without injustice, that it has neither head nor tail, since, on the contrary,
everything in it is both head and tail, alternately and reciprocally. I beg
you to consider the admirable convenience this offers all of us, you,
me and the reader. We can cut wherever we like—me my reverie, you
the manuscript, the reader his reading. For I do not keep the reader's
restive will hanging in suspense on the threads of an interminable and
superfluous plot. Take away a vertebra and the two parts of this tortu-
ous fantasy will come together again painlessly. Chop it into numerous fragments and you will see that each one can exist on its own. In
the hope that there is enough life in some of these segments to please
and amuse you, I dare to dedicate the whole serpent to you.

CHARLES BAUDELAIRE, dedication of *Paris Spleen*
(trans. Louise Varèse; 1869)

On New Year's Day, 1912, after a long silence due to illness, Natsume Sōseki
announced in the Tokyo *Asahi* newspaper that he was beginning serialization of a new novel, *To the Spring Equinox and Beyond* (*Higan sugi made*;
hereafter abbreviated as *Equinox*). Sōseki declared that although he hoped
the still largely unwritten work would embody his characteristic style, he
was also planning it as a formal experiment. While serialized novels often
relied on exciting plots to sustain reader interest day after day, Sōseki vowed
he would try something different. "I have long held the opinion that if I
took a series of individual short stories and combined them to form a single
longer work, it might be an unusually effective newspaper novel."[1] Rather

than being built around a tightly constructed plot, *Equinox* would consist of a series of loosely linked stories. If *Equinox* didn't work as a full-length novel, Sōseki noted, the reader could still enjoy the individual pieces, each wriggling with its own life—like the segments of Baudelaire's serpent.

Equinox was experimental in other senses, as well. The novel can be understood as a continuation of the project Sōseki had begun a decade earlier: his attempt to construct a universal theory of literature. The results would eventually be published in his *Theory of Literature* (*Bungakuron*, 1907). As he wrote in the preface to that work, when he set about this project of theorizing literature, Sōseki began by shutting away all works of literature. To understand literature by reading literature was "like trying to wash blood with blood."[2] Sōseki wanted to construct a universal, scientific theory of literature, and so he turned to two modern scientific disciplines, sociology and psychology. Despite being a specialist in English literature, Sōseki was a product of the elite Meiji higher education system, meaning that he enjoyed a relatively high level of scientific literacy.[3] Here I will retrace Sōseki's encounter with modern sociology, as well as explore *Equinox* as a continuation of this theoretical experiment, which will as in previous chapters involve a creative response to the modern property regime.

Sōseki's literary experiment has important ramifications today: since the 1980s, literature and literary theory have increasingly been subjected to critiques from the perspective of sociology. Exemplary works such as Pierre Bourdieu's *The Field of Cultural Production* (1993) and John Guillory's *Cultural Capital: The Problem of Literary Canon Formation* (1993) have reminded literary scholars of the need to supplement textual studies with a demystifying and disenchanting sociological perspective. Such critiques insist on the importance of reconnecting textual analysis with material reality and remind us that flows of language interact in multiple ways with social hierarchies of power and wealth. Understanding this multiplicity requires some notion of how society as a whole operates and hence it "is only intelligible from the point of view of a sociological analysis."[4]

The problem here is that using sociological knowledge to awaken us from the spell of literature requires us to place ourselves—for good reasons—under the spell of sociology. While sociology may help us find a way out from "the general and well publicized curricular crisis of the 'humanities,'" it can only lead us into the maelstrom that is the crisis of the social sciences.[5] By this, I mean the whole range of problems that we might call the politics of knowledge, as have been raised from such positions as postcolonialism, feminism, queer studies, antiracism, and ideology critique.

Moreover, while Bourdieu and others have launched admirable attempts to develop a self-reflexive sociology, to try to understand the politics of sociological knowledge through the use of sociology is to try to wash blood with blood. While I acknowledge the need for a sociological perspective in literary studies, I think it also behooves us in the humanities to offer literature as a site for critique of the epistemologies that reign in the social sciences. Literature provides a useful entryway for exploring the politics of sociological knowledge and for performing alternative possibilities.

In sum, Guillory's "sociology of judgment" should be accompanied by a judgment of sociology, one that originates from literature rather than from sociology.[6] Sōseki's theoretical project offers some hints on how to do this. Sōseki understood that any theory of literature must include a sociological dimension—yet he did not thereby choose to become a social scientist. We can rethink Sōseki's career as novelist and theorist as being in part a response from the site of literature to the knowledge produced in the discipline of sociology. Sōseki was staking a claim to a territory for literature that would exceed the grasp of other spheres of knowledge—in particular, sociology.

As we have seen, Sōseki's theoretical project began after the Japanese government sent him to England in 1900. There, Sōseki wanted to research the field of *bungaku* (literature), but he soon realized that he could not define the term adequately. Bungaku had long existed as a keyword in the classical Chinese scholarly tradition within which Sōseki received his primary education. There, it referred to the Confucian classics and other forms of canonical writing that elite males in East Asia were expected to know. This bungaku seemed utterly incommensurable with the bungaku—centered on novels depicting heterosexual romance and domestic life—that the category seemed to signify in modern Western societies.[7] Moreover, as a specifically Japanese reader, Sōseki found himself unable to locate in the English version of bungaku the supreme value that English literary theory insisted was there: as he would later recall, he felt cheated by English literature.[8] In response, Sōseki resolved to develop a new scientific definition of literature that could comprehend both the classical Chinese and modern English versions of bungaku.

He threw himself into an exhaustive survey of the disciplines of sociology and psychology. In chapter 2, I discussed the psychology that Sōseki relied on, so here I focus on the other discipline that provided the foundation for his experimental literary theory. The sociology that Sōseki read presumed a linear and hierarchical form of social evolution, and in particular defined systems of property ownership as a reliable yardstick for measuring the degree of civilization a given society had attained. We can trace Sōseki's reaction toward this sociology and its view of property in the marginal notes he jotted in the books he acquired in London, in the version of sociology he constructed in his *Theory of Literature*, and in his later fiction—which frequently derives its narrative force from the contradictions and ambiguities of property ownership. No fewer than eight of his novels, for example, revolve around questions of inheritance.[9] It seems almost to have been an obsession on his part.[10]

I argue here that Sōseki's theory and practice of bungaku formed a critical response to modern norms of property, norms that underwrote the discipline of sociology as he knew it. I look in particular at *Equinox*. The snake that is *Equinox* wriggles and twists, groping its way toward an experimental 'way out' from the ideologies of property that were hegemonic in the Meiji period. The snake, as we shall see, becomes a figure for the ability of literature to perform slippery forms of knowledge and imagination, forms that ultimately exceed the grasp of sociological knowledge.

SŌSEKI AND SOCIOLOGY

As we saw in chapter 1, in *I Am a Cat* (*Wagahai wa neko de aru*, 1905–6), the reader encounters a playful turnabout. The cat-narrator presents himself as a sort of anthropologist, studying the strange habits of the tribe known as human beings, classifying its cultural types and contrasting its savage behavior to that of the more civilized realm of felines. The cat is parodying a commonplace of Meiji-period anthropology and sociology: that a stable system of private property—one marked by clear titles of ownership and widely accepted procedures for the protection and voluntary disposition of property—provided a benchmark for measuring the degree of civilization of a given society.[11] In Meiji literature, as discussed in the introduction to this book, we see the presumption of property law as a marker of civilization in numerous works, including Kanagaki Robun and Fusō Kan's *By Shank's Mare through the West* (*Seiyō dōchū hizakurige*, 1870–76), Yano Ryūkei's *Tale of the Floating Castle* (*Ukishiro monogatari*, 1890), and Uchida Masao's *A Brief Geography* (*Yochishi ryaku*, 1870–75). This insistence on the centrality of property and commerce to civilization represented, among other things, an overturning of the orthodox pre-1868 value system of the Tokugawa regime, based on a Confucian hierarchy that placed merchants at the bottom of both the social and moral hierarchies. Whereas the Tokugawa-period model of a civilized man required a rejection of materialistic concerns, the new modern version of civilization set property and commerce as its pillars.[12]

This notion that a modern civilized society was characterized most clearly by its property systems predominated in English sociology. Not surprisingly, it was works in this tradition that formed the bulk of Sōseki's reading in sociology—and of the sociology taught in Japan following the 1893 appointment of Toyama Masakazu as the first chair in the discipline at Tokyo Imperial University.[13] Although there are surprisingly few works by Herbert Spencer in Sōseki's own library, the sociology-related texts that Sōseki did own are dominated by the schools arising from Spencer and Mill. English sociology, which mixed together classical liberalism, utilitarianism, and social Darwinism, contained, of course, a diverse range of positions. If it can be said to have a shared assumption, it was that society consisted of an aggregation of distinct individuals, and that its essence hence was rooted in the natural essence of the individual. Furthermore, taking up a line that had predominated in English thought since Hobbes, it presumed that the natural essence of the individual consisted of the selfish instinct for acquisition—that is, in the desire for property.[14] In this, it was closely aligned with the Manchester School of political economy and its presumption of what C. B. Macpherson has called "possessive individualism":

> Its possessive quality is found in its conception of the individual as essentially the proprietor of his own person or capacities, owing nothing to society for them. The individual was seen neither as a moral whole, nor as part of a larger social whole, but as an owner of himself. . . . The individual, it was thought, is free inasmuch as he is proprietor of his person and capacities. The human essence is freedom from dependence on the wills of others, and freedom is a function of possession. Society becomes a lot of free equal individuals related to each other as proprietors of their own capacities and of what they have acquired by their exchange. Society consists of relations of exchange between proprietors.[15]

Etienne Balibar points out one further fundamental presumption of possessive individualism: the existence of a distinction between two kinds of property, alienable real property and inalienable person.[16] One can sell things (with human labor categorized as an alienable thing), but one cannot sell persons: hence, for example, the strong opposition in both the utilitarian and liberal traditions to slavery and prostitution—a problem I return to in chapter 4. This distinction in turn became one of the concrete measures for distinguishing the degree of civilization of a given society—and one of the markers used to identify monstrous others.

The following passage from a textbook by Franklin Giddings, the preeminent American sociologist of the 1890s, is representative (underlined passages here and below correspond to passages underlined in Sōseki's own copies of the works quoted):

> The idea of possession, which originated in the assertion of ownership that is exhibited by animals, became, in the primitive social mind, the notion of property or of property right, which is a product of two factors; namely, the assertion of possession on the part of the individual possessing, and the toleration of his claim or acquiescence in it on the part of the community. In primitive society, property extended to simple personal belongings, to articles of adornment, to trophies of the chase or of war, and to tools and weapons.[17]

As discussed in chapter 1, this sociology hypothesized that property derived from animal instinct, and that hence property systems were not historical but rather natural in origin. This view not only tended to naturalize modern Western systems of ownership, it also—when the tenets of social Darwinism were thrown into the mixture—posited property systems as reliable benchmarks for measuring the degree of civilization attained by any given society. The system of property that had arisen in England since the Industrial Revolution, not surprisingly, was posited as representing the highest stage of development yet achieved by any human society.

A number of books contained in Sōseki's library reflect this view—for example, the English translation of a French work, Charles Letourneau's *Property: Its Origin and Development*. Like Giddings, Letourneau participates in the naturalization of property norms, arguing that property arises from an instinct for appropriation in animals and tracing the evolution of human civilizations by way of their property systems. Yet Letourneau also argues that "the unrestrained and selfish right of private property" will lead to "decadence" and "ruin," even for highly civilized societies.[18] Moreover, these darker tendencies are inherent in the very instinct for property. "But the propensity to appropriate, so praiseworthy when its object is the preservation of the individual, the family, or the group, easily degenerates into a less moral inclination, that for robbery," so that the "instinct of appropriation, by the very closeness of its connection with that of preservation, easily engenders selfish passions."[19] Letourneau sees property ownership as a double-edged sword, one that is fundamental to civilization but also potentially destructive of it.

How did Sōseki react to this sociology? Did he grow skeptical of its assumptions in the same way that he came to question British norms for literature? As a Japanese, in particular, Sōseki was forced to take up an ambiguous stance toward the discipline. Sōseki launched into his studies of sociology in order to transform himself into a knowing subject who operated within that discipline. Yet from the standpoint of Western sociology, Japan and its society were more properly positioned as the objects of knowledge. Japan's turn to the West "coincided almost exactly with the period when scientific racism dominated the natural and social sciences in Europe and the United States," so that for intellectuals like Sōseki, "the very process of Westernization involved being told that the racial inferiority of the Japanese was empirically verifiable," leaving them in an "awkward position."[20] Given the instability of his position, it would not be surprising if Sōseki began to harbor doubts about the form of knowledge he was pursuing.

In works where European sociologists turned their gaze on Asia, we find hints about Sōseki's reaction to the discipline. When Letourneau, for example, discusses the history of property in Japan and claims that feudal structures of land ownership remain unchanged to the present day and that first daughters have the same rights of primogeniture as first sons, Sōseki jots down the word *false* (*uso*) in the margins next to each claim.[21] In his copy of another work by Letourneau, Sōseki writes, "Can such a thing be? How foolish!" ("Konna koto ga aru ka. Baka o ie.") next to a passage mistakenly describing Japanese marriage practices.[22] Likewise, when John Beattie Crozier claims that Buddhism is inferior to Christianity because its disinterest in the material realm hindered the rise of modern science in Asia, Sōseki's copy contains several skeptical marginal comments, all jotted down in English. One such remark declares the argument a "specimen of sophistry & inaccurate reasoning. It is not Buddhism that has promoted science but neither can it be said of Christianity that it has helped in any way the advancement of science. On the contrary history shows that it has been a great obstacle in the evolution of it. If they at present utilise the results of science for the welfare of people, why should not the Buddhists?"[23]

In another 1890s sociological work, we find the following passage:

I believe Japan will be ruined long before Europe, for the simple reason that she has superimposed, on her own civilisation, and without being able to fuse the two, another civilisation which has nothing in common with her past, and which will presently lead her into the completest anarchy. But China, by far the superior of Japan in many respects, and notably in the matter of commercial honesty, is destined to have a powerful future. These small-skulled Asiatics, who can effect nothing but servile copies of our inventions, are doubtless barbarians, but history shows that the mightiest empires have always been brought low by barbarians.[24]

In the margins by this passage in Sōseki's copy, we find several sarcastic comments, all in English, including, "Of course. Think a little & find out its cause"; "What sorts of barbarians?"; and "What sweeping arguments are these!"

In sum, as Sōseki sought to theorize literature using Western sociology, he repeatedly encountered the problematic ways in which that discipline objectified Japan and assigned its property systems to an inferior stage of civilization. He was forced, in other words, into an awareness of the politics of sociological knowledge. Paradoxically, this questioning also put him in sync with the most recent developments in continental sociology.

Unbeknownst to Sōseki, at about the same time as he was launching into his survey of sociology in London, on the European continent a new generation of sociologists was taking shape, one that was frequently skeptical toward the English version of the discipline. The new schools that developed, mainly in France and Germany, were quite different from one another, and yet when compared to the earlier English sociology, a few common characteristics can be discerned. First, they shared a tendency to reject the view that society consisted of a composite of individuals and tended instead to argue that the various forms of human society each gave rise to a different type of individual subject. Moreover, they tended not to see property systems as the ground of social existence, but rather sought behind property systems a more fundamental stratum, a spirit or morality that was the true ground of society. The new sociology also tended to be less celebratory of contemporary Western society, and its analysis frequently focused on what it considered to be the pathologies of modern Europe. When scholars from the new schools looked to non-Western societies, they were less inclined to regard those societies as inferior, and instead sought in them alternative models that might provide hints as to how to cure the sicknesses of Western modernity.

Among German scholars, for example, Max Weber argued that the Protestant ethic, with its stress on accumulating over consuming, provided not so much the heroic endpoint of social evolution as a tragic barrenness, the famous "iron cage" of modern society. Under it, the "idea of a man's duty to his possessions, to which he subordinates himself as an obedient steward, or even as an acquisitive machine, bears with chilling weight on his life."[25] For Georg Simmel, in turn, property ownership was not the ground for human subjectivity in society, but rather a peculiar form of performance. Ownership was not so much a state into which one entered as it was an activity that one performed, one that brought the subject into existence as much as the subject brought it into existence: possession was a two-way street.[26]

Likewise, in the French tradition, Emile Durkheim would lament the lack of a public morality in modern European societies, and sought in this lack the causes for suicide and other modern pathologies. In his university lectures on the history of private property, Durkheim argued that premodern property systems were sustained by a moral, sacred basis that had been lost in modern societies, and he argued the need for a new public ethics within the modern economy, one he sought in a restoration of professional guilds. While Durkheim believed a private property system was desirable and necessary for modern society, he also believed that it was not an absolute good in itself and that it needed to be mediated by a healthy public morality.[27]

Durkheim's nephew Marcel Mauss continued this line of exploration and made the study of alternate forms of property and economy his life's work. In his classic study, *The Gift: The Form and Reason for Exchange in Archaic Societies*, originally published in 1923–24 but based on research he had already begun to publish during Sōseki's lifetime, Mauss attempted to theorize a moral economy that could serve as an alternative to modern capitalism, with its reliance on amoral exchanges and private property systems. For Mauss, it "is our western societies who have recently made man an 'economic animal,'" and the necessity of turning back to explore archaic societies and their gift economies lay in their reminding us that for "a very long time man was something different, and he has not been a machine for very long."[28]

In the eyes of these new schools of sociology, there was nothing natural or inevitable about modern property systems, nor was the human subject best considered as the owner of his own being, as the proprietor of his own experience. Sōseki did not read Mauss, Weber, Durkheim, or Simmel: their works would not have a major impact on Japan until the Taishō period.[29] Yet we can find in Sōseki parallels with the thought of those figures.

In many sections, however, *The Theory of Literature* reflects the influence of English sociology. Sōseki presumes, for example, that social collective consciousness consists of the aggregation of individual consciousnesses, so that the nature of society derives from the prior nature of the individuals who compose it.[30] Moreover, despite the outbursts described above, he at times also shows a strong tendency to accept the views of social Darwinism, and even Max Nordau's quasi-scientific theory of degeneration.[31] English sociology also provides much of the basis for book 5, *Collective F*, in which Sōseki explores the mechanisms of shifting collective consciousness in literary history. In revising his original lecture notes prior to the book publication of *Theory*, this is one of the sections to which he devoted particular care.[32]

But we also find instances where Sōseki's theory seems to counter English sociology. While collective consciousness is grounded in the consciousnesses of the individuals who make up that social body, Sōseki also clearly argues that these individual consciousnesses are in turn historically and socially determined. Our ordinary consciousness (including, implicitly, our desire for acquisition) is shaped by our historical and cultural environments, as we mimic the actions and thoughts of those around us: "It is an imitation that is forced upon us by something stronger than the individual will."[33] Sōseki argues that this compulsion to imitation is "natural" and necessary in the struggle for survival, yet his stance here resonates more clearly with Weber's "spirit" and Durkheim's "morality" than with a Hobbesean belief in an inherently acquisitive human nature.

Sōseki argues that this historicity also means that literary tastes are constantly shifting, so that someday perhaps even Shakespeare will be forgotten.[34] Unlike scientific truth, which is permanent and universal, literary truth is historical and relative. The meanings and values of literary works, in other words, are not properties that belong to those texts, but rather temporary outcomes of the fluid processes that occur when a reader's consciousness turns its focus to the text. This view in turn allows Sōseki to challenge the authority of, for example, English literary critics—since taste is relative, the literary criticism of a Japanese, even of an English poem, is as valid as that of an Englishman—a position he would expound again in his 1914 lecture, "My Individualism" ("Watakushi no kojinshugi").

More crucially, Sōseki insists that while biological organisms, sense perception, society, and scientific knowledge may all undergo progressive evolution into superior forms, such is not the case for literature and literary taste. There is constant shifting in the focal point *F* of our collective consciousness toward literature, he argues, due to the discomfort caused by the boredom or stress (*ken'en*) that arises when any given focal point stays in place for too long.[35] But the fluctuations that result are in no way arranged in a progressive form.[36] Literature may evolve through history, but it does not follow the sort of developmental model of Civilization and Enlightenment that held sway in English sociology.

In other words, we see Sōseki here distinguishing literature from English sociology, including its vision of property ownership. This tendency emerges in even more full-blown form in Sōseki's later fiction. When we read *Equinox*, in particular, we find a form of gift that has remarkable parallels to Mauss's sociology. Moreover, in Sōseki's literary version of the gift, we find not only an implicit critique of English sociology but also of the French school of Mauss and his heirs in the present day, including Guillory and Bourdieu.

EQUINOX AND POSSESSIVE INDIVIDUALISM

This notion of personal experience as property influenced not only sociology but also turn-of-the-century psychology, especially that of William James. As we saw in chapter 2, one of the standard texts that Sōseki relied on in London was James's *Principles of Psychology* (1890), a work that includes many clear examples of the doctrine of possessive individualism: James repeatedly uses metaphors of ownership to explain psychological mechanisms.

> When Paul and Peter wake up in the same bed, and recognize that they have been asleep, each one of them mentally reaches back and makes connection with but one of the two streams of thought which were broken by the sleeping hours.... The past thought of Peter is appropriated by the present Peter alone. He may have a knowledge, and a correct one too, of what Paul's last drowsy states of mind were as he sank into sleep, but it is an entirely different sort of knowledge from that which he has of his own last states. He remembers his own states, whilst he only conceives Paul's. Remembrance is like direct feeling; its object is suffused with a warmth and intimacy to which no object of mere conception ever attains. This quality of warmth and intimacy and immediacy is what Peter's present thought also possesses for itself. So sure as this present is me, is mine, it says, so sure is anything else that comes with the same warmth and intimacy and immediacy, me

and mine. . . . Whatever past feelings appear with those qualities must be admitted to receive the greeting of the present mental state, to be owned by it, and accepted as belonging together with it in a common self.[37]

For James, personal experiences and memories formed a kind of inalienable property: Peter could never acquire Paul's experience, because our own memories come indelibly branded with our personal seal of ownership, like cows in a herd: they are not transferable from one person to another.[38]

Does possessive individualism provide one of the themes in *Equinox*? As we have seen, in announcing his serialization of the novel, Sōseki declared that it would be a disjointed work, without a single coherent plot line. The book is made up of six chapters, plus a brief conclusion. The six chapters (with some variation) each present a narrative spoken aloud by some character and listened to by Keitarō. The chapters are given in chronological order of the events of telling, but with each narrative he hears, Keitarō learns about a wider range of past events, setting up a complex temporal relationship between the time of telling and the time of the narrated events.[39]

Despite this disjointed structure, critics have sought a unifying theme that would permit a coherent reading of the novel as a whole. Some have identified the inalienability of personal experience as that theme. Komori Yōichi, for example, argues that the novel "repeatedly stresses the impossibility for a bystander to report the interior or psychology of another person, so that it becomes a sort of 'metafiction' that includes a dimension of self-reflexive self-criticism."[40] Ogura Shūzō likewise, in tracing the impact of James's work on Sōseki, declares that the theme of the novel is the impossibility of anyone possessing another's personal experiences.[41]

Such interpretations demonstrate that the novel can be—and has been—interpreted through the framework of a Jamesian possessive individualism, with its assumption that personal experiences remain the inalienable property of the person who first experienced them. And the novel itself contains many passages that seem to substantiate this reading. Early on, Keitarō—the perspectival center of the narrative if not the protagonist—asks Morimoto to tell him about Morimoto's past adventures. "It's always interesting to hear about your past. And I'm really grateful, because I feel that I—who know so little about the world—profit from it whenever I hear your stories." But Morimoto, even as he offers up one of his stories "in payment for [his] supper," quashes this, as he stresses the fundamental difference between one's own experiences and those of another person.

"You, well, this may sound rude, but you've just graduated and don't know anything about the world . . . whereas I have actually stomped around on the ground of the real world. . . . It may sound funny to put it this way, but I'm sure I've piled up ten times the experience you have."[42]

We find a similar assertion in the concluding section of the novel. The narrator pronounces judgment on Keitarō:

> And so the adventures of Keitarō began with a tale and they end with a tale. The world he wanted to know had at first appeared far distant. Now, it appeared right in front of his eyes. And yet to the very end he was like an outsider, unable to enter into it and play an active part. His role was nothing more than that of a kind of investigator who ceaselessly holds a telephone receiver to his ear and listens to "the world."

As a result of all the stories he has heard, "he felt as if his own worldly experience had grown somewhat wider. Yet that experience had merely grown wider in the area it covered; it seemed not to have taken on any added depth."[43] The narrator seems to stress here the limits on one's ability to share in the experiences of another.

But Sōseki's novels also frequently toy with the idea that the personal experiences of one person might somehow be acquired by another. In *I Am a Cat*, for example, the bulk of the narrative consists not of the cat-narrator's own experiences nor of experiences that others have willingly given to him. Rather, it consists mainly of experiences he has inadvertently obtained from others—stolen glimpses (*nusumi-mi*) and pilfered conversations (*nusumi-giki*), a device widely used in the fiction of the Meiji (and earlier) eras.[44] But who properly owns these experiences? Are eavesdroppers best considered thieves, or do they have some proper claim to the experiences obtained in their illicit acts?

Kokoro (1914) is another work that treats personal experience as a sort of private property—as we will explore more fully in chapter 4. The second half of that novel consists of a letter that the character known as Sensei sends, explaining to the recipient the reasons for Sensei's mode of life and for his imminent suicide. Near the beginning of that letter, Sensei explains why he has decided now to reveal the secret of his past, which he has hitherto kept hidden. Sensei writes, "My past is my own experience—one might call it my personal property [*shoyū*]. And perhaps, being property, it could be thought a pity not to pass it on to someone else before I die." Without an appropriate person to pass it on to, however, he had resigned himself to having his experiences buried with him after he died. But now he has met the letter recipient, and declares, "Among the many millions of Japanese, it is to you alone that I want to tell the story [*monogataritai*] of my past." The passage ends with Sensei virtually naming the recipient as his heir: "Now I will wrench open my heart and pour its blood over you. I will be satisfied if, when my own heart has ceased to beat, your breast houses new life."[45]

This passage treats past personal experiences as a form of property, as did William James. But we should note a significant difference: whereas James's Peter and Paul can never own one another's personal experiences, Sensei is proposing that such experiences are an alienable form of property and that through an act of narration (monogatari) ownership can be transferred. Here we see literature being used to perform a transfer of property that was impossible, at least according to certain forms of scientific knowledge. As noted above, the narrator in *Equinox* concludes that "the adventures of Keitarō began with a tale and they end with a tale [monogatari]." In fact, exploring the function of monogatari within *Equinox* allows us to develop a different interpretation of the novel, one that situates it in a more critical relationship to the framework of possessive individualism.

There is another famous passage in *Equinox* that directly takes up the inaccessibility of another person's internal experiences. In the chapter "Matsumoto's Story," Matsumoto evaluates the character of his nephew, Sunaga Ichizō:

This man Ichizō is of a character such that whenever he comes into contact with the world, he coils up inside himself. Because of this, when he does receive some sort of stimulation, it begins to spin out of control, eating its way ever more deeply and more finely into the depths of his heart. And because there is no limit to how far it eats into him, the process just goes on and on, causing him to suffer. In the end, he becomes so tormented that he prays to be released from this incessant internal activity, and yet he seems dragged along by it, as if he were cursed and powerless to do anything about it.

The cause of this condition, Matsumoto concludes, is that "Ichizō is a man who from the start possesses nothing other than his own self," and it is this that threatens to drive him into madness. The possibility for a cure lies in the hope that "the always inward-facing direction of his life must be changed, he must somehow uncoil and open up to the outside world," which could happen only if he would "discover something great, something beautiful, something gentle—something that will steal away [*ubaitoru*] his heart."[46]

Matsumoto's judgment on his nephew can perhaps be summarized as follows: those who possess nothing outside themselves risk becoming possessed by the modern ailment of neurasthenia—they risk losing ownership over their own personal experiences.[47] It is only through external acquisitions, through being possessed by something that will "steal away" one's heart, that self-possession can be sustained. If this represents a form of possessive individualism, it is of a remarkably devious sort. Rather, the novel seems to be challenging that ideology quite explicitly. Note that Matsumoto here is narrating the internal experience of another, his nephew. As a result, that inner experience can be shared in common, not only by the direct listener, Keitarō, but also by the reader of the novel. The mode of narration in *Equinox* is consistently constructed around the implicit presence of an active listener, one whose presence dialogically shapes the contents of the speakers' narratives and whose perspectival position the reader is frequently invited to share.[48]

WALKING STICK AS GIFT

I am suggesting here that the form of self-ownership imagined in *Equinox* is remarkably complex and that the novel structures itself around an unusual open-ended economy, an incessantly spiraling form of circulation. Ichizō himself mentions that he has recently read the short story "Gedanke" (Thought) by Leonid N. Andreyev. In this Russian story (Sōseki owned a copy in German translation), the narrator compares the human mind to thousands of snakes, each angrily attempting to devour the others—a striking image for the impossibility of self-possession.[49] Moreover, the key to this economy (if that is what it is) seems to be the walking stick carved in the shape of a snake's head that Keitarō receives as a gift from Morimoto.

Several critics have argued that the snake-shaped stick is the central device holding together the otherwise scattered pieces of *Equinox*.[50] Wherever the influence of the stick extends, there an opening for narration is created, and thanks to it a bystander becomes able to possess, or at least share in, the inner experiences of some other person. In this way, the novel unfolds its narration in a mode that troubles the model of subjectivity implicit in possessive individualism: Keitarō and the reader, for example, are forced into a realization that they can function as subjects only when they act out roles in preassigned narratives—narratives whose origins and ownership clearly exceed the performing subject him- or herself.[51]

For example, in the scene where Keitarō first visits Matsumoto's house, he finds himself turned away for a mysterious reason: he is told to come again some other day, because it is raining. We should also note, however, that on this day Keitarō has not brought the walking stick with him. As Ichizō teases him subsequently, "Well, you didn't bring your stick with you that day, right?"—the absence of the stick seems another possible cause for the failure to obtain monogatari on this day.[52] On the day after the rainy day, it is sunny, and so Keitarō resolves to call on Matsumoto again. This time, however, "he took that stick from its hiding place behind a suitcase, having decided to try bringing it with him today."[53] On this day he is welcomed into the house and hears a monogatari from Matsumoto about his brother-in-law Taguchi. At the conclusion of his tale, Matsumoto comments, "What an odd stick you have. Can I see it?" and then, examining it, "Hmmm. A snake's head. It's really well done. Did you buy it?" Keitarō responds, "No, it was a gift from an amateur woodworker who carved it."[54]

Later, Keitarō will learn about the experiences that led Matsumoto to refuse guests on rainy days. This occurs via a monogatari spoken by Chiyoko, and again it seems to be the almost magical influence of the walking stick that summons up her tale. Before she launches into her narrative, Chiyoko declares, "What kind of a stick is it that Keitarō has? Please let me see it." It turns out that Keitarō has not brought the stick with him this day. It is only after he promises to bring the stick on his next visit to show her that Chiyoko at last relents and launches into her narrative.[55]

Likewise, in the chapter "Sunaga's Story," Sunaga Ichizō first confirms, "You've brought that stick again, haven't you?" before launching into his narrative.[56] The tale that Ichizō subsequently relates reveals a bit more about the strange economy that governs the world of this novel. The main thread of his tale revolves around the riddle of why, although he has no intention of marrying Chiyoko, Ichizō nonetheless finds himself burning with jealousy the moment a rival for her affections appears. It is not the case that he has no interest in women. When he passes a beautiful woman in the street, he says, "I sometimes fantasize about making her my own [lit., "becoming her owner," *shoyūsha ni natte*]." Still, he cannot understand why he feels jealous about Chiyoko, over whom he has "no claim of ownership, nor any desire to lay claim to ownership [*jibun no shoyū de mo nai, mata shoyū ni suru ki mo nai*]." Nonetheless, when the rival Takagi appears, Ichizō finds himself flustered, as if his "heart had been stolen away."[57] In sum, he finds himself fearing Takagi as a property owner would fear a thief. Moreover, as Ichizō acknowledges, his subjective reaction of jealousy arises not from some internal identity over which he can claim ownership; the jealousy only arises from outside himself, when he finds himself inadvertently situated in the sort of triangular relationship that characterizes much of Sōseki's fiction.[58]

Alongside this plumbing of the irrationality of ownership, we also find in the novel the outlines of a theory of the gift. A number of crucial turning points in the plot hinge on the question of gifts. For example, in "At the Trolley Stop," the conversation between Matsumoto and Chiyoko on which Keitarō attempts to eavesdrop revolves around the still-unfulfilled promise of a gift, a ring. Moreover, the main narrative of "Sunaga's Story" revolves around whether the Taguchi family will give Chiyoko as Sunaga's bride—and whether Sunaga would accept this gift. While narrating this tale, Sunaga describes Chiyoko's character by invoking an anecdote about a girl who refused the gift of a handkerchief offered by the artist Gabriele D'Annunzio. "If it were not Chiyoko, but rather her younger sister Momoyoko," Sunaga declares, "whatever her true thoughts, she would have offered thanks and gracefully accepted the handkerchief on the spot. But Chiyoko could never do that."[59] Likewise, when he explains his reluctance to marry Chiyoko, Sunaga laments that in marrying her he would receive a great deal, yet, "I could not reciprocate by offering her something in return that was more—or even equally—attractive."[60] Both Sunaga and Chiyoko, it seems, are troubled by the prospect of accepting gifts—largely because of fears over the obligations for reciprocity that acceptance would incur.

The key to the novel's implicit theory of the gift, however, lies with the abovementioned walking stick. In the open-ended, spiraling economy of this novel, characters begin narrating the personal experiences of others when they come under the influence of this stick. Moreover, when we look at passages that explicitly describe the stick itself, we find that it bears nearly all of the attributes that Mauss argues are characteristic of the gift, such as the copper objects used in North American potlatch societies: "they have a power of attraction that is felt by other copper objects, just as wealth attracts wealth, or dignitaries bring honours in their train, as well as the possession of spirits and fruitful alliances,—and *vice versa*. They are alive and move autonomously, and inspire other copper objects to do so."[61]

Likewise, in *Equinox*, the stick transforms into an almost magical object. A "mysterious and contradictory object," it seems alive and functions not only to elicit narrative from people but also as a kind of talisman guiding their actions.[62] The stick shakes loose other people's proprietary hold over their own experiences and allows Keitarō (and therefore the reader) to share in them. The stick, that is, opens a topos for dialogue in the form of spoken narrative, in which the speaker must share a given space and time with the listener, and in which "everything that is said, expressed, is located outside the 'soul' of the speaker and *does not belong only to him* [*sic*]."[63]

Already at its introduction into the narrative, the walking stick is associated with a violation of social norms of debt and property. The stick is left behind in Keitarō's boardinghouse by Morimoto, its original owner, when he skips town without paying his board bill. Morimoto eventually writes Keitarō a letter from Manchuria, explaining his whereabouts and offering him as personal mementos pieces of property he left behind, in case the boardinghouse landlords have not already claimed them in lieu of unpaid rent. He specifically offers the stick, because the landlords probably would not know it was his, since it was kept not in his room but in the communal umbrella stand in the boardinghouse entryway.

But Keitarō is reluctant to accept this gift. As Mauss argues, an object received as a gift is potentially dangerous, because one cannot know in advance the full extent of obligations it will entail: they can spiral out of control. Moreover, in a gift economy, the original owner retains a kind of spiritual possession over the gift object, because "by giving one is giving *oneself*, and if one gives *oneself*, it is because one 'owes' *oneself*—one's person and one's goods—to others."[64] Therefore, "the thing received is not inactive. Even when it has been abandoned by the giver, it still possesses something of him. Through it the giver has a hold over the beneficiary just as, being its owner, through it he has a hold over the thief."[65] To accept a gift is to take on the burden of potentially infinite reciprocation, and the gifted object itself contains the magical spirit of the original owner to ensure that this obligation is repaid.

In such an economy, one does not accept gifts lightly. This is the reason, perhaps, that Keitarō for a long while refuses the proffered gift: the stick remains untouched in the umbrella rack. Keitarō's mental state toward the stick at this stage is described in terms that overlap remarkably with Mauss's description of the gift. Every time Keitarō passes through the boardinghouse entryway, his eyes are drawn to the stick, so much so that he feels a "strange sensation" from it:

> And so he purposely averted his gaze when he went in and out, trying as much as possible to avoid setting his eyes upon it. But now, the whole

business of passing by the umbrella stand and deliberately pretending not to look had become distressing, and it even seemed—albeit to an admittedly slight degree—as though he were somehow under a spell cast by this odd stick. . . . His inability to muster the courage to accept gratefully that which had been expressly offered to him as a personal memento had the effect of voiding another's act of good will and hence was certainly regrettable. Yet even that was not enough to produce the sense of distress that he now felt. Put simply, the stick seemed somehow to proclaim an imminent untimely end to the floating-world destiny of Morimoto. (And most probably, the end it proclaimed was that of a sad, anonymous death in some foreign land.) The stick, as it stood in the umbrella stand, seemed to foretell of a miserable end. The head of this trunkless snake, carved by his own hands, trying without success either to swallow something down or to spit something out, always there on the tip of the bamboo pole, its mouth wide open. . . . To have been requested by a man on the verge of a sad, anonymous death that he should take up this snake's head on his daily walks as that man's personal representative: it was this thought that first summoned up the odd feeling in Keitarō. That he could neither take up this stick from the umbrella stand with his own hands nor instruct the boardinghouse owner to place it somewhere out of sight: certainly, these were exaggerated responses, and yet he also thought there was a certain karma about it.[66]

In the end, though, as Mauss notes, no one in a potlatch society has the right to refuse a gift. Accordingly, Keitarō eventually must accept the stick and the obligations it entails. On the day Keitarō carries out the mysterious mission Taguchi has assigned him (to tail Matsumoto and Chiyoko to overhear their conversation), he plots to steal the stick that already belongs to him. As he is planning his mission, he thinks about how the stick and Morimoto have become inextricably linked in his mind, and how the presence of the stick seems to link him to Morimoto.

> The two characters that made up Morimoto's name had long since become a medium transmitting an odd reverberation to Keitarō's ear, and lately this had intensified so that they had utterly transformed into a kind of symbol. From the start, whenever the man's name arose, he would always associate it with that stick, but whether he interpreted the stick as something that linked the two of them together, or whether he regarded it as a barrier that stood between and separated them, Keitarō's head was violently unsettled by this thought: even though he knew that there was a distance between Morimoto and this bamboo pole so that he could not immediately leap

from one to the other, nonetheless the two had now become one, so that Morimoto signified the stick and the stick signified Morimoto. In this unsettled state of mind, when the idea floated up by chance from the feverish flow of his blood that the stick's ownership was indeterminable, that it seemed to belong to himself just as it seemed to belong to Morimoto, he shouted, *aah, that's it!*, and from the blackness of a confused, fleeing shadow he seized on the stick.[67]

Keitarō here recalls the prophecy made earlier by a fortune-teller he visited and decides that her words referred to the stick. As a result, the stick comes to take on supernatural powers in his mind and becomes "something used in magical spells."[68]

Once Keitarō takes possession of the stick, it possesses him in turn—just as Mauss would have anticipated. When he arrives at the streetcar stop where he is to carry out his mission, he realizes that there are in fact two possible streetcar stops, and he must choose which of the two to monitor. It is the stick that rescues him from his dilemma. As he is trying to decide, a passerby bumps into him and knocks the stick to the ground. Because the head of the stick as it lies on the ground is pointing east, Keitarō decides to monitor the streetcar stop to the east. Moreover, for Keitarō—as for the previous owner, Morimoto—possession of the stick seems to liberate him from ordinary conventions of propriety and property. When he finally locates the couple he is supposed to tail, he follows them into a restaurant in his attempt to overhear illicitly their private conversation. He realizes that he is experiencing none of the ethical qualms he might normally have about stealing the private experiences of others: "He acknowledged no particular need to consult his conscience regarding the moral value of his secretly reeling in the words and actions of others, without having obtained their consent."[69] He is a kind of thief, and he even considers at one point directly approaching the man and asking his permission—thereby, apparently, to claim legitimate title to the experiences he has obtained illicitly. But he never does, because "it seemed to him that all responsibility [for his actions] lay with the stick he was now carrying."[70] On the following day, as he reflects back on the previous night, he can only explain his conduct as if he had been "intoxicated" or "bewitched" by the stick.[71] Keitarō has taken up the role of Mauss's gift recipient, possessed by the gift the moment he takes possession of it.

As we have seen, Mauss's theory of the gift represented an attempt to formulate a critical understanding of modern society, especially its institutions of property. Moreover, we have seen how *Equinox* depicts characters who seek a way out from the norms of modern property ownership and possessive individualism. Possession of the gift that is the stick elicits narrative, by which one in turn becomes able to share in the personal experiences of others.

At the conclusion of *Equinox*, the narrator reflects on the quality of such experiences, gained at secondhand via narrative. Keitarō has heard from Chiyoko the tragic tale of the death of Matsumoto's daughter. "The 'death' described by Chiyoko was different from his previous mundane imaginings; it elicited pleasure in him, like that obtained from viewing a beautiful picture. And yet tears mingled in with this pleasure."[72] Keitarō did not participate directly in the death or the experiences surrounding it, yet via narrative he has been able to share in the emotional experience of it. The narrator concludes, "In sum, all of the recent knowledge and emotions he has acquired from the human world have come to him via the vibrations of his eardrums," that is, from "the many long stories he has heard, beginning with Morimoto and ending with Matsumoto."[73] As a result, he has received the gift of unknown worlds, experiences he has been able to share in, albeit as an auditor rather than as a narrator or participant. "To the end, he was unable to enter into them. This was the source of what he lacked, and at the same time it was his greatest blessing. For what he lacked, he cursed the snake head; for his blessings, he offered up thanks to it. And, looking up into the vast skies, he wondered how this drama, which might seem to have come to a sudden ending, would continue undergoing eternal permutations forever into the future."[74] Having accepted the gift of the stick, neither Keitarō nor anyone else can know how long the obligations it imposes will continue to spin out their repercussions: the spiral of circulation remains unbounded even as the novel itself draws to a close.

In this way, we find parallels in the novel to Mauss's critique of English sociology. But we also find traces in *Equinox* that suggest a critique of Mauss's sociology—a critique made specifically from the site of literature. Jacques Derrida's reading of Mauss provides a way of getting a handle on this. According to Derrida, Mauss's sociology distorts the nature of the gift. "One could go so far as to say that a work as monumental as Marcel Mauss's *The Gift* speaks of everything but the gift."[75] Mauss's version arises from his assumption of a closed circle, of a bounded economy and the "total social fact" whose identity allows Mauss as sociologist to discover scientifically its symbolic laws.[76]

But for Derrida, a gift, if there is any, is precisely that which interrupts the circle of economy. By definition the gift, in order to be a gift, must not in any form come back to the donor: "For there to be a gift, there must be no reciprocity, return, exchange, countergift, or debt." Hence, "If the figure of the circle is essential to economics, the gift must remain *aneconomic*."[77] Rather, the gift precedes and renders possible the existence of an economic system: it is the letter that never reaches its intended addressee, the impossibility whose paradoxical presence sets into motion the economic system of exchanges.

A social formation organized by the gift takes a spiraling, open-ended form, and in it, the role of a third party is crucial. Gift exchanges between two parties have a tendency to decay into simple bartering, a closed-circle economy in which goods of equal value are exchanged. By contrast, a third party guarantees that the gift keeps moving along an unending chain, that it never comes back in the same form to the original donor, that its value remains contingent and incalculable.[78] The gift establishes an erotics of sociality with others, in which one constantly gives oneself away with no guarantee of anything like equal value in return. A gift that stops moving, that is not continuously passed on through an endless string of third parties, risks being transformed into capital or some other form of property, whereupon it would lose its quality of being a gift.

In fact, as Derrida argues in rereading Baudelaire's "Counterfeit Money," a gift could only take place if the donor and donee were both unaware of it, because an awareness of giving or having been given would already amount to a return on the gift. Gift giving, then, is an experience that cannot be owned. A self-aware donor could only be a subject that sought "through the gesture of the gift to constitute its own unity and, precisely, to get its own identity recognized so that that identity comes back to it, so that it can reappropriate its identity: as its property."[79] Such a return would destroy the gift, render it into something else. And yet it is also true that a gift by definition cannot be a mere random occurrence, because there can be no gift without an intention to give: there must be a free intention on the part of the donor to give. Paradoxically, for the event of a gift to occur, there must be an impossible coming together of intention and accident.

As such, a gift can only be an interruption of the circle of time, of expectation, of identity. The gift is impossible—and yet not unthinkable or unnameable. As Derrida's argument continues, the impossibility that is the gift becomes increasingly bound up with narrative and writing. Language itself becomes the "given"; we receive it "from out of a fundamental passivity" so that it "gives one to think but it also steals, spirits away from us. . . . It carries off the property of our own thoughts even before we have appropriated them."[80]

In unpacking the peculiar nature of this impossible possibility, Derrida frequently invokes examples from literature, in particular fiction. Literary fiction is like the gift in that it starts from an impossible possibility, the assertion, "I am lying." Encountering this phrase, a reader cannot know finally if it is true or false: more precisely, if it is true, then it must also be false. Literary fiction begins with this sort of impossible structure: it is a lie that truthfully admits to being false. Out of this impossibility, the time and space of narrative open up and are presented—like a gift—to the reader. According to Derrida, the novel presents a more fundamental critique of the common sense of modern property than does Mauss's sociological theory of the gift.

In sum, literature is a site for working out the impossibility of the gift. As readers, we encounter a literary text as a given. Literature announces itself as fiction; it is the lie that announces itself as a lie, and therefore, impossibly, is true. The movement of this impossibility opens up the time and space of narrative. Given this time, we readers enjoy the impossibility of borrowing the experiences that properly belong to others, the characters and narrators.

For Derrida, then—and, as I am arguing, for Sōseki as well—literature is not bound by the rational, a priori laws of the social totality. Literature for a sociologist—as in Bourdieu's famous reading of Flaubert's *Sentimental Education*—amounts to locating the closed-circle structure of the text, its "upside-down economy" of social norms and the "circular causality" pertaining between authorial position in society and his literary perspective, so that to call a novel experimental means precisely that its procedures can be verified through repeated demonstrations conducted in the laboratory of social structure.[81] But for Derrida, literature is an open-ended spiral, and its pleasures lie not in the domain of the repeatable but rather of the unprecedented. *Experimental* in the realm of literature means something quite different from what it does in the sciences: it refers to the singular, that which cannot be repeated. Literature gives its pleasure from "the sudden coming of the new, of that which cannot be anticipated or repeated."[82]

In literature, we take possession of that which both common sense and science tells us we cannot possibly own: we appropriate the experiences of others, even when that experience is the experience of the impossibility of appropriating the experience of others. *Equinox* is precisely this sort of fiction. In it, Ichizō's assertion is typical: "I am lacking in the qualifications necessary for a character in a novel."[83] In *Equinox*, the characters repeatedly compare themselves to characters in fiction and proclaim as a result that they themselves are nothing like characters in novels: *Equinox* is more antinovel than novel.[84] It presents us with a nested box of compounding impossibilities: in a novel that is not a novel, we obtain the experiences of others which by definition we cannot obtain, experiences whose original owners do not even own them. As a result of this impossibility, the time and space of the narrative open up and are presented—like a gift—to the reader.

When we combine this reading of *Equinox* with our previous consideration of Sōseki's critique of Western sociology, perhaps we can conclude as follows. It may well be that a "sociological reading of a text breaks the spell" of the literary.[85] The problem is, of course, that to awaken from this spell one must fall under the spell of sociological reason. But the gift that is literature "would be that which does not obey the principle of reason: It is, it ought to be, it owes itself to be without reason, without wherefore, and without foundation."[86] In *Equinox*, Sōseki experimented with ideas that have remarkable parallels to those found in Mauss's sociology—but then Sōseki went beyond, to critique that sociology from the position of literature.

Sōseki, then, clearly understood the need to critique literature from the perspective of sociology, but he did not neglect the need to critique sociology from the perspective of literature. Sōseki does not simply reject sociology: that science, after all, provided the starting point for his own attempt to theorize literature. But if sociology produces its knowledge by following the established rules for normal science, literature produces knowledge (and pleasure) by calling into question those same rules, by probing the impossibilities that ground the knowledge of normal science, by moving forward into the unmapped territory of the unprecedented that is revolutionary science—the realm of the genius that Sōseki explored at length in his theory.[87] On this unmapped territory, one cannot rely on naturalized concepts such as property to ground identity; rather, the very writing of the literary text is aimed at destabilizing identity, at pulling the ground out from underneath it. This is, I think, the direction in which Sōseki's walking stick—and Baudelaire's snake—would take us, and it is one of the most important legacies of Sōseki's theoretical project for us today.[88]

In writing *Equinox*, the genre Sōseki employed was that of a collection: "a series of individual short stories," as hinted in his newspaper preview quoted at the beginning of this chapter, that were "combined . . . to form a single longer work." This choice of genre seems related to the questions of the relation of sociology to literature that I have explored here. A figure we encountered in chapter 2 as one of Sōseki's teachers provides a window for unpacking this connection. Motora Yūjirō was among the first Japanese to engage with the new modern discipline of sociology. He received his PhD from Johns Hopkins University in 1888, studying under G. Stanley Hall—a seminal figure in the rise of American psychology. Hall studied at Harvard with William James and at Leipzig with Wilhelm Wundt and later served as president of the American Psychological Association. But Motora's dissertation, "Exchange Considered as the Principle of Social Life," clearly belongs not to the field of psychology, but rather sociology—its final three chapters are an extended attempt to define what Motora calls "The Domain of Sociology."[89] There is no evidence that Sōseki read Motora's dissertation, but it opens another avenue for exploring the sociology of property and its relation to literature.

As his title suggests, Motora explores exchange as the primary mechanism binding society together. "Strictly speaking, it is only through the action of exchange, that man can become a member of society."[90] He proposes an expansive definition of *exchange*: it includes not only commodity exchanges but also gift exchanges (including the notion that moral esteem constitutes a return even in cases of seemingly pure gift giving), emotional relationships such as friendship, and our relations to the state and its imposition of coercive "positive law": "If we sacrifice our freedom to obey a law or rule, we must receive some benefit by doing so," he writes.[91] Such positive laws become necessary because humans in society always operate under the condition of limitations: "as population increases in the world, they can not [sic] use land so freely as the ancient nomads use [sic] to do. There must be limitation, and thus, the idea of property came [in]to existence."[92] Property in turn requires the existence of a state: "From the peculiar relations under which we live in society, the necessity arises of distinguishing the property of one person from that of another. Not only so, but we must have some security to maintain this distinction. We find this security in the organization of political institutions."[93]

Motora questions the distinction commonly drawn in early sociology between social statics and social dynamics. Physics, he argues, has demonstrated that all seemingly static matter actually consists of dynamic force. Physical science studies force and movement in nature, which arises independent of human consciousness, whereas sociology studies social movement, which is always mediated by individual human consciousness. Social movement in turn is composed primarily of exchange: "It is a transference of ownership from one person to the other, or a service of one person to the other, or any other activities. . . . When we say a social movement proper, we mean neither movement in space, nor social agitation, but the transference of the ownership from one person to another person, or sometimes, it may mean the change of social constitution."[94] Property at rest, not immediately subject to exchange, might seem to suggest the existence of social statics, which would then lie outside the domain of sociology: "it is clear that society has nothing to do with the relation of man to his property, so long as it is not transferred."[95]

But even in seemingly static property ownership, a kind of kinetic social force is at work. When a person claims something as their property, they cannot do so on their own subjectively, but must objectively mark it in a socially recognizable manner to distinguish their property from that of others, thereby excluding others from using it.

> Property, then, may be said to have two predicates. This property belongs to a person A, and it belongs to no one else. It is on this double relation, that the social nature of property, depends. As we have seen above, property may be used by an owner, according to his will. Thus it is private, but at the same time it bears a negative relation to society. The negative relation is no less important than the positive. It becomes more evident when this right is violated. The violation is considered as an offense, not only against the owner, but also against the whole of society. Here we see that the property of a person, A, can be such not by the power or will of the person A, alone, but [because] the whole of society agrees upon it and grants it as his property. This is accomplished through the instrument of the authority of the government. . . . The preservation of property without transferring it, has much similarity to the balance of power—the statics. Both in this case and in physics, it is not an absence of power, but it is the action of power, that keeps a thing in its position. So in this negative function of society or of the government, there is an activity, through and through.[96]

Motora's emphasis on the centrality of exchange foreshadows the later work of Mauss and other sociologists discussed above. It also seemingly anticipates a more recent attempt to rethink human society: Karatani Kōjin's *The Structure of World History: From Modes of Production to Modes of Exchange*. Karatani provides an original and systematic rereading of Marxist versions of world history, approached not from the perspective of modes of production, but rather of what Karatani calls modes of exchange. The task Karatani sets for himself is a thought experiment: to understand what he calls "Capital-Nation-State," the dominant form of modern societies, as well as the possibilities that exist for superseding it. While sympathetic to Marxist analysis, Karatani argues that Marxist thinkers (although not necessarily Marx himself) have failed to adequately consider the role of state power. His goal is to produce a model that accounts for state power and its ideological counterpart, nationalism, alongside the determinative economic force of capitalism.

Like Motora, Karatani distinguishes between several different modes of exchange. Mode A is the form of gift exchanges that Mauss argues were definitive of archaic societies, but which Karatani stresses exist in all social formations that arise following the adoption of fixed settlement and the abandonment of nomadic primitive communism. Mode B arises with the emergence of the state: it involves an exchange of submission to the state by its subjects in return for receiving protection from the state. Mode C is commodity exchange, the sort that is central to Marx's critique of capitalism. Finally, there is Mode D, a "return of mode of exchange A in a higher dimension." Mode D first emerges in the communistic practices of early universal religions that arise in resistance to state power and market economies; it indicates a form of exchange that "can be called by many names— for example, socialism, communism, anarchism, council communism, associationism" and that rather than getting fixated on any specific meaning should best be considered as a kind of unknown, an X.[97] Mode D takes the form of a Kantian regulative ideal, an ideal that can never be actualized in reality but that nonetheless provides an index toward which our actions are directed.[98] All four modes of exchange are present in every society, Karatani argues, but in any given society one mode is dominant and gives primary shape to that society. Under Karatani's model, private property first emerged in tandem with Mode A as a consequence of the sedentary revolution, when the abandonment of constant nomadic movement made possible the pursuit of agriculture and the stockpiling of wealth.[99]

Karatani first rose to prominence as a literary theorist—indeed, his early work as a literary scholar focused on Natsume Sōseki. While he has since switched his focus from literature to critical theory, literature and aesthetics continue to occupy an important role in his theorization of world history. *The Structure of World History* includes an extended meditation on the role of aesthetics and aesthetic philosophy as critical attempts to alleviate the "destruction of community at the hands of capital-state."[100] Mode D, the regulatory ideal toward which revolutionary movements yearn, appears first in the form of universal religions, which arise as critical moments in societies dominated by Modes B (state power) and C (commodity exchange). But we also see its presence in other domains, including the aesthetic and literary, which share a certain orientation with universal religions: "Mode D does not appear only in religion. It also appears in such forms as philosophy, literature, and the arts."[101] In his subsequent work, Karatani would focus in particular on Mode D in the ancient Greek philosophy of isonomia.[102]

Modes of exchange are, of course, a way of rethinking Marx's structure of world history, which centered on modes of production. Karatani appropriates a Marxist schema of history as a series of stages of development, insisting on two crucial caveats. The stages are all universal and hence should not be limited to specific geographical areas: "what Marx calls the Asiatic social formation is not limited to Asia in any strict sense"; it is rather universal.[103] Second, "it is crucial to realize that the various social formations—clan, Asiatic, ancient classical, and Germanic—are not successive linear historical stages but instead exist simultaneously and in mutual interrelationship. Because each social formation exists in a world of mutual interrelationships, none can be considered in isolation."[104] The various social formations defined by their dominant mode of exchange are structural formations, not historical stages in a teleology of development that assumes a Eurocentric movement of progress from Africa to Asia to Europe, and they each have to be understood within the world system in which they exist.

Karatani's rejection of a teleological model stands in striking contrast to Motora's theory of exchange. Not surprisingly, Motora's theory of sociology is fundamentally teleological: society progresses constantly toward higher and higher stages of development. Whereas natural forces move in an aimless manner, Motora maintains, human consciousness shapes social movement so that it is always moving toward some predetermined goal.

There is a spirit of progression inherent in the nature of man. No matter what is the level to which life has risen, man desires to attain a higher one. The aspiration of the poet and artist for perfection, that of the statesman for an utopia, that of Divine perfection in religion, and that of a man of science for facts as they are; these are of the essence of human nature and give impulse to the activity of man from within. These are absolute stimuli of the social movement. They are not the result of social organism, but social organism, on the contrary, tends to be moulded . . . by these ideas. They influence society, only through the agency of consciousness of individual persons, and thus of their desires.[105]

For Motora, exchange is not only the primary mechanism holding the social organism together, it is also the primary engine by which the human desire for progress is realized.

As we have seen, for Karatani literature can be one of the sites where the effects of Mode D can be detected. Motora, by contrast, excludes literature and the other arts from the domain of sociology.[106] When we turn to Sōseki's theory of literature, we note that Sōseki defines literature as being in part a sociological problem. But as we have seen above, while Sōseki accepts a teleological model for explaining social development, akin to Motora, he rigorously excludes the domain of literature from that model. Literary history does not, he insists, unfold along a single linear trajectory from primitive to advanced. Following my reading of *Equinox* above, we can also posit that literature for Sōseki is a site for experimenting with Karatani's nonteleological Mode D, an expression of a yearning for a return to a social formation characterized by the return of Mode A, a gift economy, in a higher dimension.

We see the rejection of teleological form not only in Sōseki's theorization of literary history but also in his literary works, which are characterized by open-ended narratives that defy closure around some tidy conclusion. Sōseki's suspicion toward the novel genre, even as he wrote what were called novels, is an expression of this. As he groped his way forward, experimenting with techniques for writing full-length works of prose fiction that did not obey the teleological form of novelistic temporality, he played with multiple genres—including, with *Equinox*, the collection as a form.

The collection is, of course, one of the oldest literary genres in East Asia. The remarkable prominence of collections in the classical Japanese canon would lead Earl Miner to identify a dominant "principle of collection" that would have "a major, enduring effect on subsequent Japanese literature."[107]

Likewise, traditional Chinese culture produced numerous literary collections that Sōseki knew well, works that often claimed the status of history but that, as Judith Zeitlin notes, "are not arranged chronologically and freely mix fact and fiction," so that in them "the idea of history" seems not linear or progressive but rather "closer to an encyclopedic compilation of narratives past and present organized around a central theme."[108] In writing *Equinox* as a collection, Sōseki was invoking East Asian literary traditions that dated back centuries.

But in 1910 the collection as a genre and technique also defined the cutting edge of the modern. In an era in which "the belief in evolution, progress, and history itself was wiped out," artists around the world engaged in the kind of radical artistic experimentation we now call, somewhat paradoxically, modernism.[109] Many of their works experiment with the genre of collection as a strategy for escaping the control of a linear, progressive time. We might consider, for example, the collages produced by Picasso and Braque, the fictional assemblages of story fragments into longer works such as Gertrude Stein's *Three Lives* (1905), poetic montages like T. S. Eliot's *The Waste Land* (1922), or Debussy's rejection of the linear logic of the symphony to produce "music without a destination" in such compositions as *La Mer* (1905).[110] Sōseki's appropriation of the genre of collection in *Equinox* provided him an avenue for experimenting with literature as a shared experience that exceeded the teleological temporalities of sociology proper. I have argued here that this involved imagining alternative forms of owning and sharing that deviated from sociological models of economy and property. As Sōseki was well aware, this choice of genre put him in sync with the most antimodern modernist currents of global artistic practice in his day.

CHAPTER FOUR

The Tragedy of the Market

Younger Brothers, Women, and Colonial Subjects in Kokoro

> The reader probably knows that no promise or writing given to a slave is legally binding; for, according to Southern laws, a slave, *being* property, can *hold* no property.
>
> HARRIET JACOBS, *Incidents in the Life of a Slave Girl* (1861)

> Unlike inheritance *ab intestato*, bequest is one of the attributes of property: the ownership of a thing cannot be looked upon as complete without the power of bestowing it, at death or during life, at the owner's pleasure: and all the reasons, which recommend that private property should exist, recommend *pro tanto* this extension of it. But property is only a means to an end, not itself the end. Like all other proprietary rights, and even in a greater degree than most, the power of bequest may be so exercised as to conflict with the permanent interests of the human race.
>
> JOHN STUART MILL, *The Principles of Political Economy* (1848)

Judging from the underlining and marginal comments left behind in books he owned, Sōseki possessed at least some interest in the question of slavery. The markings around a passage discussing the situation of emancipated American slaves from his copy of Benjamin Kidd's *Social Evolution* (1898), for example, suggest an engaged reader. Kidd's racist argument—that regardless of any humanitarian efforts made to achieve equality, as a matter of scientific principle the superior Anglo-Saxon race will naturally come to dominate "inferior" races—does not sit well with Sōseki. Kidd cites W. Larid Clowes's *Black America* (1891) (Sōseki underlines the title in the footnote citation) on the refusal of postbellum Southern whites to accept as equal anyone with even a trace of "African blood" as proof of this "law" of social evolution. Next to this passage, Sōseki jots, "This is of the same nature as prejudice against *eta*. It is not a matter of *natural selection*, but rather of *racial prejudice*."[1]

Kidd's argument continues: "The cardinal principle of the political creed of 99 per cent of the Southern whites is that the <u>white man must rule at all costs and at all hazards</u>." Sōseki responds to the phrase he has underlined with another marginal outburst: "How remarkably arrogant! It is absurd to claim that this is caused by nature." Kidd proceeds to assert that we must accept such domination by superior races as inevitable. We have no choice but to accept as fact, he argues, "the nature of this rivalry which compels us to make progress whether we will or not, its tendency to develop in intensity rather than to disappear, and our own powerlessness either to stay or to escape its influence." To which Sōseki rebuts in yet another marginal aside, "I don't buy this theory" (Kono setsu o kikan).[2]

Sōseki's interest in slavery transcends simple disgust at Western racism. His copy of Charles Letourneau's *Property: Its Origin and Development* (1892) contains some two dozen underlined passages discussing slavery. In a section titled "Genesis of Private Property," Sōseki underlines as follows in a passage discussing the earliest emergence of private property among primitive tribes:

> <u>The only exchangeable values were, at first, children and women.</u> They might be exchanged, for frequent raids allowed of their being replaced if necessary; but <u>slaves constituted the earliest capital admitting of important accumulation, and the institution of slavery only developed when difficult and toilsome work, especially agricultural work, needed to be done.</u> Before this, folks preferred to kill, and often to eat the conquered; but when agriculture had acquired a certain amount of importance, slave labour was joined to that <u>of women</u>. . . . <u>From this time forth the contention between rival tribes was no longer merely a struggle for existence; its object was often to gain riches, to capture slaves, exchangeable values.</u> The robbery of neighbours was the grand source of power and wealth. At the same time the family, first maternal, then paternal, disengaged itself from the confused relationships of the primitive clan, and capital, generally very ill-gained, was transmitted from mother to son, from uncle to nephew, finally from father

to son. Hence arose the institution of hereditary castes, and the individual separated his private interests more and more from those of the community. According to a commonplace dear to economists, the first origin of private property was individual work. Ethnographic sociology, on the contrary, brings numerous proofs to attest that <u>private property of any degree of importance had its origin in violence and usurpation.</u> The captive spared was at first the most important sort of capital, and the earliest agricultural work was done, far from spontaneously, by women and slaves.[3]

As with the situation of animals discussed in chapter 1, the issue of slavery presented a scandalous problem for nineteenth-century theorists of property.[4] On the one hand, as Letourneau acknowledges, the slave was undeniably a crucial early form of property, perhaps the prototype for all subsequent forms of ownership.[5] On the other hand, the notion that human beings could not properly be owned became one of the defining traits of a modern, civilized society. As Cheryl Harris argues, "Slavery produced a peculiar, mixed category of property and humanity—a hybrid possessing inherent instabilities that were reflected in its treatment and ratification by the law."[6] Civilization, in other words, was in many ways grounded in the very form of property it could not acknowledge and whose troubling shadow lingered over other forms of ownership—for example, the modern legal fiction of corporate personhood—that were posited as hallmarks of enlightened societies.[7] This capacity to trouble modern definitions of property may have attracted Sōseki's interest to questions of slavery.

Sōseki's fiction itself contains no extended discussions of slavery.[8] But his novels frequently revolve, explicitly or implicitly, around other human subjects who are situated ambiguously within modern regimes of ownership. In this chapter I will take up his 1914 novel *Kokoro* and weave together two different approaches to the work. The first is to think about the novel in relation to the modern property regime that arose in Japan during Sōseki's lifetime, that messy assemblage of legal codes, everyday practices, and disciplinary knowledge that we have been examining in this book. As we have seen in previous chapters, one of the clearest instantiations of this regime was the 1898 Meiji Civil Code, still today in modified form the basis for Japan's family and property law.[9] The Civil Code was a milestone in Japan's ongoing project to achieve parity with the modern world powers in an increasingly integrated global political economy; its enactment was, for example, a key component in Japan's successful campaign to have the Unequal Treaties abolished, a goal realized in 1899. In rereading *Kokoro*,

I look particularly at the status of human characters placed in a kind of double bind within Japan's modern property regime: namely, younger brothers, women, and colonial subjects. Like the ambiguous figure of the slave, each of these was defined as being potentially both a subject and object of ownership—that is, as being simultaneously a possession and a possessor. As Jeff Nunokawa argues about female characters in British Victorian fiction, "Like the slave auction with which it is persistently linked, the marriage market is often less a scandal of possession than a scandal for possession."[10] That scandalous quality is one of the things that makes women, along with younger brothers and colonial subjects, interesting as fictional characters.

The second approach I try to weave into my analysis is something critics have long noted about *Kokoro*. Like so many of Sōseki's works, *Kokoro* is a novel about being unable to speak.[11] James Fujii has provided one of the most forceful articulations of this reading: *Kokoro* "refuses or is unable to address the imperialist dimensions of Japanese modernity." For Fujii, this "refusal to admit any meaningful consideration of events outside Japan's borders" is linked to repeated instances in the work of "broken communication" and an "inability to express feeling."[12] This use of fictional aphasia as a literary trope appears in the opening lines of *Kokoro* and carries all the way through to its final sentence: impeded speech forms a kind of leitmotif across the work.

I want to push this reading of the novel a step further. When confronted by a novel that thematizes an inability to give voice to the essential, shouldn't we step back and ask what this silence is trying to say? In other words, what is *Kokoro* signifying in its insistence on repeatedly marking the presence of the unspeakable? The answer, I suggest, has much to do with the new property regime. Appearing at a moment in which new mechanical recording technologies made it possible to alienate the human voice from the body of the speaker, even transforming it into a novel form of property whose ownership status provoked considerable legal debate, in *Kokoro* the inability of Sōseki's characters to speak carried considerable significance.[13] Whereas in the previous two chapters I focused on Sōseki's response to ways in which property became an object of knowledge in modern academic disciplines, here I turn my focus toward Sōseki's relation to the historical situation of 1914 Japan, specifically the institutionalization and expansion of the modern property regime in the first two decades of the twentieth century.

The Meiji Civil Code makes a fascinating companion text to the novels of Sōseki, as Japanese scholars have noted.[14] As is well known, the code defined citizenship, ownership, and legal status primarily in terms of the unit of the family rather than the individual. Even today, the primary document of Japanese citizenship is not the individual birth certificate, but rather the family registry. When we read the text of the Civil Code, we find a markedly paranoid stance: an attempt to imagine in advance and head off all possible conflicts that might arise from unclear lines of succession or blurred claims to ownership. The family head, a position normally passed down from father to eldest son, is legally the owner of the family's property, but what if he wants to abolish the family? (The answer: Article 762.) And what happens to a wife's property when she gets married? (Article 801: "A husband manages his wife's property.") Can the adoption of a son as presumptive heir to the family head position be annulled, and if so under what circumstances? (Article 862.) Under what conditions can a family head disinherit the presumptive heir from his position? (Article 975.) Can the legal heir to the family head position refuse that position? (Article 1020.)

The authors of the Civil Code wrote in seeming horror of deviations, of muddy ambiguities that might trigger crises that left ownership and lineage up for grabs. They clearly favored what Carol Rose calls "crystals": "hard-edged doctrines that tell people exactly where they are" in networks of ownership and kinship. By contrast, Sōseki the novelist seems to delight in ambiguous mud: unanticipated complexities that erupt and throw ownership into confusion.[15] Such moments become prime material for building fictional narratives. When we read through the Civil Code, we repeatedly find in bare bones the outlines of Sōseki's fictional plots—including that of *Kokoro*.

As anyone who has read *Kokoro* knows, it is a novel about property: about inheritance and disinheritance, about thieves and the fear of theft, about stolen affections. This goes beyond mere thematic content; as Ken Ito has argued, "the inheritance dramatized in *Kokoro* must be approached not only on the level of story, but on the level of discourse," that is, as an integral part of the narrative structure of the work.[16] The novel repeatedly depicts ways in which the transmission of both tangible and intangible property from one generation to the next is disrupted or corrupted. Like Joyce's *A Portrait of the Artist as a Young Man*, published two years later,

Kokoro presents not so much a modern inheritance plot as a modernist disinheritance plot.[17] At least eight different last wills appear explicitly or implicitly in the novel, only one of which seems to be carried out without a hitch.[18] In other words, Sōseki in *Kokoro* as elsewhere seems interested in the sorts of stories that become possible when the modern property regime falls into confusion. In the novel we find Sōseki once more constructing a fictional experimental world in which the established property norms falter and possible alternative norms flicker into view. To paraphrase Viktor Shklovsky, here Sōseki toys with a literary dimension where property might change hands along alternative lineages, from uncle to nephew rather than from father to son—or from mother to daughter.[19] And in the novel, these crises in ownership appear in tandem with moments of literary aphasia, of an inability to speak.

Originally serialized in the *Asahi* newspaper from April 20 through August 11, 1914, *Kokoro* presents itself as—among other things—a reflection on the end of an era. In its closing pages, the character known as Sensei vows that he will commit suicide in the wake of the 1912 death of the Meiji emperor out of loyalty to what he calls the "spirit of Meiji," a spirit that he believes will pass away with his generation. This sense of fin de siècle in the novel corresponded well with the historical moment of its publication. Early in 1914, the empress dowager, widow of the Meiji emperor, died, and her state funeral in late May once again placed the city of Tokyo in official mourning, re-creating the physical setting of 1912 Tokyo that would be depicted in the novel. As the newspaper audience read *Kokoro* in its daily installments that month, it must have seemed that—once again—the Meiji period was ending.

In the West, too, the period of the 1910s has been widely theorized as marking the end of an era. In Henri Lefebvre's formulation,

> The fact is that around 1910 a certain space was shattered. It was the space of common sense, of knowledge (*savoir*), of social practice, of political power, a space thitherto enshrined in everyday discourse, just as in abstract thought, as the environment of and channel for communications; the space, too, of classical perspective and geometry, developed from the Renaissance onwards on the basis of Greek tradition (Euclid, logic) and bodied forth in Western art and philosophy, as in the form of the city and town.[20]

This sense of ending is often linked to the outbreak of World War I—an event that also shaped the world in which *Kokoro* was first read: the conflict broke out in the opening weeks of July.[21] On August 8, 1914—three days before the final daily installment of *Kokoro* was published—Japan decided, at Britain's request, to enter the war. As we saw in the previous chapter, World War I has since been widely theorized as marking the end of a historical era and the beginning of the fractured and decentered world of modernism.[22] Even at the time, it was perceived by Sigmund Freud and others as marking a disillusionment that called into question many of the West's confident assumptions about historical progress and civilization.[23] The moment of *Kokoro*'s publication, then, was perceived by both contemporaries and later historians as marking the end of something. The fundamental modes of space and time by which people understood their place in the world were shifting, and this would have enormous ramifications in the practices and beliefs surrounding ownership in Japan and elsewhere.

YOUNGER BROTHERS AND THE BURDENS OF INHERITANCE

To unpack this in relation to *Kokoro*, as I have already suggested, I will look at three types of figures that present potential moments of confusion over property ownership. The first figure is that of the younger brother. Sōseki himself was a younger brother and was keenly aware of the alienability that this position implied.[24] Under the Civil Code, the eldest son (for example, Sensei in *Kokoro*) typically inherited the family property, including the family estate. When the eldest son assumed the position of family head upon the retirement or death of his father, his younger siblings all in a sense belonged to him, even as they were destined eventually to leave the family and set up their own new single-generation households. Hence, alongside the more conventional "traffic in women," we often find in Meiji-era literature a "traffic in men," as families negotiate the ownership of superfluous younger brothers.[25] *Grass on the Wayside* (*Michikusa*, 1915), Sōseki's most autobiographical novel, focuses on Kenzō (based on the author himself), a younger brother given up for adoption to a childless couple, and his troubling relations with his adoptive parents, who treat him as a prized possession—as, that is, a kind of slave: "The couple did everything in their power to make Kenzō exclusively theirs. They regarded him no doubt as their possession by right. And the more they pampered him, the more possessive they became. He did not mind so much being owned physically, but even his childish heart grew fearful at the thought of becoming emotionally enslaved to them."[26] Kenzō's subsequent adult anxieties over his familial and ethical duties blur into contractual disputes over property and inheritance, and he finds that his past lives on in the present primarily in the form of bad debt.

As legally incompetent subjects, younger siblings had to receive permission from the family head to get married. Moreover, a second son, such as the student who narrates the first half of *Kokoro*, could expect to inherit little from his father and instead had to seek his own way in the world—in this case, by heading to the university to receive an elite education that would presumably prepare him for a career as a government official. Or, like the character K in the novel (or Sōseki himself), he could be sent out for adoption to another family that lacked a first-son heir.

In *Kokoro*, Sensei repeatedly urges the student to clarify what property he as a younger brother can expect to inherit from his father. At one point, the two men go for a long stroll and come across a path leading up a hill. They pause, wondering if they can follow it. In other words, they wonder whether they are facing a parcel of private property: "At length the little path opened out at a point below a large house shrouded by the fresh young leaves of an overgrown garden. We quickly realized that this was no private dwelling—the sign attached to the front gate bore the name of a plant nursery. Gazing at the gently sloping path, Sensei suggested we go in for a look."[27] They do enter, but can't shake the sense that they have violated property norms. Later, they encounter a boy, the son of the family that owns the tree nursery, who chides them for not obtaining permission to tour the nursery: they should have at least paid their respects at the family house before entering the property. Sensei hands the boy a coin in a playful gesture of payment.

These seem minor details, yet when we trace through the conversation that Sensei and the student pursue while walking through the nursery, those details take on deeper significance. It is during this walk that Sensei most clearly addresses the issue of the student's property. "It's none of my business, of course, but in my opinion," he instructs the student, "if there's anything to inherit you should make sure that matter's completely attended to before it's too late. Why not arrange things with your father now, while he's still well? When the worst happens, you know, it's inheritance that causes the biggest problems."[28] From this point on, the narrative increasingly revolves around the tangled issues of property: inheritance, broken wills, theft, and the guilt of ownership.

Such questions would not be so urgent if the student were an eldest son. The eldest son is supposed to inherit the family estate and become the family head—which is why, as Nishikawa Yūko notes, protagonists from late nineteenth- and early twentieth-century Japanese fiction are rarely first sons: their life course is determined in advance, and hence uninteresting.[29] But we should also note that Sōseki repeatedly depicts first sons who choose not to become masters of the (often rural) family estate and who instead liquidate the lineage's property.[30] In *Botchan*, for example, the hero's older brother liquidates the family's estate and hands his younger brother a sum of cash to pay for his education. Likewise, in *The Gate*, Sōsuke relies on his uncle to liquidate his family property after his father's death. And in *Kokoro* itself, we learn that Sensei too declines to take over the old family estate after his parents die. He entrusts everything to his uncle, and after the uncle squanders much of the estate, Sensei intervenes and has a friend negotiate a cash liquidation of what remains of the family property:

> My friend disposed of everything as I had asked. Naturally, it took some time after my return to Tokyo to finalize it all. Selling farm land in the country is no easy matter, and I had to be careful lest others take advantage of me, so in the end I settled for a lot less than the market price. . . . Sadly, the inheritance my parents had left me was greatly diminished. . . . Still, the proceeds were more than enough for me to survive on as a student—indeed, I used less than half the interest from it.[31]

This tendency for fictional first sons in the late Meiji period to liquidate the family estate, particularly its landed property in the rural ancestral hometown, is one sign of the novel's historical situation—the moment Lefebvre describes as the shattering of a previously lived understanding of space. Lefebvre is writing primarily about Europe, but his work is helpful for understanding the world in which *Kokoro* appeared. Lefebvre argues that the rise of modernity's abstract conception of space required a radical change in the status of land: "The process begins, as we have seen, with the land, which must first be wrenched away from the traditional form of property, from the stability of patrimonial inheritance. This cannot be done easily. . . . The entirety of space must be endowed with exchange value. And exchange implies interchangeability: the exchangeability of a good makes that good into a commodity."[32] By around 1910, land had increasingly become just another commodity, freely alienable, its worth calculated primarily in terms of exchange value rather than any sentimental or use value it might also hold. This change in the status of land is connected, according to Lefebvre, with the rise of urban centrality, in which the city comes to dominate the countryside—so that, for example, landed property near the center enjoys a higher exchange value than that located farther away.

While there are significant differences between Meiji Japan and the European experience that Lefebvre is describing, nonetheless in broad outlines, we can see much similarity. The process whereby land increasingly became measured in exchange value had already begun in the Tokugawa period, but rapidly accelerated after the Meiji Restoration. As we have seen, one of the first major reforms introduced by the new government came with the 1873 Land Tax Reform, which launched a new taxation system: taxes would now be paid in cash rather than kind, and they would be calculated not in relation to actual crop yield but rather the exchange value of the land. Prior to the Meiji period, land had not been considered "as simply a commodity but as one element embedded in a variety of economic, political, and social networks."[33] With the Meiji reforms, however, for the first time since 1643, land in Japan legally became alienable property (though there had been an informal, de facto market in real estate before this).

These changes in real estate property law led to much dislocation in the countryside—which in turn led to a rapid increase in migration to urban areas from the 1890s on. From the late 1880s, a massive wave of rural peasants migrated to Japanese cities and became urban laborers.[34] The urban expansion led to the discovery of new social problems. One predictable result of urbanization was a relative decline in the amount of rice produced in Japan. Rising food prices in Japan became a key social problem throughout the 1910s, leading ultimately to the Rice Riots of 1918. With fewer Japanese engaged in farming, and a rapidly swelling population of urban laborers, rice shortages became common. One of the countermeasures adopted by the Japanese state was to increase Japan's imports of rice from its colonies, most notably Korea. Already in 1910, nearly 5 percent of the Korean rice crop was being exported to Japan; by 1920 the figure would rise to 22 percent.[35] The increasing integration of Korean agricultural production into a global commodity market was abetted by the 1910–18 Land Cadastral Survey—a paradigmatic instance of modern colonial enclosure that, as I argue below, also casts a shadow over *Kokoro*. As a scholar of eighteenth-century British literature—the literature, that is, of the age of enclosure that saw rural landholding in England violently reorganized to meet the dictates of an increasingly global system of mercantile capitalism and imperial dispossession—Sōseki may well have sensed similarities to the transformations Japanese landowning practices underwent in his own lifetime.[36]

The world in which the characters from *Kokoro* move reflects this new system of commodified land where the exchange value of land is largely determined by proximity to urban centers. In it, nobody wants to get stuck living on the family estate in the country: not the student who narrates the first half, not the student's older brother, not Sensei, not K. Despite the sentimental value attached to the rural family home, they all want to liquidate their family's rural landed property in order to acquire the capital that will enable them to live in the urban center.

Moreover, this confrontation with the new land property system is associated in the novel with an inability to speak. In the first section of the novel, as we've seen, Sensei repeatedly urges the student to speak to his father about the status of their family property—but the student hesitates. Then, in the middle section of the novel, after the student returns to his hometown and he and his older brother anticipate their father's impending death, they hold tense conversations about who should assume responsibility for the family home (and their mother) in the countryside. The student tells us that his ailing father was "of the firm belief that there would be no change in the house, and that my mother would remain there until the day she died," yet the father also expects his younger son to find a job in far-off Tokyo, insisting that the student should find "some good work and become independent" because, as the father lectures, "You really should not have to rely on anyone from the day you graduate." The student muses: "I found this contradiction rather funny, but it also pleased me, since it meant that I could go back to live in the city."[37]

With the status of the family estate unresolved, the two brothers find speech increasingly difficult. "Essentially we were awaiting our father's death, but we were reluctant to express it that way." Finally, the elder brother suggests that the younger son take over the family house after the father's death. The younger son, well versed in the strictures of the Civil Code, pushes back: "The elder son's the one who ought to come back," he reminds his brother.[38] The father, though, "still did not speak of how he wished his estate to be managed after [his] death." Unable to bring themselves to ask him directly, the brothers turn to an uncle, whose response is of little help: "It would be a great pity if he died leaving things he wanted to say unsaid, but on the other hand, it doesn't seem right to press things from our side," he tells them.[39] To speak openly about the family property seems somehow patricidal, and so in the end, what needs to be said is left unsaid, and the father falls into a coma with the issue of property still unresolved.

This is when the letter from Sensei arrives, announcing his intention to commit suicide. The younger son resolves to abandon his father on his deathbed and race to Tokyo to ascertain whether Sensei is still alive. He sees his family members, but cannot bring himself to speak and tell them what he is about to do. He instead heads for the train station. "Once there, I penciled a letter to my mother and brother, holding the page against the station wall. It was very brief, but I judged it was better than simply running off without apology or explanation, so I gave it to the rickshaw man and asked him to hurry and deliver it. Then, with the vigor of decision, I leaped onto the Tokyo-bound train."[40]

One of the quirks in the structure of *Kokoro* is that this passage, located exactly at the midpoint in the novel, is chronologically the last event to take place in the story: everything on the pages that follow consists of flashbacks to earlier times. For the reader, in a sense the student never gets off that Tokyo-bound train. But we can extrapolate a probable outcome to this abandonment of his dying father: it will likely lead to the student's disinheritance. By running off to Tokyo without speaking to his family (though he does dash off a note), he manages to evade the position of heir to the family estate, a position that he clearly doesn't want. For this younger brother, the failure to speak what must be said opens an escape hatch, a way out that allows an escape from the tragic burdens of ownership.

WOMEN WHO TRAFFIC

Things work differently for women, the second kind of figure suspended in a seemingly impossible position within the modern property system. Under liberal capitalism, "Women are property, but also persons; women are held both to possess and to lack the capacities required for contracts."[41] Like the younger brother, a woman is a subjected subject under the Meiji Civil Code: she can own things, but she is also in a sense owned.

This ambiguous status was particularly foregrounded in conventional Japanese marriage practices. Through this traffic in women, daughters were often exchanged between families as if they were a kind of commodity. Sōseki had encountered Western sociological studies of this practice that used the language of ownership. In Charles Letourneau's *The Evolution of Marriage and of the Family*, for example, he came upon the following passage linking Japanese sexual mores to a woman's status as property of her family: "It is not the chastity of woman, as we understand it, but her subjection, that Japanese morality requires. The woman is a thing possessed, and her immorality consists simply in disposing freely of herself."[42] The marginal comment jotted in next to this passage in Sōseki's copy: "What a stupid thing to say" (Baka o ie).

But Sōseki's objection here is likely directed against the assertion that sexual chastity was not expected of unmarried Japanese females, rather than the notion that they were possessed by their family. As we have seen, many of his novels revolve around triangular relations in which one man seizes ownership rights over a woman from another man through an act of betrayal. In these narratives, women are figured as a kind of property to be trafficked among men—and *Kokoro*, with its narrative of how Sensei betrayed his friend K to obtain his wife, provides an exemplary instance.[43] In this sense, Sōseki's novels resemble much Victorian British fiction, in which the wife was figured as "a brand of property supposed immune from loss," a possession that, unlike a slave, was fundamentally inalienable and thereby functioned ideologically as a fantasy form of secure ownership. Owning a wife seemed to offer a kind of security that other commodities, always in danger of moving away from their owners via exchange, failed to provide. Such texts associate "the institution of marriage with the stabilization of possession," making women into "a form of estate that replaced insecure marketplace property."[44] As Gayle Rubin notes, this tendency is one of the legacies that capitalist societies inherit from earlier forms of society organized around Maussian gift economies.[45]

Yet even when he portrays marriage as a mode of ownership over the wife, Sōseki is generally more interested in the insecurities that this form of possession introduces. One of the lines by which he develops this interest can be seen in his apparent fascination with women who own things. We can think, for example, of the money that Mineko lends to Sanshirō in *Sanshirō* or that Kiyo lends to Botchan in *Botchan*.[46] Likewise, we can think of the aunt who, after her husband's death, holds the title to Sōsuke's family property in *The Gate*, and the troublesome mother-daughter duo who usurp family property in *The Poppy*. Or again, the intense competition between the wife and younger sister of the protagonist in *Light and Dark* to supply the money he requires to make up a budgetary shortfall. *Kokoro* belongs to this lineage of novels depicting women as owners. This theme comes to the foreground in the delicate negotiations Sensei undertakes with Okusan, his future mother-in-law, for the hand of "Ojōsan," his future wife. But in these negotiations, Sōseki twists standard expectations, so that it is the woman who acts with "masculine clarity" and who played "the male far better than" Sensei. Okusan is the owner of her daughter, and she agrees to transfer her to Sensei—though she also says that she would never force her daughter to accept someone she didn't want to marry.[47]

Likewise, that daughter, Sensei's wife, Shizu, is narrated simultaneously as both possessor and possession. Here, too, this instability in the property regime is linked to an inability to speak. To sketch in what I mean, let me take up two passages from the novel. The first occurs near the end of part I, when the student pays what turns out to be his final visit to Sensei to take his leave before he travels back home to be with his dying father. Sensei and his wife speak about death and inheritance:

> He [Sensei] gave his fan a few boisterous flaps, then turned to his wife. "I'll give you this house when I die, Shizu."
>
> She laughed. "And the earth under it too, if you don't mind."
>
> "The earth belongs to someone else, so we can't do much about that. But I'll give you everything I own."
>
> "Thank you. But I couldn't do much with those foreign books of yours, you know."
>
> "Sell them to a secondhand dealer."
>
> "How much would they come to?"
>
> Instead of replying, Sensei continued to talk hypothetically about his own death. He was firmly assuming he would die before his wife.[48]

What is being imagined here, of course, is a household headed by a woman, one who would own its properties—an unusual situation in late Meiji Japan, yet one permitted under numerous sections of the Civil Code. Moreover, we are told elsewhere that Sensei's wife, who was raised in another household headed by a woman, has inherited her mother's property, as well—this is the one instance in the novel of a successfully executed last will and testament.

In Shizu we find a prototypical Sōseki figure: a woman whose hold over property forms an implicit, and sometimes explicit, challenge to patriarchal norms of ownership in modern Japan.[49] This contradicts the triangular narrative that dominates the second half of the novel, in which Sensei narrates her as if she were a piece of property, the object of an ownership dispute between two men. Shizu may not possess a voice (her name itself means "silence"), yet she does possess property: she functions as a legal subject, one with a proper name (unlike the other characters in the novel), a status that renders her absence as a speaking subject all the more palpable.[50] The novel performs into being, that is, a strange lacuna, an impossible speaking position that nonetheless exists. We see this tendency to problematize a woman's voice elsewhere in the novel, too: Sensei is troubled by the question of whether or not his mother's last words, as reported to him by his uncle—that he should depend on that uncle in the future and that he should go to Tokyo—really constituted her last will, her final bequest to him.[51]

The second passage I will discuss occurs early in part III, "Sensei's Testament," at the beginning of the long letter that Sensei sends the student, explaining the reasons for his mode of life and his eventual suicide. As I discussed in chapter 3, Sensei writes, "My past is my own experience—one might call it my personal property [shoyū]. And perhaps, being property, it could be thought a pity not to pass it on to someone else before I die." Without an appropriate heir to pass it on to, however, he had resigned himself to having his experiences buried with him after he died. But now he has met the student and declares, "Among the many millions of Japanese, it is to you alone that I want to tell the story of my past." As many critics have noted, this passage ends with Sensei virtually naming the student as his heir: "Now I will wrench open my heart and pour its blood over you. I will be satisfied if, when my own heart has ceased to beat, your breast houses new life."[52]

In this passage, personal experiences are treated as a sort of property, a view that was in accord with the science of psychology that Sōseki knew— for example, William James's *Principles of Psychology* (1890), a work discussed at length in chapter 2. In James's version of possessive individualism, personal experiences form a kind of inalienable property. To return to a passage already discussed in chapter 3, Peter could never acquire Paul's past experiences, because the memories of each come permanently branded with their unique seal.

> When Paul and Peter wake up in the same bed, and recognize that they have been asleep, each one of them mentally reaches back and makes connection with but *one* of the two streams of thought which were broken by the sleeping hours. . . . The past thought of Peter is appropriated by the present Peter alone. He may have a *knowledge*, and a correct one too, of what Paul's last drowsy states of mind were as he sank into sleep, but it is an entirely different sort of knowledge from that which he has of his own last states. He *remembers* his own states, whilst he only *conceives* Paul's. Remembrance is like direct feeling; its object is suffused with a warmth and

intimacy to which no object of mere conception ever attains. This quality of warmth and intimacy and immediacy is what Peter's *present* thought also possesses for itself. So sure as this present is me, is mine, it says, so sure is anything else that comes with the same warmth and intimacy and immediacy, me and mine.[53]

From the multiple streams of consciousness that exist, we can always pick out the memories that belong to us and to us alone because they come indelibly branded with our mark of ownership, like cows in a herd. The passage from *Kokoro* quoted above likewise treats past personal experiences as a form of property, but with a significant difference: Sensei is proposing that they are an alienable form of property and that through an act of narration or speaking (*monogatari*), ownership can be transferred. To reiterate a point I made in chapter 3, here we see literature being used to imagine a transfer of property that was impossible, at least according to certain forms of modern knowledge.

This passage also foregrounds the fact that the earlier version of the will spoken to his wife was a lie. Sensei promised to leave Shizu all of his property, but betrays this vow in his letter to the student. The very last sentence of the novel consists of Sensei's commandment to the student never to reveal to Shizu the secret of Sensei's past: "While she remains alive, I therefore ask that you keep all this to yourself, a secret intended for your eyes only."[54] In other words, despite Sensei's promise to leave all of his property to his wife, here he identifies one possession that she must never own. The student's acquisition of ownership over Sensei's personal experiences, his assumption of the position of Sensei's heir, comes with a condition: in order to own these experiences, he must not speak of them to the woman around whom they revolve. To acquire this property, the student must remain silent.

This mirrors the powerful aphasia that struck Sensei himself with regard to the circumstances surrounding the acquisition of his wife. "Again and again I would decide to summon my courage and confess everything to her. But at the last minute some power not my own would always press me back."[55] The condition of inheriting Sensei's property, it seems, is that one also take possession of (or be possessed by) Sensei's inability to speak. Once again, the novel links ownership to an inability to give voice to that which must be spoken. But as we next explore, the novel also holds out the possibility for sidestepping such a tragic denouement.

The final ambiguous ownership position I want to examine is that of the colonial subject. *Kokoro* is unusual among Sōseki's fiction in that, unlike most of his novels and stories, its pages include no direct reference to Japan's expanding empire.[56] In fiction prior to *Kokoro*, Sōseki had frequently portrayed the effect of the colonies on Japan, especially in the form of fantasies and imagination—the rubber plantation in Singapore, for example, that Keitarō dreams about in *To the Spring Equinox and Beyond* (*Higan sugi made*). In such works we find an explicitly colonial imagination: those who suffer under class hierarchies and from uneven development within Japan proper (such as Morimoto in *Equinox*, Nami's husband in *Kusamakura*, or Kobayashi from *Light and Dark*) consider going abroad to colonial and semicolonial space, where the racial hierarchies of empire will assign them membership in the ruling elite. The dream is of an unpeopled country, a place where land is available free for the enjoyment.[57] This dream, however, would become considerably more complicated after 1910.

Perhaps that is why *Kokoro* avoids discussing the empire. The passing mention that Shizu's father died as a soldier, presumably in the 1894–95 Sino-Japanese War, and the figure of General Nogi, a military commander during both the Sino-Japanese War and the 1904–5 Russo-Japanese War, are the only indirect references to empire I can detect in its pages. This silence is the source of James Fujii's abovementioned critique of the novel as evading the issue of empire, part of an important lineage of criticism that takes Sōseki to task for his complicity in Japanese imperialism.[58] But is this silence simply an evasion? Or is it instead a way of saying something? I'd like to push Fujii's reading of the novel a bit further by bringing in the question of property: perhaps the inability to speak marks an indirect attempt to own up to something that cannot be said directly. In other words, perhaps the silence here is a guilty silence, a silence that is trying to signal the presence of a tragic, unspeakable secret.

This guilt is bound up with ownership. A leitmotif runs through the novel: anyone who takes possession of property also acquires—directly or indirectly—a burden of guilt. I argue here that this guilt can also be understood, in part, as imperial guilt, one associated with both the violent acquisition of new colonial possessions and the imposition of new norms of property in those territories. Sōseki scholars have often made much of his 1900–1902 journey to London and its impact on his work, but—as Fujii has charged—they rarely note the impact of his 1909 journey through semicolonial Korea and Manchuria, recounted in the travelogue *Mankan tokorodokoro* (Travels in Manchuria and Korea, 1909), nor attempt to situate *Kokoro* within its historical moment of imperial expansion.[59] In a certain sense, the empire is the unspeakable of this text, and yet, as I will attempt to demonstrate, that secret leaves its guilty traces throughout the novel.

Guilt permeates *Kokoro* like a poisonous miasma. In some instances, the guilt that haunts characters has an identifiable cause. Sensei's wife, kept ignorant of the backstory that Sensei confesses in his letter to the student, worries that she might somehow be the cause for Sensei's withdrawal from the world.[60] K himself is driven to his death out of guilty fear that he has betrayed his own ideals. General Nogi commits ritual suicide to atone for his guilt at having lost his flag in battle decades earlier in the Satsuma Rebellion of 1877. The student narrator will likely be burdened by future guilt after having abandoned his own father on his deathbed. Even characters who have done nothing wrong seem to be infected by this guilt. In a delirium brought on by his fatal illness, the student's father inexplicably cries out to beg forgiveness from General Nogi—whom he has surely never met. And of course the ending of *Kokoro* is dominated by Sensei's overpowering sense of guilt over his betrayal of his friend K, a guilt that finally drives him to suicide.

To exist in the imaginary world of *Kokoro* is, it seems, to harbor guilt. This has led critics to speak of the novel as an expression of modern alienation—which it surely is. But we can also understand this guilt in more specific terms. As I have already suggested, guilt in *Kokoro* is associated with ownership. In the world depicted by the novel, anyone who takes possession of property also acquires—directly or indirectly—a sense of guilt. Pierre-Joseph Proudhon's assertion that property is theft seems to haunt the novel, so that whenever a character acquires ownership over something, it invariably comes with a burden of guilt attached. To acquire possessions, the novel implies repeatedly, is to commit a violation of ethical norms—and thereby to acquire an often suicidal guilt.

Hence, the guilt that permeates *Kokoro* is bound up with acts of acquisition. But I want to suggest that this guilt can also be understood, in part, as an imperial guilt, one associated with both the violent acquisition of new colonial possessions and the imposition of new property regimes in those territories. In a sense, the empire is the unspeakable of this text, a secret that haunts the novel even as it can never be directly addressed.

We can link this guilt-in-ownership to the actual practices and discourses surrounding property in the Japanese empire of 1914. The period of *Kokoro*'s original serialization coincided with that of the Land Cadastral Survey in Japan's new colony of Korea. As we have seen in earlier chapters, since the dawn of the Meiji period, the Japanese state shared the widespread presumption that private property systems formed a yardstick for measuring the degree of civilization attained by any given society. Hence, as its empire expanded, Japan held up its 'civilized' modern property systems as evidence of its right to rule over backward neighboring countries, all justified under the "ideology of improvement" that characterizes settler colonies around the globe.[61] As its empire expanded, Japan undertook to introduce new property regimes based on the Meiji Civil Code into each of its colonial possessions—with, for example, the Former Natives Protection Law in Hokkaido and the Okinawa Prefecture Land Reorganization Law, both in 1899, which replaced existing communal land systems with private property regimes.[62]

Japan's 1910 annexation of Korea was likewise justified on the grounds that Japan would civilize its neighbor, including its property systems. The Land Cadastral Survey was the first major policy that attempted to realize this goal. Implemented from 1910 to 1918, the survey "mapped all plots of land, classified it according to type (upland, dry land agriculture, paddy, etc.), graded its productivity and established ownership. The survey created a reporting system that required all owners to claim and prove title to their land."[63] The effort was part of a massive reorganization of the Korean countryside meant to rationalize taxation and property systems. Such surveys formed one of the most common technologies of rule in modern empires around the globe, stretching back to the British dispossession of Ireland in the seventeenth century.[64] Like other colonial land registration schemas, one of the unannounced goals of the Korean survey was to erase traces of other culturally specific practices of land ownership and usage. The survey also aimed at facilitating the penetration of Korea by Japanese settlers and at accelerating the integration of Korean agricultural produce, especially rice, into the export market.

There is some controversy among historians as to the extent to which the Survey can be held responsible for the massive economic dislocation suffered by rural Korea under Japanese colonialism. Conventional wisdom, especially among Korean historians, has stressed the disruption of Korean society, arguing that Japanese settlers and corporations exploited the new system to displace Korean farmers and acquire their lands. The period clearly did see much flux, as many impoverished rural Koreans moved to cities or emigrated to Japan, Manchuria, and elsewhere in search of better economic prospects. The Government-General of the colony became the largest single landholder in Korea (holding nearly 40 percent of all of Korean land by 1930), and the notorious Oriental Development Company, a semigovernmental corporation designed to facilitate Japanese settlement in Korea, emerged as a major force in Korean landholding.[65] Murai Osamu argues that the infamous massacre of Koreans by vigilante groups in Tokyo following the 1923 earthquake can be at least indirectly linked to the survey. Koreans were present in large numbers in Japan by 1923 due to the changes in the labor market brought about in part by the survey—and the violent opposition to the survey and other elements of colonial rule. The persistent opposition to the survey finally exploded in 1919 with the anticolonial March First movement, which Murai suggests provoked Japanese anger over Korean "ingratitude"—an anger that is, I think, intimately bound up with the imperial guilt that haunts *Kokoro*.[66]

Other historians have downplayed the direct impact of the survey. Edwin Gragert notes the Land Cadastral Survey carried on reform work begun in the last days of the Yi dynasty (1392–1910), even before Japanese annexation, so that it cannot be said to have initiated radically new policies and procedures. Moreover, careful scrutiny of landholding records demonstrates that there was little change in landholding patterns during the course of the survey. Large-scale changes, Gragert argues, did not take place until the 1930s and were the result not so much of the survey as of the onset of the Great Depression, which depressed rice prices and led to numerous foreclosed mortgages on agricultural lands. Gragert acknowledges the economic stresses faced by rural Koreans in the early decades of the colonial period, but argues that these should be understood more in terms of the impact of broader market forces rather than as the direct result of the survey.[67]

Hence, the Land Cadastral Survey did not necessarily represent the first introduction of private property norms into Korea. As Gragert notes, "not only was private landownership legally recognized throughout the Yi dynasty, it was also a widely accepted principle and practice."[68] In terms of developing a legal framework for landed private property, Korea for much of the Yi dynasty may well have been 'ahead' of pre-Meiji Japan. But the survey undoubtedly accelerated the transformation of the status of land into a pure commodity measured by its exchange value—the abstraction of land that Lefebvre identifies as a global phenomenon occurring around 1910. Between 1914 and 1929, nearly one-half of all land in Korea changed hands, a sign of "how marketable land had become since the Yi dynasty and how successful colonial Japan had been in removing obstacles to the buying and selling of land."[69]

While the notion of land as alienable private property might not have been unknown in Korea, the notion that property titles required recognition by the colonial state as the sole arbiter validating ownership was new—ownership had to be verified by registration with the colonial government. In other words, to own land in colonial Korea required first that one acknowledge one belonged to the Japanese empire—to accept, that is, the massive dispossession that the annexation represented. As Bhandar notes, "There is an undeniable relationship between the sovereign assertion of control over territory and the mechanisms through which the state organizes individual property ownership, which is primary to the overall apparatus of governance that characterizes the colony. The concept of possession in one register is taken as analogy in another."[70]

Not surprisingly, this provoked strong resistance. Initial attempts to reform landownership in Korea and facilitate Japanese settlement during the protectorate era (1905–10) led to open armed rebellion in Korea, which was suppressed by brutal military force under Itō Hirobumi. This led to Itō's assassination in Harbin in 1909 by a Korean nationalist, an incident that Sōseki introduces in his 1910 novel *The Gate* (see chapter 2). The formal implementation of the survey in the years after the annexation in 1910 continued to provoke resistance, sometimes violent resistance.

Gragert argues that in the years 1910–19, the Japanese reading public saw little evidence of unrest in Korea.[71] But when we turn to newspapers published in Japan during *Kokoro*'s serialization in the spring and summer of 1914, we find considerable evidence of the unrest. While *Kokoro* never directly mentions Korea or the Land Cadastral Survey, the pages of the *Asahi* newspaper from April 20 through August 11, 1914 (the period of the novel's serialization) include on an almost daily basis reports from the new colony, including the progress of the Land Cadastral Survey and violent resistance against it. From April 16 through May 1, for example, *Asahi* ran a fifteen-installment series of columns under the title "On the Politics of the Governor-General" ("Sōtoku seiji ron"), generally sympathetic to the goals of Japanese colonization of Korea but highly critical of what the author (using the pseudonym Keijō Kōdō 京城耕堂) saw as counterproductive heavy-handed measures taken by the colonial regime, including the Land Cadastral Survey. *Asahi* also carried reports on violent protests in April and May 1914 against the survey, including such headlines as "Koreans Riot Again" or "Violent Mob Erupts in Chōsen."[72] These contradicted an article that had appeared on May 11, 1914, announcing the successful completion of the survey.[73] Later that summer, *Asahi* ran a series of articles (July 14–22) on the problem of "bandits" in Manchuria: code word for armed resistance to Japanese rule on the continent.

In sum, the extension of modern property systems to the empire, especially Korea, and the violent response that this solicited characterize the historical moment in which *Kokoro* first appeared and literally forms part of the 1914 print media context in which the novel first appeared. I want to suggest that this might be part of what lies behind the guilty silence that dominates the novel. Property ownership, and in particular the ongoing violent imposition of the modern property regime in colonial Korea, seems to be one of the things that must not be spoken.

Pushing further, if we read Sōseki's narrative of ownership, theft, and aphasia allegorically, it might cause us to reread the "spirt of the Meiji era" that Sensei invokes at the end of the novel:

> I had almost forgotten the expression "to die with your lord." It's not a phrase that is used in normal life these days. It must have lain there deep in my memory all these years, decaying slowly. Reminded of it by my wife's jest, I replied that if I were to die a loyal follower's death, the lord I was following to the grave would be the spirit of the Meiji era itself. I was joking too, of course, but as I spoke it seemed to me that this old, disused expression had somehow gained a new meaning.[74]

Is the unspoken, unspeakable truth behind "the spirit of the Meiji era" something to do with property, something to do with Korea? Sensei in his youth believed himself to be the victim of a theft, his uncle's usurpation of Sensei's rightful inheritance from his father, and this reinforced his sense of determination to retain undisputed possession of his own selfhood.

> True enough, my uncle's betrayal had made me fiercely determined never to be beholden to anyone again—but back then my distrust of others had only reinforced my sense of self. The world might be rotten, I felt, but I at least am a man of integrity. But this faith in myself had been shattered on account of K. I suddenly understood that I was no different from my uncle, and the knowledge made me reel. What could I do? Others were already repulsive to me, and now I was repulsive even to myself.[75]

At the end of the Meiji period, looking back over his life and his relations with K, Sensei comes to the discovery that he was the thief all along—a realization that when given voice inevitably takes the form of a suicide note.[76]

Reading this as an allegory for the modern property system, perhaps we can summarize "the spirit of the Meiji era" as it appeared in 1914: Japan entered the Meiji period believing itself to be the potential victim of violent dispossession, that it lay in mortal danger of having its sovereignty usurped by the Western powers. But at the end of the Meiji period, having achieved parity with the Western powers as a competing empire (a parity symbolized by Sensei's swimming partner at the opening of the novel, a mysterious Westerner who never reappears), Japan in the figure of Sensei looks back over the violent wreckage of the past, culminating in the annexation of Korea in 1910, and realizes itself to have been the thief. That this violence was implemented in practice through forced reform of the landed property system, first in Japan and later in its colonies, adds to the dark portrait. The elaborate procedures followed in 1910 to make the annexation of Korea appear a legitimate transfer of ownership cannot conceal the fact that this amounted to robbery.[77] The violence that resulted from the subsequent Land Cadastral Survey and the disruption of Korean society generated by the forced transformation of land into a readily exchangeable commodity could only further goad Japanese guilt, even if that guilt could not be openly acknowledged. We can read the novel, that is, as constructed around a real kernel too devastating to address openly, yet so overbearing that its taint can be found on every page. Possession is the secret that must not be voiced: possession requires silence. To speak of the essential here would be suicidal, to lose the ability to possess not only colonial others but also the self.

Moreover, the novel is constructed, as I have suggested, around the notion that possession leads to guilt—tragic guilt. In particular, possession of Sensei's secret (about how he betrayed K in order to win possession of his wife) leads to guilt, which is clearly one of the reasons Sensei makes his dying request that the secret be kept from his wife: he is trying to protect her from the sort of guilty conscience that has destroyed his own life. The student in reading the letter acquires not only the secret but also the guilt—and we recall that his act of reading the letter is simultaneous to his own act of betrayal, abandoning his own father's deathbed, an action that could lead not only to his disinheritance but also to his own burden of guilt. As critics have noted, the novel is structured around a series of repetitions, and the student seems bound to repeat the experiences of Sensei once he has taken possession of the secret and the guilt it entails.

THE COMEDY OF THE COMMONS, THE TRAGEDY
OF THE MARKET

In part, then *Kokoro* belongs to the genre of tragedy. Sensei's guilty secret, once he defies his own aphasia and commits it to language, leads him to a tragic death. If we take his suicide as the defining event in the novel, then the work clearly is a tragedy. But a revisionist generation of critics in the 1980s and '90s returned to *Kokoro* and turned the novel on its head. They shifted its center of gravity away from the latter half toward its first half, centering the narrative not on Sensei's tragic death, but instead on the student's subsequent survival, his apparent ability to escape the guilt of ownership and aphasia. It is the student as narrator, after all, who survives to tell us everything. This new interpretation set off a lively debate among Japanese critics that, as I have discussed elsewhere, largely turned around questions of propriety and ownership of the text.[78]

If we focus on the first half of the novel, we might be tempted to classify its genre as comedy or even romance. We can't simply ignore the latter half, however, which does gesture toward the genre of tragedy. Sensei's tragic flaw seems nothing other than his inflexible determination to own properly: to appropriate his familial inheritance, his wife, his very self. His story instantiates the tendency for a "will to possess property, inseparable from the necessity of transmitting property" to finally consume "those who live by its principles."[79]

Garrett Hardin's classic 1968 essay introduced a widespread tendency to think about alternatives to private property systems as leading inevitably to the "tragedy of the commons."[80] But is tragedy necessarily the genre of the commons? Carol Rose, for example, has argued cogently for a "comedy of the commons."[81] We could make the case that the first half of *Kokoro* consists of precisely such a comedy. Moreover, as I have argued throughout this book, Sōseki's theory of literature posited it as a domain for experiences that were inherently shared—as a kind of commons. In engaging with literature, readers are all in a sense free riders, taking our pleasures at will, with little or no regard for the rights of others, in accordance with what Sōseki called "self-centeredness" (*jiko hon'i*), a practice of reading he spelled out most fully in his 1914 lecture, "My Individualism" ("Watakushi no kojinshugi"). And yet, in the domain of literature our self-centered acts of reading do not deplete the commons that is the text. Far from it: they often enrich it with new possibilities—as did, for example, the revisionist readings of *Kokoro* in the early 1980s.

Accordingly, in looking at the darker second half of the novel, I'd like to suggest we are dealing with a tragedy of the market, the tragedy of private property.[82] Sensei's tragic end—the tragedy that dare not speak its name—is the result of his doomed efforts to achieve clear title of ownership. This drive for appropriation is potentially a self-destructive mission that leads to violence, whether directed against colonial subjects in Korea or against the suicidal eldest son brooding alone in his home in Tokyo.

One of the most wretched instantiations in the novel of this tragedy of the market can be found in Sensei's relation to his own parents' graves. When he first begins to suspect his uncle of absconding with his proper inheritance, Sensei credits the realization to his deceased parents.

> Then it occurred to me that perhaps my dead parents had suddenly cleansed my dulled eyes and given me a clear vision of the world. Deep inside, you see, I felt that my parents continued to love me as in life. Even though I was already well acquainted with the real world by then, the strong superstitious beliefs of my ancestors coursed deep in my blood. No doubt they still do.
>
> I climbed the nearby hill alone and knelt before my parents' graves, half in mourning and half in gratitude. I prayed to them to watch over me, feeling as I prayed that my future happiness lay in those hands buried beneath the cold stone. You may laugh, and no doubt I deserve it. But that is who I was.

He eventually decides, "I owed it to my dead parents to obtain a detailed understanding of the house and property that I had until then left for my uncle to look after."[83]

As we have seen, he subsequently decides to liquidate what remained of the family estate and move permanently to Tokyo. One of the features of the new property system, especially its land registration scheme, is that in rendering land into a pure commodity, it abstracts away any history, personal or shared, or social relationships in which that land might have been previously tangled up. Under the new regime, whether in colonial Korea or metropolitan Japan, when you purchase title to land you erase the entire history of previous ownership: to hold fee simple title is to be free of any lingering entanglements from the past. Sensei realizes this only too well. He writes, "I had decided to leave my native home forever. . . . Before I left, I paid a final visit to my parents' graves. I have not seen it since, and now I never will."[84]

The cost of accepting the alienable commodity status of the land was to lose himself as a familial being caught up in multiple social relationships. As Bhandar notes, the modern landed property system, fee simple titles registered with the state, is a key technology in rendering land into a purely fungible property: "the system of title by registration renders prior ownership interests irrelevant; that which is recorded on the document archived in the state registry becomes the proof of ownership, not the historical memory, social use, kinship ties, or other relations that were bound up with land use and ownership for centuries prior to becoming more fully commodified."[85] Under its sway, "land was viewed as a commodity entirely divorced from the people living on it."[86] It was precisely the imposition of this imperial technology that Korean subjects were violently protesting in 1914.

Having mobilized this new technology designed to facilitate the alienation of landed property, Sensei finds himself alienated, along with his family's former holdings. After liquidating the family's estate, Sensei can visit K's grave in the city, but not that of his own parents. His flawed insistence on owning himself and his property leads to utter alienation and death. Sensei's story is the tragedy of the possessive individual, one that Sōseki takes care to balance against the comedy of the younger brother and the woman. Sōseki also signals by way of silence the existence of an even more radical alternative, one that Sōseki himself might not have been able to speak directly: the rebellious colonial subject who resists dispossession of his or her familial lands. Sensei silently accepts the erasure of the past that his contemporaries in Korea refused to remain mum about.

CONCLUSION

Who Owns Sōseki? Or, How Not to Belong in World Literature

It took a considerable period of time to acknowledge proprietorship in artistic, literary, and scientific work, beyond the peremptory action of selling the manuscript, the first machine, or the original work of art. In fact, societies are not very interested in recognizing the heirs of an author or an inventor—a benefactor of humanity—more than certain limited rights over the things created by the one that owns those rights. One likes to assert that they are the product of the collective mind as much as of individual mind. Everyone wishes them to fall into the public domain or join in the general circulation of wealth as quickly as possible.

MARCEL MAUSS, *The Gift* (trans. W. D. Halls; 1923–24)

Thus, the author writes in order to address himself [*sic*] to the freedom of readers, and he requires it in order to make his work exist. But he does not stop there; he also requires that they return this confidence which he has given them, that they recognize his creative freedom and that they in turn solicit it by a symmetrical and inverse appeal. . . . Art here is a ceremony of the *gift* and the gift alone brings about its metamorphosis. It is something like the transmission of titles and powers in the matriarchate where the mother does not possess the names, but is the indispensable intermediary between uncle and nephew. . . . Thus, reading is a pact of generosity between author and reader.

JEAN-PAUL SARTRE, *What Is Literature?*
(trans. Berand Frechtman; 1948)

When literary texts circulate beyond their original readerships, they find themselves opened to new ways of reading—and sometimes to new ways of being opened. If, like me, you are a native speaker of English and first learned Japanese as an adult, after the physical habits of reading had inscribed themselves as second nature onto your body, you will sometimes find yourself making a silly mistake when you pick up a Japanese book: you open it from the wrong side. In a sense, you demonstrate that the text doesn't belong to you, nor you to it. But that unconscious blunder also signals other possibilities, lines of escape from the domains of proper belonging.

Such a misreading will in either event bring you face-to-face with the modern property regime. If you mis-open a Japanese book this way—for example, Sōseki's *Theory of Literature* (*Bungakuron*, 1907)—one of the first things you encounter is the copyright notice, just as when you open an English book the proper way. Except you are looking at the back matter of the Japanese book, rather than its front matter. This inverted gesture provides an apt figure for my project in this conclusion: to read Sōseki backward, starting from the copyright notice. I will use it to launch a meditation on how his theory of literature might help us rethink two contemporary problems: the expanding domains of intellectual property and the category of world literature. This misreading may represent a kind of trespass on his works, but I argue that it is consistent with Sōseki's theory and practice of literature, and moreover that it helps us link those meaningfully to issues that concern us today, particularly the tendency for modern property systems to generate new forms of ownership and for world literature to reproduce problematic norms for belonging.

Modern ownership regimes necessarily do more than simply fixing stable lineages of ownership. They also have to elicit movement and fluidity: property systems, particularly under capitalism, exist for the sake of enabling exchange, distribution, circulation. They play a crucial role in directing such movements so that surplus value always flows back to the designated owner, where it supposedly belongs. This process takes place by various forms of enclosure, one of whose names is canonization, and another of whose names is intellectual property.

In the face of these tendencies, we need strategies for reimagining and reinvigorating the commons, a playful but serious practice that Sōseki understood well. Otherwise, as Sōseki's cat reminds us, we might well end up paying for the air that we breathe. In this conclusion, I explore ways in which Sōseki's theory of literature encourages forms of reading that poach literary texts from existing canons and release them into new commons, moving them from an economy defined by scarcity to one defined by plenitude. This involves both actual property systems (particularly those of intellectual property law) and more metaphorical schemas of belonging, such as those that define canons of world literature. Belonging and ownership are not exactly the same thing, and yet each of the two concepts has a pronounced tendency to show up in the other's definition, especially when mediated by other categories of identity, such as race and gender.[1] In bringing them together here, I will suggest ways in which Sōseki's theory and practice of literature remain relevant to the way we practice and think of ownership and belonging today.

WRITING AS PROPERTY, WRITING AS GIFT

In parallel with North America and Europe, Meiji Japan participated in "an expanding universe of property."[2] This involved an explosion in new forms of ownership, including intangible forms of property—copyrights, trademarks, stocks, and bonds—as well as the emergence of new types of owners, including the legal fiction of corporate personhood. Capitalism can never sit still; it must constantly seek out new commons that it can enclose into private property, properties that can in turn be launched out onto the market as commodities in order to generate surplus value through exchanges. Sōseki the historical figure participated in this process in multiple ways: he was a copyright holder, as well as a significant investor in stocks, especially in the rapidly expanding financial sector. At the time of his death, he held sixty shares in the Bank of Taiwan and forty shares in Dai Ichi Bank, valued together at the time at 15,400 yen, equivalent today to roughly 46 million yen ($421,000).[3] Sōseki in his last years apparently earned enough on his stock holdings (in addition to his *Asahi* salary and publishing royalties) to enjoy a comparatively luxurious lifestyle.[4]

In short, he was a serious investor who threw himself into the new, increasingly global, systems of intangible ownership. But he also dealt with these emergent phantasmal forms of property more playfully in his fictional narratives. In *I Am a Cat* (*Wagahai wa Neko de aru*, 1905), Meitei (Waverhouse) confuses tangible stock certificates with the intangible properties they represent: "I myself once used to own eight hundred and eighty-eight and a half of them [shares in the Tokyo Tram Company]. But I'm sorry to say that the vast majority have now been eaten by insects, so that I've nothing but one single half-share left. If you'd come up to Tokyo a little bit earlier, I would gladly have given you some ten shares that, till very recently, the moths had not yet got at." His interlocutor avers that quality stocks are the safest investment, because they only go up in value. Meitei agrees, asserting, "Quite right: even half a share, provided one holds it for roughly a thousand years, will end up making you so rich you'll need three strongrooms." He laments via an egregious pun the failure of Kushami (the character loosely modeled after Sōseki himself) to understand the modern economy: to him, "stocks [*kabu*] are no more than some vague kind of gillyflower [*kabu*]."[5] A few pages later, Meitei continues to riff off the difference between tangible and intangible property, expounding on how the classical Greeks valued knowledge over gold, whereas he dismisses Kaneda, the nouveau riche villain, as simply a walking paper currency, an "animated banknote," while his daughter is "nothing but a circulating promissory note."[6]

In a more serious vein, the plot of *And Then* (*Sore kara*) revolves in part around the 1907–8 Greater Japan Sugar Refining Company scandal. The scandal exploded when newspapers reported that the company had bribed Diet members as part of a plot to cover up its financial manipulations in paying out dividends to shareholders based on bogus bookkeeping. The goal of the bribes was to get the government to buy up all outstanding shares in the corporation, thereby papering over the concealed red ink.[7] It was, in short, an early attempt at enacting a pattern often seen in modern capitalist economies of privatizing gain (even when that gain was utterly fictional) while shifting risk onto the public. Protagonist Daisuke's rejection of his family and his inheritance revolves around his disgust at the family's involvement in the corruptions of emerging finance capitalism and its manipulation of unreal forms of property.

Questions of literature as intellectual property also appear in Sōseki's fiction. The novella *Nowaki* (*Autumn Storm*, 1907) thematizes the problematic relationships between writers, literature, and money. Likewise, the semiautobiographical *Grass by the Wayside* (*Michikusa*, 1915) repeatedly discusses the status of writing as property that can be owned and alienated—and in a manner that often troubles the distinction between commodity exchange and gift giving. Witness, for example, the scene where Shimada, the former adopted father of the protagonist Kenzō, offers to make a gift of an antique calligraphic scroll to Kenzō—who wants nothing to do with this gift, not only because he is convinced the scroll is forged but also because he is certain that Shimada will later insist on monetary compensation for it.[8] Or Shimada's belief that one who writes and publishes a book leaves behind a valuable property—a source of future income—to his heirs when he dies.[9] Or again, the rather bizarre attempt in the closing chapters by Shimada to sell back to Kenzō an utterly innocuous letter that Kenzō wrote (at Shimada's explicit request) years earlier, when the legal ties between the two were officially severed. Shimada seems to believe the letter has great value, but in Kenzō's eyes, it is a worthless scrap of scribbling: "That's just a scrap of paper," he declares to Shimada's intermediary. "It's of no use to anybody, him or me."[10] Kenzō in fact does provide Shimada with money, but insists that it be considered a pure gift, provided with no expectation of any reciprocation.

The novel further depicts the impact writing has on Kenzō's own finances. A friend who edits a magazine has asked Kenzō, a university professor, to contribute a piece of writing to his journal.

> For him [Kenzō], who up until then had no need to produce anything but his tiny, detailed research notes, it was nothing more than his first attempt at working his brain in a new and different field. He simply abandoned himself to the feeling of enjoyment that followed the trail of his writing brush, wherever it led. In his heart, he expected no recompense whatsoever. When the editor set the manuscript fee in front of him, he felt pleased to have stumbled into this unexpected reward.[11]

Kenzō receives thirty yen in payment for his story. He presents part of this as a gift to Otsune, his former adoptive mother (Shimada's ex-wife). Kenzō hopes to make this too a pure gift, one that involves no subsequent entanglements, but he quickly realizes that his gift to Otsune has launched a new economic cycle: she will expect to receive five yen every time she visits him in the future. Kenzō by the end of the novel is deliberately writing more pieces for publication in order to earn money: this is how he acquires the hundred yen he eventually presents to Shimada. (If we connect this fictional character to Sōseki's own life, the work he composed at this point was what would become the first chapter of *I Am a Cat*.)[12] Kenzō has found that his writing produces a valuable form of intellectual property, one that he can exchange on the market to generate income.

THE THEORY OF LITERATURE VERSUS THE THEORY OF COPYRIGHT

Kenzō's ability to exchange his scribblings on paper for cash reflects not only the situation of the rapidly expanding publishing industry in early twentieth-century Japan, but also a shifting environment for intellectual property rights.[13] Literature was increasingly taking on the status of intangible asset, one whose value was determined by a globalized regime for intellectual property. Sōseki was an eager participant in that new legal regime, even as his theoretical and fictional writings often sought to poke holes in these novel forms of ownership. We see the latter tendency in particular when we compare the position that Sōseki expounded in *Theory of Literature*, based on lectures he delivered at Tokyo Imperial University in 1903–5, with the theory of copyright expounded in the same historical moment across town at Hōsei University in a lecture course delivered by Mizuno Rentarō (1868–1949), Sōseki's former classmate.[14] Sōseki's theory diverges from Mizuno's explanation for how a literary work could be properly owned in ways that help us understand our own relationship to Sōseki, as we encounter his writings far from his time and place, as they enter the domain of world literature.

To explore these issues, I will proceed by reading *Theory of Literature* backward, starting from the copyright page. When we examine the copyright notice in the first edition of *Theory of Literature*, several items call attention to themselves. The author is listed as Natsume Kinnosuke, which in 1907 had been Sōseki's legal name for less than twenty years, following his formal return to the Natsume family registry in 1888, after his adoption was legally annulled: when he enrolled at the Preparatory School as Mizuno's classmate, his legal name was still Shiobara Kinnosuke (the result of the familial machinations that would later provide the plot material for *Grass by the Wayside*). Natsume Kinnosuke is also the name by which he signs the work's preface, although when the *Yomiuri* newspaper previously published that essay, it listed the author's name as Natsume Sōseki.[15] Likewise, in the first-edition printing of *Theory of Literature*, the author listed on the title page and spine is Natsume Sōseki, but the author listed on the first page of the body of the work, after the table of contents, is once again Natsume Kinnosuke. There seem to be two authors here.

Returning to the copyright notice itself, we find a prohibition against reproduction announced by four Chinese characters distributed across the four corners of the text box containing the publication data (see figure C.1). Inside that box are two legal seals, one small and red reading "Natsume," the other larger and purple belonging to the publishing house, Ōkura Shoten. In other words, we find the equivalent of two signatures claiming ownership over this publication.

In sum, a logic of bifurcation seems to shape this work and its ownership. Moreover, if we probe further into the text of *Theory of Literature*, this

明治四十年五月二日印刷
明治四十年五月七日發行

著者　夏目金之助
發行者　大倉保五郎
印刷者　石川金太郎
印刷所　秀英舎
發行所　大倉書店

文學論奥付
正價金二圓二十錢

許 / 不 / 製 / 複

名著復刻　漱石文学館

FIGURE C.1 Copyright notice in *Theory of Litera-ture*, first edition.

issue of authorship becomes even more complex, because Sōseki acknowledges in the preface that he did not actually write much of the manuscript. His original lecture notes on which the book was based sat untouched for several years, he notes, until a publisher contacted him about the possibility of bringing them out in book form. Sōseki was himself too busy at the time and so entrusted the compilation of the manuscript from his lecture notes to a former student, Nakagawa Yoshitarō.[16] In other words, behind the Sōseki/Kinnosuke and the Natsume/Ōkura divides lies yet another claimant, Nakagawa Yoshitarō, who at some level can assert ownership over *Theory of Literature*. To further complicate matters, much of the actual text belongs to none of the above: an unusually large proportion of this book consists of extended quotations from literary and critical works written by others, not all of which were in the public domain at the time *Theory of Literature* appeared.

It is an old move in Sōseki studies to distinguish between two personae, Kinnosuke and Sōseki. Given the logic of bifurcation that structures his theory of literature—and, as we will see below, Mizuno Rentarō's theory of copyright—I will adopt this convention and distinguish between Kinnosuke as the legal person who owns the copyrights, and Sōseki as the aesthetic and theoretical position worked out in a series of texts that bear that signature. Typically in first editions of his fiction in book form, Sōseki's name appears on the cover and title page, while Kinnosuke's name appears in the copyright notice.

Under the terms of late Meiji intellectual property law, Kinnosuke was the copyright owner of *Theory of Literature*. This jibed with the terms of his 1907 contract with the *Asahi* newspaper, which paid him a generous monthly retainer of 200 yen plus twice-annual bonuses, requiring him to serialize his novels initially in *Asahi*, but allowing him to retain ownership of their copyrights for the purposes of subsequent book publication. The contract also enabled him to negotiate freely with any publishing house over terms for bringing out his nonfiction works—including *Theory of Literature*.[17] Part of the story here, then, is how well Kinnosuke exploited the new system of copyright and royalties that was replacing the old system of manuscript fees paid to authors on a flat per-page basis.[18] The rapid expansion of commercial publishing since the 1890s and the slowly increasing prestige of writing as a profession were both preconditions and results of this transformation.[19] The phrase "pure literature" (*jun bungaku*) as Sōseki uses it in the preface to *Theory of Literature* primarily distinguishes literature in the narrow sense (fiction, poetry, etc.) from literature in the broad sense (writing and scholarship in general), but from the 1890s on, that phrase increasingly also began to signify literature that possessed elite aesthetic value in contrast to the commodity value of commercial mass literature (*taishū bungaku*).[20] And yet the new modern copyright regime ensured that both types of literature enjoyed the status of property that could be owned, exploited, and alienated.

Other writers could only envy the way Kinnosuke turned to his advantage the new system for literary intellectual property. During this period, the image of the starving genius writer, whose dire poverty bespoke a heroic refusal to compromise with the market, became a fixture of public imagination. The suicide of novelist Kawakami Bizan in 1908, for example, prompted *Asahi* to run a story under the subheading, "The problem of writers' livelihood and society" that traced through his scant manuscript fees and compared them to his living expenses.[21] In this treacherous new environment, one characterized by a "delicate balance" between writers and publishers, Kinnosuke made out pretty well.[22] It is estimated that Kinnosuke's total lifetime earnings from royalties alone were in the range of 25,000–27,000 yen. In the year 1906, between salary, manuscript fees, and royalties, he earned approximately 4,944 yen.[23] By contrast, in 1897 Shimazaki Tōson received only 25 yen in manuscript fees for his first poetry anthology, and his contract transferred the copyright for that work to the Shunyōdō publishing house.[24] Moreover, in the years during which he wrote his debut novel *Broken Commandment* (*Hakai*, 1906), Tōson had a monthly income of only 15 yen, a salary so low that family members suffered from malnutrition.[25] Seemingly unable to work the new royalty and copyright system to his benefit, he relied on private patrons and finally resorted to self-publication of his novels in order to secure a livelihood. Tōson in 1925 looked back with envy at Kinnosuke's ability to work the new system, even as he was careful to deny any pecuniary desires on Sōseki's part: "As an author, Sōseki was known for having especially high royalty rates. The royalties Sōseki earned from his writings reached 20 percent or more of the recommended price for his books. That Sōseki, who by nature was indifferent to questions of money, was able to make such strong demands was probably a matter of pride. Moreover, only an author such as Sōseki, who had so many readers, could have made such a demand."[26]

Kinnosuke's remarkable financial success depended on the new legal regime for managing intellectual property. Following the breakdown during the Tenpō era (1830–44) of the publishing guild system that regulated copyright practices during the Tokugawa era, the Civilization and Enlightenment movement of the 1870s and '80s saw numerous calls for a copyright system that would situate Japan at the leading edge of intellectual property systems being developed primarily in the West.[27] Fukuzawa Yukichi, himself a frequent victim of pirated editions, wrote in 1873, "If exclusive rights for sales are not returned to the author, no one will expend the effort needed to compose works. If no works are made public, we will lose the path along which we can progress toward Enlightenment."[28] Following the issuance of the first Meiji Publication Regulations (*Shuppan jōrei*) in 1875, early versions of copyright laws recognizing specific rights for authors were promulgated in 1887 and 1893. These early copyright laws helped construct modern notions of literature and authorship, such as we find in a successful 1889 lawsuit filed by the Hakubundō publishing firm and Shiba Shirō (penname: Tōkai Sanshi) against Hattori Bushō and his publisher for a work that infringed on Shiba's political novel, *Kajin no kigū*

(Chance encounters with beautiful women).[29] This process culminated in 1899 with Japan's signing onto the Berne Convention for the Protection of Literary and Artistic Works (1886, revised 1896) and the promulgation of the new 1899 copyright law, the text of which was authored primarily by Mizuno. Amended several times, this law would remain the basis of Japanese copyright until 1970.[30]

This development of copyright was an important link in the process of modernization of Japan's property law system. As we have seen, these efforts culminated in the 1898 promulgation of the Meiji Civil Code, a measure that helped prod the Western powers to abolish the Unequal Treaties and accept Japan as a modern world power. The enactment of the new copyright law in 1899 and Japan's signing onto the Berne Convention in the same year were in many ways the capstone in this effort. Mizuno Rentarō, author of the new copyright law, would participate in the implementation of modern property regimes in imperial Japan in other capacities, as well. From 1919 to 1922, he would serve as second in command to the governor general in colonial Korea, where he became an architect of the so-called Cultural Policy, designed to mollify Korean resistance to Japanese rule, especially to the Land Cadastral Survey, the attempt to modernize colonial taxation systems by rationalizing the land ownership regime that I discussed in chapter 4.

But for our purposes, the relevant phase of Mizuno's career is his earlier work as a legal scholar. In 1905, he taught the first university course on copyright law ever offered in Japan.[31] I have already noted how a logic of bifurcation seems to run through Sōseki's (or Kinnosuke's) *Theory of Literature*. A similar pattern marks the theory of copyright that Mizuno outlines in his lecture course. Modern copyright is best considered a "composite right," he argues, a sometimes messy combination of two distinct kinds of rights: property rights and intellectual or moral rights.[32] Each of the two aspects is a necessary condition for understanding copyright, yet neither on its own is sufficient to explain the range of rights and duties that inhere in modern copyright law, Mizuno explains.

These two aspects are reflected respectively in two Japanese terms frequently used as translations for *copyright*: *hanken* (reproduction right) and *chosakuken* (authorial right), although Mizuno himself does not distinguish the terms in this way. Mizuno begins his exploration historically, tracing the rise of copyright back to ancient Roman legal codes. The narrative he presents is explicitly progressive, providing an instance of the use of developing property systems as a reliable measure for the degree of civilization attained by a given society. It also claims universal validity: "the development of copyright always follows the identical form of development, whether in Orient or Occident, in ancient times or today."[33] Societies that fail to develop copyright systems will be trapped at an uncivilized stage, unable to progress beyond it.[34] Looking at classical Rome and Greece, Mizuno finds elements foreshadowing copyright, but not copyright itself. It is only with the rise of modern technologies of reproduction that copyright per se begins to emerge in fifteenth-century Europe. Here, though, it arose primarily as hanken—that is, in the form of a limited monopoly granted to publishers to ensure that they could recoup expenses incurred in the preparation and dissemination of works that were of public benefit. Mizuno refers to this historical stage in copyright as one characterized by "the doctrine of patents" (*tokkenshugi*).

The second stage is characterized by what Mizuno calls "the doctrine of rights" (*kenrishugi*). Hanken gives way to, or rather is supplemented by, *chosakuken*: the grounds for copyright protection shift to the creative mental labor of the author who produces the work. As the product of intangible labor, a work emerges as something inherently owned by that author: under modern copyright systems, protection is extended to all works that are expressions of mental labor. The third and final stage in Mizuno's historical narrative is the globalization of copyright: through a series of at first bilateral and then subsequently multilateral international treaties, copyright protection expands from being national to being global in scope, as represented by the Berne convention. With its new modern copyright regime, Japan (and, implicitly, Japanese literature) had joined the world.

Mizuno proceeds to unpack the complexities of the composite right that is copyright. It includes elements that make it a kind of property right, and yet unlike other property rights, it mainly concerns the question of controlling the reproduction of what is owned. This derives from the fact that copyright is also a kind of intellectual right (*droit intellectual*), a new kind of right that has become increasingly important under conditions of modernity, in particular the rise of technologies of reproduction.[35] This new intellectual right derives from the notion of personality—that is, from a Lockean form of possessive individualism. "The thought of a person can only be known by that person and is not something that can ever be known by another person."[36] Accordingly, this right remains with the original author even after the property rights of a copyright are transferred to a new owner. If you own a house, you may modify it at will, but if you own the copyright to a work produced by another, you are not free to reproduce that work in altered form—for example, to alter the text or publish it under your own name.

In sum, Mizuno argues that copyright is an aggregate of two distinct rights, neither of which is adequate on its own to explain the existing legal practice. Pirated editions, for example, infringe only on the property rights of authors, but not on their intellectual rights, while a redacted edition of a work on which copyright is expired infringes only on the intellectual rights of the author, not on his or her property rights. The property right aspect of copyright expires after a limited period, while the intellectual right aspect of copyright is permanent.

This insistence on the complexity of copyright is perhaps the most striking feature of Mizuno's theory. To bring his discussion closer to Sōseki, I should note that Mizuno argues that copyright applies only to those expressions belonging to the categories of scientific or artistic work: written texts, paintings, sculptures, musical scores, and the like. Other sorts of original products such as inventions or designs are protected not by copyright but rather patents or trademarks. Two conditions are required to qualify a work for legal copyright protection. First, the work must be the product of original mental or spiritual labor: the product of original mental labor is automatically granted copyright, even without official registration, while something that is not the product of such labor can never qualify for copyright.[37] Second, the product expressing this original thought must belong to the domains of either science (*Wissenschaft*) or art (*Kunst*). It must take as its aim, that is, either truth or beauty.[38]

Mizuno's realm of works qualified to enjoy copyright protection overlaps precisely with the domains of experience that Sōseki takes up in his *Theory of Literature*: science and literature. For Mizuno, the two realms are equivalent: both deserve copyright protection because both originate with creative mental labor carried out by a unique person and because a public benefit is gained in encouraging the production of such works. By contrast, Sōseki's theory revolves around the task of distinguishing between the two realms, scientific and literary. He seems to operate from the assumption that only after we have carefully defined what distinguishes the literary from the scientific can we then draw a useful transversal linkage between the two domains, to create a scientific theory of literature.

Another key difference between Mizuno and Sōseki lies in where they locate the labor that produces the experience that is literature. Sōseki's theory, in foreshadowing reader-response theory, decenters the author from the privileged position in literature.[39] This is not to say that Sōseki ignores the author.[40] We find, for example, many passages in *Theory of Literature* where Sōseki makes value judgments about the relative quality of various writers. Moreover, in his explication of the varieties of *f*, Sōseki notes that we must consider not only the *f* that arises in the reader's mind, but also that in the mind of the author—and of the characters depicted.[41] Nonetheless, the $(F + f)$ formula by which Sōseki expounds the nature of literature, as his examples repeatedly demonstrate, is primarily a description of what goes on in the reader's mind. Literature begins not solely with the labor of the author-producer but also with that of the consumer-reader. In this shared production, the author sits explicitly at the mercy of his or her readers and their social situation:

> To take an example close at hand from our own country, the focus of contemporary consciousness during the time of the Restoration forty-odd years ago consisted of the three concepts of "expel the barbarian" (*jōi*), "support the government" (*sabaku*), and "duty to the Emperor" (*kinnō*). Let's say hypothetically that there was a man in that period who surpassed Shakespeare in expressive power; still, this period-level F would have no room to accommodate such a person. Even if a second Matthew Arnold were to appear to elucidate the principles of "Sweetness and Light" (a famous essay advocating literature in education), he would probably be unable to move any of his listeners. The consciousness of the age would not allow for this. That not even a great sage or genius can defy the force of an age (*ikioi*) exemplifies the principle of the focus of consciousness F of a given age.[42]

Sōseki argues that literary taste is constantly shifting, so that someday perhaps even Shakespeare will be forgotten.[43] Unlike scientific truth, which is permanent and universal, literary truth is historical and relative. The author's right to intellectual integrity that is so central to Mizuno's theory of copyright is sidestepped in Sōseki's theory—at the level of both content and form, given the ruthless way in which Sōseki cuts up the works he cites in order to reduce them to the disconnected fragments that he quotes.

Again, it is not that the author has no role to play in Sōseki's theory. Book 3 of *Theory of Literature* is devoted to distinguishing the stance of a literary author from that of a scientist: a literary author is one who relates to the world primarily through the faculty of emotion, rather than intellect or will. This is a question Sōseki would develop at greater length in his 1908 lecture "The Attitude of a Creative Author" ("Sōsakuka no taido"). But in that work, Sōseki insists on the hybrid (or, to use Mizuno's phrase, the composite) nature of literary works, as well as of their authors:

> To take another example, here we have a man. He goes to school. At this time, we must regard him as one member of the faculty. Next he takes up a writing brush. Here, we properly recognize him as taking his place among the ranks of authors. Next he returns home. Now we must classify him as husband or parent. This is a single person, yes, yet he has the character of being woven together out of a variety of types. A work is of the same nature.[44]

The author, then, is not a single unified point of origin, the self-owned personality that underwrites Mizuno's theory. Instead, the author is a point of intersection of multiple lines, including feedback from readers. Atsuko Sakaki aptly describes this view of authorship, rooted in earlier literary practices: "Literary composition as practiced among men of letters in premodern Japan rested on a shared reading knowledge and the acceptance of the inseparability of one text from those that preceded and followed it. A work became 'literary' because of its indebtedness to other texts," not because of its creation by a single unique author.[45]

According to Sōseki, what distinguishes an author considered great is not some singular property intrinsic to his or her person, but rather a particularly good match between the author's stance and the shared worldview of a specific historical and cultural audience. To reiterate a point I discussed in chapter 2, Sōseki would argue in the 1907 lecture, "Philosophical Foundations of the Literary Arts" ("Bungei no tetsugakuteki kisō"):

> When literary art achieves perfection, those who come into contact with it will find themselves falling into perfect correspondence [*kangentaki kanka*] with it—assuming the times are right for this. This perfect correspondence is the ultimate effect that the literary arts can bestow upon us. The times are right for this when the ideal manifested within a work of literary perfection is in agreement with our own ideal, or, again, when our own ideal finds itself being pulled along by the work toward something new, something deeper or more extensive, and thereby undergoes a moment of awakening, a moment of enlightenment.[46]

When the ideal pattern of consciousness expressed through a work harmonizes with that of readers in their own historical moment, it allows the reader the pleasure of losing their self in the world of the work, of surrendering ownership in the self to a collaborative joint production. But a reader from a different time or culture might be unable to achieve this correspondence with the work, because this reader is out of sync with the author's stance. Neither reader is especially correct or mistaken: success or failure in achieving correspondence is the result of historical contingency.

For Sōseki, in sum, the meaning and value of a literary work are not properties that belong to that text or to its author, but rather temporary outcomes of the fluid processes that occur when a reader's consciousness encounters the author's text. This view in turn allows Sōseki to challenge the authority of, for example, English literary critics. Since taste is relative, the literary criticism of a Japanese, even of an English poem, is as valid as that of an Englishman—a position he would expound again in his 1914 lecture "My Individualism" ("Watakushi no kojinshugi").

The experience of literature that Sōseki theorizes here parallels the notion of reading as poaching that Michel de Certeau describes in *The Practice of Everyday Life*.[47] For de Certeau, as for Sōseki, the reader confronts the spatial grid of a written text and through the labor of reading translates that space into time. We can know whether the text is literary only retroactively, through the quality generated through this temporal experience of reading. This is a special kind of theft: the reader "insinuates into another person's text the ruses of pleasure and appropriation: he poaches on it, is transported into it, pluralizes himself in it like the internal rumblings of one's body. . . . A different world (the reader's) slips in the author's place."[48] What Sōseki calls "perfect correspondence" is what de Certeau describes as the nomadic experience readers undergo as they lose themselves in the text, "oscillating in a nowhere between what he [*sic*] invents and what changes him."[49] We are in the domain of literature when this experience of reading generates something beyond the denoted meaning of the text—an excess that in Sōseki's theory is marked by f in the $(F + f)$ formula that defines literature.

THE ENCLOSURE OF CONNOTATION

The connections between Sōseki's and Mizuno's theories are also relevant to recent developments in intellectual property. As we have seen, Sōseki's $(F + f)$ formula situates f as the attribute that distinguishes the experience specific to literature. This f holds down multiple meanings: it refers to emotions, but also to the temporal fringes of perception—the advancing and receding edges of the wave of consciousness. It is simultaneously the location of poetic language and tropes, and the site of connotation, as opposed to the denotation proper, which is marked by F. As such, f is highly fluid and changeable: its qualities differ from reader to reader, culture to culture, and moment to moment. It does not belong solely to the text itself.

To whom, then, does *f* belong? The answer in Sōseki is ambiguous: *f* is produced on multiple levels in the ever-changing interaction between author, written text, and readers—all of which are, in turn, networked to their historical moments. Connotations are not properties of texts, but rather qualities arising out of contingent experiences in which specific readers encounter specific texts at a specific place and time. As one scholar of intellectual property puts it,

> some words have core definitions (definitions that can be found in a dictionary), and a set of connotations that depend on their history, derivation, and identification with users. These peripheral meanings are often highly individualized to the speaker, the listener, and possibly to the method by which they interact or perceive one another. When such words are used, they become infused with the listener's own frame of reference. The result is that the expression as perceived can have much greater impact on the recipient's thinking than the words that were actually transmitted.[50]

One recent tendency in intellectual property law is the expansion of ownership rights beyond denoted meaning to include connotations. So far, this has become an explicit feature not so much of copyright per se as of other forms of intellectual property, especially trademark and publicity rights, but given the history of capitalism and its ever-expanding sphere of enclosures, it seems quite possible that literary connotations will eventually be subjected to legally recognized ownership claims. While the author may be dead in literary theory, he (this is a gendered system) continues to walk around as something like an undead zombie in the legal codes of intellectual property. There, the author is increasingly permitted to claim ownership of the "surplus value" produced by consumers in their creative engagements with such cultural signs as trademarks, even in cases where there is no possibility that such uses might produce confusion about the source of goods.[51]

> The trademark owner is invested with authorship and paternity; seen to invest "sweat of the brow" to "create" value in a mark, he is then legitimately able to "reap what he has sown." The imaginations of consumers become the field in which the owner sows his seed—a receptive and nurturing space for parturition—but consumers are not acknowledged as active and generative agents in the procreation of meaning. The generation of new, alter-

native, or negative connotations are ignored, denied, or prohibited because patrilineal rights of property are recognized as exclusive: no joint custody arrangements will be countenanced.[52]

In this gendered subordination of reproduction to production, consumers are banned from engaging in parodic uses of trademarked symbols that might damage the goodwill that is believed to inhere in those marks, a goodwill that is defined as a form of property belonging to the trademark holder. Likewise, creative adaptations of intellectual properties—for example, the common abbreviation of McDonald's to Mickey D's or the invention of neologisms such as "McMansions" using the prefix "Mc"—are increasingly defined as secondary connotations that belong to the owner of the trademark. This tendency toward enclosure threatens "to deprive us of the optimal *cultural* conditions for dialogic practice."[53] In terms of Sōseki's theory, moreover, this blurring of the distinction in legal status between denotation and connotation, the absorption of the reader's *f* into the author's *F* as a private possession, means not so much the death of the author but the erasure of literature as a distinct realm of shared human experience.

While the grounds for such extension of copyright and trademark principles lie with an increasingly inflated Romantic ideology of the author as assumed source for all potential denoted and connoted meanings of a work, in actual practice, these new legal codes mean that authorship is being redefined "in order to establish capital's right to ownership" of the work; "the 'original' moment here is thus that of investment."[54] In other words, capital itself increasingly takes on the rights of personality.

Sōseki's own afterlife becomes tangled up in this tendency. While Kinnosuke's copyrights expired in 1946, thirty years after his death, Sōseki's works subsequently emerged as a new frontier in the expansion of intellectual property claims. In 1979, Reader's Digest Japan announced that it was bringing out an edition of reproductions of the first editions of Natsume Sōseki's works. At that point, several parties requested court injunctions to halt the project, claiming that the new series infringed on their property rights. They argued that the new series was in fact a reproduction of an earlier reproduction series they had published in 1975 and that the new publications hence infringed on their copyright as editors of that series. The 'theft' was detected because some of the distortions of printed characters that were a result of the earlier reproduction process also showed up in the later reproduction series. Essentially, the plaintiffs here were claiming that distortions of form introduced through the process of mechanical reproduction themselves constituted an expression of authorial creation, and hence of creative labor that justified claims of ownership.[55]

The various cases were settled out of court a few months later in a manner that demonstrates the retroactive nature of much modern property law. Under the modern property regime, courts and other juridical institutions are frequently stuck in the muddy position of having to explain after the fact where ownership rights lie even as they have to pretend that those ownership rights had always existed in crystal-clear form in the legal code.[56] Reader's Digest Japan agreed to recognize a "right of reproduction" that was held by original publishing houses such as Iwanami and promised that it would no longer market reproductions without first obtaining the permission of the owners of this newly coined intellectual property right. The court, in accepting this resolution, provided the first legal recognition of this right in Japanese law.[57] The incident was a crucial stage in the development of the principle that the typesetting of a book itself constituted an act of creative mental labor, and that therefore a legitimate intellectual property right was held by a publisher in the physical form of a book, even after authorial copyright had expired. And with that, another patch of the public domain was enclosed, transformed into private property.

Multiple historical ironies emerge here. Intellectual property owners are mobilizing the Romantic ideology of authorship not to protect the integrity of authorial creation but rather to maximize return on corporate investment. The ideologies of literature and authorship that underwrote the development of modern copyright in eighteenth- and nineteenth-century Europe originally emerged in response to the growing commercialization of literature and the frustrations of elite writers at their inability to make a satisfactory impact on the expanded readership.[58] Advocates proposed copyright protection as a means for allowing writers the freedom to pursue artistic creation without having to compromise themselves to market demands. This doctrine, which stressed the value of a literary work as arising solely from the self-owned personality and mental labor of its author, was developed to protect authors from the commercialization of literature, but today the same ideology is being invoked to protect the investment of the publishing house.

Sōseki's theory of literature troubles the Romantic ideology of authorship that underwrote such copyright laws. As we have seen, the defining feature of literature was *f*, the emotional factor that emerges in the reader's mind, even as it cannot be said to belong solely to the reader. Nonetheless, on the copyright page of *Theory of Literature*, Kinnosuke asserted his legal ownership over the work in which he expounded this nonproprietary theory. Moreover, as I noted above, the Ōkura Shoten publishing house also asserted its proprietary rights on the same page, and it is the latter that enjoy expanding legal protection today, even as Kinnosuke's legal proprietary rights have expired. It is a situation that would have perplexed both Kinnosuke and Sōseki. This development would also likely have struck Mizuno Rentarō as atavistic, a retreat backward down the progressive teleology of civilization that he valued so highly.

A legal theft is taking place: the village commons is again being enclosed. But those of us who would join the Village Green Preservation Society also have tools at our disposal, tools that we can poach from Sōseki's theory. Kinnosuke is dead, his copyrights expired, but Sōseki's texts have entered their afterlife, where they provide moving targets for poachers, grave robbers, and shameless translators. Poaching is not, as Brian Massumi reminds us, a matter of subtraction but rather of addition, and as Thomas Lamarre argues, it is addition—the plus symbol that lies at the heart of $(F + f)$—that serves as the pivot in Sōseki's theory.[59] If certain entities claim legal ownership over proliferating connotations, the fs that we readers generate through our experiences of literature, and if the juridical system validates that act of dispossession, we should of course protest the injustice, but we should also keep poaching in our everyday practice, by which we "produce without capitalizing."[60] As they enter the canon that we call world literature, Sōseki's writings become available for new forms of poaching—but also to new claims of belonging particular to that notion of world literature. It is to these that I turn next.

SŌSEKI AND THE PROPERTIES OF WORLD LITERATURE

Sōseki's is not the only modern literary estate to end up embroiled in an ownership dispute. Franz Kafka, who in chapter 1 provided me with a kind of foil for Sōseki, has also in recent years become the object of fierce battles, both literary and legal, with multiple parties claiming property rights over his manuscripts. In this situation, as Judith Butler argues, each claim "effaces other modes of belonging, or rather, non-belonging." The resulting legal chaos is particularly perplexing in Kafka's case, because—as with Sōseki—the "very question of where Kafka belongs is already something of a scandal given the fact that the writing charts the vicissitudes of non-belonging, or of belonging too much."[61]

In a similar spirit, let me consider to whom and where Sōseki belongs. As I've argued across the pages of this book, his fiction and literary theory engage in an extended, playful exploration of the ambiguities of the modern property regime. In that Sōseki was creating these works within, alongside, and in reaction to the emergence of a global capitalist regime of ownership, I conclude here predictably that he was writing our story all along, one that transcends his place (Japan) and time (the early twentieth century). Today, his fictional commons has, in other words, a place in the celebrated category we call world literature.

But the concept of world literature is tangled up in its own issues of property and belonging. In her manifesto *Against World Literature*, Emily Apter has rejected overly celebratory notions of the critical possibilities of world literature, noting that "one reason why literary studies falls short as anti-capitalist critique is because it insufficiently questions what it means to 'have' a literature or to lay claim to aesthetic property."[62] In this final section, I outline the alternative form of world literature that Sōseki implicitly and explicitly points to, one that I think does undertake a rigorous questioning of what it means to belong and to own. This in turn will suggest an answer to the question of who owns Sōseki.

There is evidence that Sōseki gave considerable thought to his own position in world literature. In 1907, for example, he sent a copy of his debut novel *I Am a Cat* to a Mr. Young in New York City, including the following English-language inscription: "Herein, a cat speaks in the first person plural, we. Whether regal or editorial, it is beyond the ken of the author to see. Gargantua, Quixote, and Tristram Shandy, each has had his day. It is high time this feline King lay in peace upon a shelf in Mr Young's library. And may all his catspaw-philosophy as well as his quaint language, ever remain hieroglyphic in the eyes of the occidentals!"[63] I have repeatedly returned to this striking epigraph in my own attempt to understand Sōseki.[64] He imagines his own novel sitting comfortably on a bookshelf alongside the works of Rabelais, Cervantes, and Sterne—that is, he imagines his work as belonging to a world literature.

Yet at the same moment, he expresses the ironic desire to "ever remain hieroglyphic in the eyes of the occidentals." Here is my novel, he seems to say, but I hope you can never read it. This suggests something about Soseki's own implicit theory of world literature, outlined in the theoretical project he pursued in tandem with writing *I Am a Cat* and that would appear in 1907 as his *Theory of Literature*. Sōseki approaches the problem of world literature from a position much like that of a nameless stray cat who wakes up to find itself unexpectedly surrounded by the celebrated classics of European literature. The nameless cat cannot assume it knows what constitutes a great work, or even what makes something literature in the first place: it has to theorize literature without standing in the privileged position of a person who presumes to know, the position of one who can assume that he or she belongs. This opens possibilities for a vision of world literature unlike the one that has emerged in our own day, one characterized by different notions of what it might mean to belong or to own.

Edward Said described the "genuinely profound scholarship of the people who believed in and practiced *Weltliteratur*" as something that "implied the extraordinary privilege of an observer located in the West who could actually survey the world's literary output with a kind of sovereign detachment."[65] This sense of "sovereign detachment" was itself, of course, a historical product, the legacy of a long history of imperialism. No one can claim an external, objective position outside the unequal historical relationships that pertain between cultures: we are all products of those relationships, and our perspectives grow out of them. This means that different readers in different places and times respond to literary texts differently. Or, in Said's phrasing, "interpreting Jane Austen depends on *who* does the interpreting, *when* it is done, and no less important, from *where* it is done."[66]

So what happens when a nameless stray cat—or a neurasthenic Japanese scholar and budding novelist—picks up Jane Austen in 1907 Tokyo and tries to work out from it a theory of literature? What you get is something like Soseki's *Theory of Literature*. In fact, Jane Austen is one of the authors he most frequently cites in it. As we have already seen, the project began with Soseki's stay in London in 1900–1902, when he was sent by the Japanese government to study English and English literature. Halfway through his stay, he came to several troubling realizations: first, that he didn't really much like or understand English literature. "I was bothered by a notion that lingered at the back of my mind—that somehow I had been cheated by English literature."[67] Second, and more troubling, that he did not even know what literature was. He did not specialize in classical Chinese literature, but read it with pleasure. By contrast, he was supposed to be an expert in English literature, but failed to enjoy it: "For my sense of like and dislike between the two to be so widely divergent despite my having roughly equal scholarly abilities must mean that the two were of utterly different natures. In other words, what is called 'literature' in the realm of the Chinese classics and what is called 'literature' in English must belong to different categories and cannot be comprehended under a single definition."[68] Sōseki had stumbled onto the problem of world literature: what is the category that includes both ancient Chinese classics and nineteenth-century British domestic novels? Significantly, Sōseki does not use the expression "world literature," but simply "literature." He sees that category as commensurable with that of science: a universal that, while taking different forms in different places and times, nonetheless can be defined by certain abstract principles that remain valid in all cultures and eras.

Sōseki further realized that he could not simply read more literature to solve this problem. The solution required finding a new perspective, a new methodology. As we saw in chapters 2 and 3, he sought this new perspective in the rising modern sciences of psychology and sociology, ultimately arriving at the $(F+f)$ formula: any time the waveform of our consciousness is defined by both its cognitive focal point F and the affective fringes f that attend to that focal point, we are in the realm of literature.

Sōseki's approach seems to foreshadow many recent theories of world literature in fascinating ways—but also to differ significantly from them. Most recent theories of world literature start with a canon of texts or authors that have achieved global circulation and try to figure out what it is about those texts or authors or the field of literature that has caused these specific texts and authors to be canonized, while others are forgotten. They start, that is, from what Said called the "extraordinary privilege" of one who knows already what texts constitute the canon of world literature, and then proceed to borrow methodologies from other disciplines such as sociology to figure out the rules and hierarchies that structure that canon. But Sōseki starts from a position of not knowing what the canon is: like a stray cat thrust into an unknown world, he starts from a position of ignorance. As a result, his theory shows relatively little interest in comparing the literary value of different texts. For Sōseki, something either is or isn't literature: either it generates $(F+f)$ or it doesn't. Any work that generates the experience of $(F+f)$ belongs equally to the domain of literature (though he also acknowledges that the intensity of that experience can vary due to multiple factors).

Moreover, as we have seen, $(F+f)$ is not a formula for describing the structure of literary texts or canons. As the long passage about the experience of looking at St. Paul's Cathedral quoted in chapter 2 demonstrates, $(F+f)$ is not an account of the structure of the building itself, but rather of what goes on in the mind of a person looking at it: $(F+f)$ describes a segment of consciousness. Without the act of reading, and the stream of consciousness that unfolds across time with it, there can be no literary substance, no $(F+f)$. To reiterate the argument I've made across these pages, the $(F+f)$ of literature names a site for the possible merging of the streams of consciousness of the reader, the characters in the work, and the author. If $(F+f)$ fails to emerge in the mind of the reader encountering the text, then that text falls outside the domain of literature, even if it is authored by Shakespeare. For Sōseki, world literature is not something that takes place inside literary texts, genres, or fields of cultural practice: it takes place inside readers' minds as they encounter literary works.

This helps us see the political stakes of his theory. Sōseki specifically uses this approach to justify non-Western readings of Western texts: he is legitimating his own indifferent response to British literature, his sense of having been cheated. If Japanese readers happen to arrive at a different understanding of an English poem from what a British critic finds, the Japanese readers are equally correct, insofar as they are accurately reporting the $(F+f)$ that they experience (or fail to experience) while reading the work. Sōseki envisions the field of world literature not so much as a closed canon, but rather as a commons to which all readers have equal access rights.

This is related to a second quirk of Sōseki's approach. He seems to be producing a theory of world literature that does not presume the need for translation. David Damrosch and others have defined world literature as consisting of that body of texts that have been translated into foreign languages and traveled far from home to be read in different cultural and historical contexts.[69] But Sōseki seems to be pursuing a different model, starting from the nuts and bolts of his scholarly practice. When you flip through the pages of the original Japanese version of his *Theory of Literature*, you immediately notice the large number of extended quotations from foreign literature, mostly in English, presented without modification within the Japanese text: Sōseki refuses to translate them.[70] Moreover, Sōseki structures his theory around mathematical notation, charts, and graphs—all modes of expression that that transcend the need for translation, since they belong to no single national language. He seems deliberately to be constructing a theory of world literature that avoids resorting to translation.

Throughout his career, in fact, Sōseki seems to have avoided translation. We can begin with the above English-language inscription to Mr. Young in *I Am a Cat* and its assertion, "may his catspaw . . . language ever remain hieroglyphic in the eyes of the occidentals." Sōseki may have been imagining his novel as a part of world literature, but clearly this did not involve translation of that work. There is ample other evidence of his dislike of translation. As I have explored elsewhere, he evidenced a rather cool attitude toward such writers as Rabindranath Tagore, who rode a wave of English translation to become the first Asian writer to win the Nobel Prize in Literature in 1913.[71] We also see Sōseki repeatedly responding with skepticism to requests to allow his own works to be translated. In a July 2, 1906, letter to Takahama Kyoshi, he mentions that an English translation of *I Am a Cat* has been sent to him for approval: "But to someone born human, I have to think there is much greater human value in writing even a single page of one's own than in translating something like *Cat*."[72] In May 1916, he would express reluctance to approve publication of a German-language translation of his *Kusamakura*.[73] Two months later, in a letter to Kuriyagawa Hakuson, in response apparently to a query about translating his works into English, he would demur, "Among my works, there is not a single one that I would like to have read by Americans."[74]

Sōseki's discomfort with the idea of translation no doubt arose in part from his complex responses to his traumatic stay in London. But beyond whatever inferiority complexes toward English he may have harbored, it also seems clear that he possessed a clear-eyed view of the emerging politics of world literature. As Aamir Mufti has argued, the very idea that each nation should have its national literature, and that compiled together they form a broader category called world literature, one mediated by translation, is a product of Orientalism and the European drive to know the non-European world in order to better dispossess it. World literature emerges by way of a kind of enclosure, in which the space of the globe is transformed into "a *plane of equivalence*, a set of categorical grids and networks that seek, first of all, to render legible *as literature* a vast and heterogeneous range of practices of writing from across the world and across millennia, so as to be able, second, to make them available for comparison, classification, and evaluation. World literature is therefore fundamentally a concept of exchange or, in other words, a concept of bourgeois society."[75] Such exchanges, mediated by translation into global languages such as English, guarantee that the idea of a national literature written in the local vernacular is not antithetical to world literature, but rather complicit in it. They mediate, in short, an enormous system of belonging that had arisen since the eighteenth century to encompass more and more of the globe, and Sōseki wanted nothing to do with it. Sōseki's theory of literature challenged dominant narratives of national literary history that were taking shape in the late Meiji by severing literary texts from the national home ground that social Darwinist thought claimed provided their only authentic explanatory key.[76] Moreover, he seems to have realized that to belong to this mode of world literature, increasingly mediated by translation into

English, was to accept an inferior position within a global hierarchy. If translation was part of the great game, Sōseki seems to have intuited that there was no way for a Japanese novelist in 1907 to win at it. Sōseki, it seems, was driven not so much by a fear of untranslatability as by the fear that literature was only too translatable, and that for a cat coming from the periphery, this was not an advantageous thing.

How does one approach the problem of world literature without the presumption of a canon and without the assumption that translation is necessary? As we have seen, Sōseki believed that one first had to step outside of literature to gain a perspective on it: he turned to the social and natural sciences, specifically sociology and psychology. This involved, among other things, a shift from qualitative to quantitative data. In this, Sōseki anticipated recent theories of world literature by such figures as Pascale Casanova and Franco Moretti, who likewise have sought a more rational, scientific approach to literary criticism.[77] Their works share with Sōseki a tendency to mobilize mathematical formulas, as well as graphs, charts, and maps to define problems. As we saw in chapter 2, Sōseki's $(F+f)$ formula, particularly in its psychological guise, was grounded in experimental results from laboratory work done by such figures as Wilhelm Wundt, who sought finer and finer gradations of measurement for sensation and perception. Sōseki seems to assume that, given the appropriate laboratory equipment, both F and f could be accurately measured and quantified. He argues, for example, that we should think of Romanticism and realism not as qualitatively different schools but rather as relative poles on a sliding scale of quantifiable degrees of narrated content and mode of expression. He provides in book 4 of *Theory of Literature* (in a section not included in the English translation) a chart to show how this might be expressed in the form of numerical data.[78]

Why was quantitative data so attractive to Sōseki? This was probably at least in part because the scientific discourse of $(F+f)$ provided him with a way out of the existing language for theorizing literature.[79] Numbers, that is, provided a mode for speaking about literature outside the vocabulary of classical Chinese rhetoric with its insistence on ethics and morality—just as it also provided a vocabulary outside the notions of beauty and aesthetic value that dominated British literary criticism. The shift to quantitative data allowed Sōseki to decenter the authority of morality and beauty in theorizing literature: both have a place in literature, he argues, but neither can claim absolute authority. By appealing moreover to the universal nature of mathematical formulas, Sōseki was also able to create an alternate ground of authority for his own judgments regarding literature—about, for example, not liking British literature very much. Quantitative data was a kind of language this stray cat invented to authorize him to speak about literature, a language in which all speakers are supposed to be equal.

The turn toward quantitative data is connected to another element of Sōseki's theory that foreshadows more recent theories of world literature. Like Casanova, who employs Pierre Bourdieu's sociology, and like Moretti, who adopts evolutionary theory from the natural sciences and world systems theory from sociology, Soseki argues we have to get outside of literature to understand it and hence turns toward science. Yet in Sōseki, this turn is connected to another axiom from his theory: his insistence that literature or literary substance, $(F+f)$, is not science, or (F). Sōseki paradoxically turns to science to identify that which by definition is not science. In this paradoxical, transversal move, world literature becomes an object for scientific knowledge, and yet that object does not exist within the domain of science.

In part, this reflects a difference between spatially and temporally oriented approaches. Many recent theories of world literature explicitly recast the problem of world history in terms of space rather than time: Moretti, for example, uses graphs and maps in an attempt revise the format of literary history from a narrative that unfolds along a timeline to a spatial category that is best understood geographically via an atlas.[80] Likewise, Casanova's *World Republic of Letters* resituates the temporality of world literary history as a spatial problem: instead of advanced or belated moments, she talks about core and periphery in a spatial structure, writing a "spatialized history" that presumes the field of literature exists as a kind of closed space.[81] As a scientist examining this bounded domain, she takes up a position outside of it, from which she can analyze the kinds of exchanges and hierarchies that structure the space. This spatially external position provides the distance that enables her to critique and disenchant existing narratives of world literary history.

But for Sōseki, literature primarily unfolds in time. As I discussed in chapter 2, $(F+f)$ represents a waveform; without the unfolding of time as a continuous flow, $(F+f)$ cannot exist. Without activation through the stream of the reader's consciousness, literature exists only in potential and cannot be distinguished from its polar opposite, science. Moreover, as we have seen, Sōseki insists that this temporal unfolding of literature— whether in an individual's stream of consciousness or in the shared consciousness of an epoch—does not follow a linear, developmental model: it is not an evolutionary process that progresses to higher and more complex forms. "Taste in literature never tarries long in the same place. It must always develop and change," but "it is natural to assume that when we compare the F of one period to the F' of the next, the latter does not necessarily represent an advance or improvement over the former."[82] Sōseki rejects a universal, civilizational teleology for literary history. In his view, the literary history of each country will unfold according to its own specific conditions and circumstances. As he argued in his 1908 lecture "The Attitude of a Creative Author," "We cannot simply take as our standard the final point reached by Europeans through the many transformations of their own history. This is especially the case in terms of literature."[83]

This insistence on provincializing European literary history is another tendency that Sōseki shares with recent theories of world literature. Many recent scholars of world literature, including Casanova and Moretti, see their own theoretical positions as postcolonial and critical of previous Eurocentric literary history. Yet insofar as they leave out the agency of readers, insofar as they presume that literary substance is something bracketed off inside literary texts and inside the space of literature, they presume to read from a position of sovereign detachment. They implicitly position their own readings at the end of history, as if theorizing from a position outside the cultural relations that have been generated through the history of imperialism. Assuming that literary works exist as fixed entities, they see the task of the critic as being to analyze that fixed content.

By contrast, Sōseki's theory assumes that literary history is not finished. Insofar as time continues to unfold, insofar as readers continue to take up and interact with literary texts, the story of literature is not ended. Sōseki understands that the future will likely see readers producing versions of $(F+f)$, literary substance, that we cannot imagine from our current position. Literary history and the literary past remain open-ended, and the future of literary history cannot be assumed to take the form of a continuous development out of the present. Readers and translators who betray the expectations of authors and texts in ways that exceed our ability to imagine are entirely possible: this may well be one reason Sōseki was so cool to the idea of having his own works translated.

For Sōseki, any approach to world literature was inherently situated. To understand the structure of world literature, one has to start reading from one's own place and time and move outward from there, creating one's own world. One has to read in a self-centered manner, what Sōseki called *jiko hon'i*. As he argued in the 1914 lecture, "My Individualism," "A Westerner, for example, might say a poem was very fine, for example, or its tone extremely good, but this was his view, his Western view. While certainly not irrelevant, it was nothing that I had to repeat if I could not agree with it. I was an independent Japanese, not a slave to England, and it was incumbent upon me *as* a Japanese to possess at least this degree of self-respect."[84] If an English reader and a Japanese reader take up the same novel by Jane Austen and react differently, it does not mean that one is mistaken. Such differences are the inevitable result of cultural and social differences and of individual circumstances. The $(F+f)$ generated by a given text in a given reader at a given moment is influenced by the historical and cultural background of that reader, as well as by the reader's individual circumstances. In other words, it depends on who reads Jane Austen, where and when.

For Sōseki, literature was a domain that was fundamentally dialogical, carried out in proximity to others. $(F+f)$ cannot be said to belong to the author, the text, or the reader, but is generated in common between them. What counts as literature will always remain fluid in the continual unfolding of consciousness across time, individual and social, and in the fluid relations that arise between readers, writers, and fictional characters. In that sense, Sōseki's theory situates literature as "a continuing and changing practice which already substantially, and now at the level of theoretical redefinition, is moving beyond its old form."[85]

Whenever we engage in such relationships via texts and $(F+f)$ fleetingly emerges through these relations, we partake of literature. Ownership of the f that distinguished the experience of literature from (F), the experience of science, cannot be assigned to any of the three participants (reader, author, fictional character), even as each of those three was in turn a site of relationality, a node in the multiple networks that define their historical and social moment. Affective f is, as Hardt and Negri remind us, a form of commons.[86] In this sense, for Sōseki the experience of literature is a mode for engaging in sociality, in which sociality names a form of "proximity quite distinct from the possessive attachment languages of belonging."[87] In a sense, the entire *Theory of Literature* project and its subsequent development were for Sōseki a working out of what it meant to read literature in which you do not belong: "I was bothered by a notion that lingered at the back of my mind— that somehow I had been cheated by English literature."[88]

For Sōseki, literature is a project of reimagining and reengaging the commons. It is a site for playful subversion of the norms and practices of enclosure that define modern capitalism and its property systems. The commons in this sense should not be understood as a given thing or substance, but rather a fluid and ongoing site of practice that must be renewed in every moment and whose outcome is uncertain: commons as a verb rather than a noun.[89] Literature is a practice of generating differences through the ongoing intersubjective production of $(F+f)$, differences that hint at other models for owning or sharing beyond what the market offers in the form of private property and possessive individualism. Literature for Natsume Sōseki is a practice less of owning or belonging to than it is a mode of being with.

NOTES

Note: *SZ* is used throughout as an abbreviation in citations for Natsume Sōseki, *Sōseki zenshū*, 29 vols. Tokyo: Iwanami Shoten, 1993–99.

INTRODUCTION

1 Modern property regimes, Carol Rose argues, rest on an ambiguous ideological foundation akin to an oil and water mixture, at times claiming to arise from principles involving collective wealth enhancement and preference satisfaction, but at other moments grounding itself in shared notions of what is proper. Elsewhere, she describes modern property regimes as a cobbling together of crystal-clear rules and ambiguous muddy standards. Rose, *Property and Persuasion*, 49–65 and 199–225.

2 "Inheritance plots usually involve a tangible form of property: a family portrait, a set of diamonds, a country seat. In the sense that inheritance necessitates the transfer of property, novels interrogate the ideology of ownership as an inherent legal right, with ramifications for both personal and national belonging. Fictional narratives often conclude that property ownership is an insoluble puzzle." Hepburn, "Introduction," 3–25. This passage appears on 5.

3 Hardt and Negri, *Commonwealth*.

4 According to Ishihara Chiaki, a strong awareness of the Meiji Civil Code is one of the key characteristics that distinguishes Sōseki's domestic novels from those of previous decades. Ishihara, *Sōseki to Nihon no kindai*, 1:25–27 and 43–46.

5 On the Tokugawa-era economy and economic thought, including the increasing awareness of the importance of circulation and market forces (albeit with little discussion of the property system underlying this), see the essays included in Smits and Gramlich-Oka, *Economic Thought in Early Modern Japan*.

6 On the impact of the new taxation system on the property regime of Japan, see Brown, *Cultivating Commons*; Dunn, "The Property Rights Paradigm"; and Sato, "The Emergence of 'Modern' Ownership Rights."

7 The ban was modified in 1723, but outright sale of land in the sense of fee simple ownership remained under de jure restrictions. See Kwon, *State Formation, Property Relations, and the Development of the Tokugawa Economy*, esp. 57–65.

8 See Hein, "Shaping Tokyo"; and Matsuyama and Itō, "Meiji-ki ni okeru Yotsuya Samegahashi no toshi kūkan kōzō." I am grateful to Susan Burns for introducing me to these sources.

9   On the history of the gold standard and its impact on modern Japan, see Metzler, *Lever of Empire*.

10   Suzuki, *Re-inventing Japan*, 27.

11   On the colonial land property system in Taiwan, see Ching, *Becoming "Japanese,"* esp. 86–87 and 135–36.

12   Bhandar, *Colonial Lives of Property*, 4.

13   On the political measures imposed to quell potential dissent after the abolition of the property qualification and the granting of universal male adult suffrage, see Rin, *Shōwa ideorogii*, esp. 13-111.

14   Tateiwa, *Shiteki shoyūron*, 30.

15   Pels, *Property and Power in Social Theory*, 2 and 21.

16   Hardt and Negri, *Commonwealth*, 4.

17   Karatani, *The Structure of World History*.

18   Radin, "Property and Personhood," 957. See also Dayan, *The Law Is a White Dog*.

19   Balibar, *Citizen Subject*. For a productive reading of another Meiji author in relation to Balibar's notion of citizen-subject, see Yoda, "First-Person Narration and Citizen-Subject."

20   Macpherson, *The Political Theory of Possessive Individualism*. For a critique of the unresolvable aporia that lie at the core of the notion of possessive individualism, see Balibar, "'Possessive Individualism' Reversed."

21   Quoted in Kamei, *Transformations of Sensibility*, 256–57. The following discussion is based on Kamei, *Transformations of Sensibility*, 255–87.

22   Quoted in Kamei, *Transformations of Sensibility*, 259–60. This four-stage narrative of the rise of civilization was a product of eighteenth-century discourses in early English liberalism and became integral to the expansion of the modern property system across the British Empire as well as in the US dispossession of Native American land. See Purdy, *The Meaning of Property*, 38–39 and 67–86.

23   See, for example, the "Natsume Sōseki" entry (Uchida Michio), *Kodansha Encyclopedia of Japan* (Tokyo: Kōdansha, 1983), 5:349–51.

24   For example, Mary Layoun argues that "Sōseki's texts themselves raise a darkly despairing and contradictory objection, not to modernization and the foreign, not to nationalism and the leap from a feudal state to a monopoly capitalist one, but to the stultifying social and cultural effects of the specific direction that modernization, nationalism, foreign 'importation,' and capitalism took." Layoun, *Travels of a Genre*, 116–17.

25   Takayoshi, "A Note on the Political Thought."

26   Quoted in Takayoshi, "A Note on the Political Thought," 82. Takayoshi's translation.

27   For a passionate defense of liberal property norms as the basis for a radical form of egalitarian sociality grounded in an attempt to achieve an integrated balance between negative and positive notions of freedom, see Purdy, *The Meaning of Property*.

28   Anthropologist David Graeber, for example, argues that human relationships are grounded simultaneously in three distinct moral principles—communism, hierarchy, and exchange—each of which implies a different schema of ownership. See Graeber, *Debt*, esp. 89–126.

29 Balibar, "'Possessive Individualism' Reversed."

30 Rose, *Property and Persuasion*, 5. See also 37–38, 127, and 144.

31 Hegel, *Elements of the Philosophy of Right*, 81–82.

32 Rose, *Property and Persuasion*, 25. On property's reliance on narrative, see 286–94.

33 For feminist analyses of the concept of property and its relationship to narrative, see Rose, *Property and Persuasion*; and Dickenson, *Property, Women and Politics*. On the rhetorical ambiguity of legal practice, see Dayan, *The Law Is a White Dog*.

34 See Best, *The Fugitive's Properties*.

35 Williams, *Culture and Society*, 35.

36 Williams, *Marxism and Literature*, 50. I should note that Sōseki's own definition of literature (*bungaku*) was somewhat different, as we will explore at length in chapters that follow.

37 Frederic Jameson, *Marxism and Form*, 85.

38 Jameson, *Marxism and Form*, 87.

39 Jameson, *Marxism and Form*, 89.

40 Jameson, *Marxism and Form*, 90.

41 Poovey, *Genres of the Credit Economy*, 299.

42 Sedgwick, "Paranoid Reading and Reparative Reading," 136.

43 Fisher, *K-Punk*, 580.

44 Natsume, *The Miner*, 55; *SZ* 5:41.

45 Natsume, *Kusamakura*, 12. Alan Turney's translation of the passage brings out the relation to property even more vividly: "Three feet away from the canvas, you can look at it calmly, for there is no danger of becoming involved. To put it another way, you are not robbed of your faculties by considerations of self interest." Natsume, *The Three-Cornered World*, 24. For the original, see *SZ* 3:13.

46 Karatani, *The Structure of World History*.

CHAPTER ONE: FABLES OF PROPERTY

1 Sebald, *The Civil Code of Japan*, 45.

2 Haraway, citing the work of dog trainer Vicki Hearne, speaks of dog obedience training as "a place to increase the dog's power to claim rights against the human." These rights, "rooted in reciprocal possession," have lasting impact on both partners. "Possession—property—is about reciprocity and rights of access. If I have a dog, my dog has a human; what that means concretely is at stake." Haraway, *Companion Species Manifesto*, 53–54.

3 See, for example, Karatani, *Sōseki-ron shūsei*, 197–260; Fujii, *Complicit Fictions*, 103–25; and Itahana, "*Wagahai wa neko de aru* ron."

4 Putz, "Nachwort," 657.

5 I was alerted to the relevance of the Shklovsky essay by Kimata, "*Wagahai wa neko de aru.*" See "Art as Device," in Shklovsky, *Viktor Shklovsky*, 73–96.

6 Sōseki's personal library, as preserved at Tōhoku University, includes eight titles by Tolstoy, all in English translation, but no version of *Kholstomer*, which is also known

in English as *Strider*. Sōseki's fiction and critical writings contain numerous mentions of the Russian novelist, but again, there are no references to this specific work.

7 Berger, "Why Look at Animals?," 16.

8 Fisher, *K-Punk*, 765–66.

9 For a critical history of the legal status of dogs and other animals as property in Anglo-American law, see Dayan, *The Law Is a White Dog*, esp. 209–52. On early American legal disputes over ownership of animals in hunting and whaling disputes, see Rose, *Property and Persuasion*, 12–13 and 17. On "living property," see Favre, "Living Property." On animals as potential owners, see Foster, "Should Pets Inherit?"

10 Bond, *Paddington Helps Out*, 70–71. Knut, the polar bear narrator of the last segment in Tawada Yōko's *Yuki no renshūsei* (*Memoirs of a Polar Bear*, 2011), 233–35, likewise finds himself mystified to learn that zoos can claim ownership rights over their animals (and the profits derived from them).

11 Lippit, *Electric Animal*.

12 I have in mind Borges, "Kafka and His Precursors."

13 Natsume, *I Am a Cat*, 1:27–28. For the Japanese original, see Natsume, *Sōseki Zenshū* (hereafter abbreviated as SZ), 1:8.

14 Letourneau, *Property*, xi.

15 Letourneau, *Property*, 2.

16 Natsume, *I Am a Cat*, 2:14–15; SZ 1:141.

17 For example, Sōseki would take up Oliver Goldsmith's 1770 poem "The Deserted Village," a lamentation over the impact of enclosure and engrossment on the countryside, in his 1893 essay "Eikoku shijin no tenchi sansen ni taisuru kannen" (English poets' ideas of nature) and in his *Bungaku Hyōron* (Literary criticism, 1909). See Matsui, *Natsume Sōseki as a Critic of English Literature*, esp. 28–32. On Goldsmith's poem in relation to enclosure and how in it, "the social forces which are dispossessing the village are seen as simultaneously dispossessing poetry," see Willliams, *The Country and the City*, 74–79. On enclosure and dispossession as crucial components of capital accumulation as seen in eighteenth-century literature, see Rosenberg and Yang, "Introduction."

18 Walker, *The Sublime Perversion of Capital*.

19 This sequence can also be read as a parody of the wartime fanaticism that swept over Japan during the Russo-Japanese War: the cat compares his own actions to those of war hero Admiral Tōgō Heihachirō. See Hintereder-Emde, "Erkenntnis geht durch den Magen."

20 The burglar's face is said to resemble remarkably that of Kangetsu, for example, while the cat goes off on a long tangent (discussed below) in which he refutes the notion that the fact that no two human faces look alike serves as proof of the omnipotence of God, arguing that it equally well serves to disprove that omnipotence, since it shows God unable to produce two identical faces.

21 Natsume, *I Am a Cat*, 2:7; SZ 1:183. This foreshadows Kangetsu's interminable story in the last chapter, which draws its comic impact from the speaker's refusal to abbreviate any detail, no matter how irrelevant, in recounting his purchase of a violin.

22 We see this in how "the feline interlocutor/amanuensis constantly disrupts the narrative flow with reflections upon the instrumentality of writing itself." Jacobowitz, *Writing Technology in Meiji Japan*, 252.

23 Andō, "Wagahai wa 'We' de aru."

24 Similarly, in chapter 11, Beauchamp's theft of cigarettes from the man with whom he shares a room at an inn results, when the pilfering is discovered, not in punishment, but rather in the gift from the victim of several dozen cigarettes.

25 James A. Fujii has argued similarly that *Neko* can be read as contesting in its very narrative form the "new private subject" operating in a chronotope dominated by private space that was emerging as dominant in late Meiji literature and national/imperial ideology. Fujii, *Complicit Fictions*, 104.

26 Natsume, *I Am a Cat*, 3:318; *SZ* 1:531.

27 Natsume, *I Am a Cat*, 3:362–63; *SZ* 1:564.

28 As Andō notes, the cat violates the typical contract with the reader in a first-person narration when he claims access to the unspoken thoughts of Kushami-sensei. The cat later, in chapter 9, papers this over with a ridiculous claim that cats can read human minds; rather than rejecting this implausible claim, the reader accepts it precisely because its comicality adds to the pleasure of the reading experience. Andō, "Wagahai wa 'We' de aru," 36–39.

29 James, *A Pluralistic Universe*, 309.

30 Natsume, *I Am a Cat*, 1:21; *SZ* 1:3.

31 Komori, *Sōseki o yominaosu*, 8–11.

32 Andō, "Wagahai wa 'We' de aru." Itahana reads the narrative device of the cat in terms of a Bakhtinian polyvocality and heteroglossia in which a single utterance bears multiple accents and voices: see Itahana, "*Wagahai wa neko de aru* ron."

33 This habit of coining nicknames is shared with the nameless first-person narrator of *Botchan*, written at the same time and also first published in *Hototogisu*.

34 Natsume, *I Am a Cat*, 1:46; *SZ* 1:21.

35 See "The Nature of Pronouns" and "Subjectivity in Language" in Benveniste, *Problems in General Linguistics*, 217–22 and 223–30, respectively. It should also be noted that Benveniste takes language as being definitive of the human: "language provides the very definition of man" ("Subjectivity in Language," 224); what would the linguist make of a talking cat? For another reading of *Neko* by way of Benveniste, see Fujii, *Complicit Fictions*, 103–25.

36 Benveniste, "Subjectivity in Language," 224–25.

37 Benveniste, "The Nature of Pronouns," 219, and "Subjectivity in Language," 226.

38 According to Benveniste, in Japanese and other East Asian languages, "the use of periphrases or of special forms between certain groups of individuals" replaces "the direct personal references. But these usages only serve to underline the value of the avoided forms; it is the implicit existence of these pronouns that gives social and cultural value to the substitutes imposed by class relationships" ("Subjectivity in Language," 226). For critiques of Benveniste's ahistorical and universalizing assumptions about the categories of person and pronoun, see Sakai, *Voices of the Past*, 69–72; and Yoda, "First-Person Narration and Citizen-Subject."

39 "My master said nothing, but blew out smoke-rings as if in confession of his own [*wagahai*] lack of such audacity." Natsume, *I Am a Cat*, 1:44; *SZ* 1:20.

40 Benveniste, "The Nature of Pronouns," 219.

41 Benveniste, "The Nature of Pronouns," 220.

42 Maeda Ai, however, argues that in *Neko* language is frequently used for purposes other than opening intersubjective communication. Despite the loquacity of the various characters in the work, their incessant dialogues often seem to create no communication, no intersubjective I-Thou relations. It is language spilled out for the pleasure of its own sake—for that shared world of storytelling and its pleasures. Maeda, "Neko no kotoba, neko no ronri."

43 An intriguing study of *Bungakuron* that rethinks the project in part by returning to the class notes taken by Sōseki's students at the original university lectures appeared just as I finished working on this book, too late to fully integrate its contribution into my argument: Hattori, *Hajimari no Sōseki.*

44 *SZ* 16:161, Bourdaghs translation.

45 *SZ* 14:251, Bourdaghs translation.

46 Murphy, *Metaphorical Circuit*, 24–54.

47 In English it is discussed in Foster, *Pandemonium and Parade*, 119–25; and it is mentioned briefly in Figal, *Civilization and Monsters*, 38–39.

48 Kanda, "'Kagaku' to iu shinkō."

49 "Hearing Things," in Natsume, *Ten Nights of Dreams, Hearing Things, The Heredity of Taste*, 67; *SZ* 2:88–89.

50 Legal scholarship too has its own ghosts and hauntings. "Just as reason can abide quite comfortably with the unreasonable, I believe that ghost stories can be set alongside legal narratives. If, as I argue, the law creates persons much as the supernatural creates spirits, then such newly invented entities are not what we assume. A series of metamorphoses, both legal and magical, transform persons into ghosts, into things and into animals. But these terms—person, ghost, thing, animal—which we assume to have definite boundaries, lose these demarcations." Dayan, *The Law Is a White Dog*, xvii; see also 1–38 for a history of legal cases that have granted ghosts legal status in disputes over property. Dayan concludes that "specters are very much part of the legal domain" (12).

51 James, *Principles of Psychology*, 1:291, italics in the original.

52 James, *Principles of Psychology*, 1:293.

53 Michaels, *The Gold Standard and the Logic of Naturalism*, 7–9. The fundamental text on possessive individualism is Macpherson, *The Political Theory of Possessive Individualism.*

54 Natsume, "Hearing Things," 76; *SZ* 2:96.

55 Natsume, "Hearing Things," 84; *SZ* 2:103.

56 "What interests Kafka is a pure and intense sonorous material that is always connected to *its own* abolition—a deterritorialized musical sound, a cry that escapes signification, composition, song, words—a sonority that ruptures in order to break away from a chain that is still all too signifying. In sound, intensity alone matters, and

such sound is generally monotone and always nonsignifying." Deleuze and Guattari, *Kafka*, 6. I am grateful to Scott Aalaard for pointing out to me this connection between Sōseki's use of sound and Kafka.

57 Natsume, "Hearing Things," 98; *SZ* 2:114.

58 Matsumoto, "Researches on Acoustic Space."

59 In the final chapter of *I Am a Cat*, Kangetsu (Coldmoon) describes a sublime experience of loss of selfhood while sitting on a mountaintop. His friend asks him if the locale might be haunted by foxes or tanuki. Kangetsu describes his feeling at the time in the following terms: "I couldn't even tell whether I was my own self or not." Natsume, *I Am a Cat*, 3:305. I am grateful to Alex Murphy for the information about Terada's acoustic research. See for example Terada, "Acoustical Investigation of the Japanese Bamboo Pipe, Syakuhati."

60 James, *The Varieties of Religious Experience*, 233.

61 James, *Essays in Psychical Research*, 196, 198, and 202.

62 Reprinted in James, *Essays in Psychical Research*, 203–15. This quotation appears on 204.

63 Sōseki discusses Myers and James in his 1911 memoirs, *Omoide no koto nado*: "Life after death. A strange concept indeed. Even after we die our individuality continues, is active, and, if the opportunity arises, communicates with people on earth. It seems that FWH Myers, well-known for his studies of spiritualism, believed this as did [Oliver] Lodge who dedicated his work to Myers." Sōseki goes on in the same passage to discusses Fechner and James's interest in this area: "James, by analyzing and then synthesizing the contents of consciousness, came to the conclusion that there is a large universal consciousness which embraces and is aware of all the small consciousnesses. The small consciousnesses thus embraced, however, are aware only of themselves and, like the peacefully grazing horses and cattle, are utterly oblivious of the whole of which they are but a part." Natsume, *Recollections*, 62. Sōseki, incidentally, owned a copy of Myers's *Wordsworth*, a work of literary criticism. On parapsychology and spiritualism in Japan, see McVeigh, *The History of Japanese Psychology*, esp. 97–106.

64 On the ethicality of Myers's version of psychology and parapsychology, see Gandhi, *Affective Communities*, 135–41.

65 Kafka, "Investigations of a Dog," 159.

66 Natsume, "Hearing Things," 113–14; *SZ* 2:126.

67 Natsume, "Hearing Things," 114, translation slightly modified; *SZ* 2:126.

68 For accounts of other forms of the uncanny and monstrous generated through modern discourses of science and imperialism in Japan, see Figal, *Civilizations and Monsters*; Foster, *Pandemonium and Parade*; and Nakamura, *Monstrous Bodies*.

69 Derrida, *Specters of Marx*, 6.

70 "One never inherits without coming to terms with [*s'expliquer avec*] some specter, and therefore with more than one specter." Derrida, *Specters of Marx*, 21.

71 Natsume, "Hearing Things," 115; *SZ* 2:127.

72 Earlier versions of material in this section previously appeared as "Novelistic Desire, Theoretical Attitude, and Translating Heteroglossia: Reading Natsume Sōseki's *Sanshirō*

around Naoki Sakai," in *The Politics of Culture: Around the Work of Naoki Sakai*, ed. John Namjun Kim and Richard F. Calichman (London: Routledge, 2010), 21–39.

73 Girard, *Deceit, Desire, and the Novel*.

74 Karatani, "Sōseki's Diversity," 126.

75 Vincent, *Two-Timing Modernity*, 86–151; and Dodd, "The Significance of Bodies in Sōseki's *Kokoro*." For a similar reading of Sōseki's 1907 novella *Nowaki*, see Reichert, *In the Company of Men*, 167–98.

76 The so-called *Kokoro* debate is summarized in English in Sakaki, *Recontextualizing Texts*, 29–53; and in Bourdaghs, "Introduction." In Japanese, see Oshino, "*Kokoro* ronsō no yukue."

77 Rubin, "The Traffic in Women."

78 Deleuze and Guattari, *Anti-Oedipus*, 72.

79 Nihei, "Nanji no me no mae ni totte." The embedded quotation is modified slightly from Jay Rubin's translation: Natsume, *Sanshirō*, 200.

80 It could also mean "the fourth son of a man who was himself a third son," though Sanshirō in fact clearly seems to be a first son. See Ishihara, *Sōseki no kigōgaku*, 240n19. Critics have also linked the name to the real historical figure of Ishikawa Sanshirō, the preacher at Hongo Central Church, identified in the novel as Mineko's house of worship. See, for example, Freedman, *Tokyo in Transit*, 79.

81 Natsume, *Sanshirō*, 13–14; *SZ* 5:288.

82 Natsume, *Sanshirō*, 9; *SZ* 5:282.

83 For a reading of this sequence in terms of forms of gendered subjectivity that were generated through literary depictions of Japan's rapidly expanding train and streetcar network, see Freedman, *Tokyo in Transit*, esp. 90–96.

84 Natsume, *Sanshirō*, 11; *SZ* 5:284.

85 Butler, "Who Owns Kafka?"

86 Natsume, *Sanshirō*, 54; *SZ* 5:346.

87 Natsume, *Sanshirō*, 119; *SZ* 5:446.

88 Komori, *Sōseki o yominaosu*, 141–55.

89 For alternate readings of the triangular logic behind this passage, see Dodd, "The Significance of Bodies in Sōseki's *Kokoro*," 482–90; and Washburn, *Translating Mount Fuji*, 97–98.

90 Natsume, *Sanshirō*, 66; *SZ* 5:364–65.

91 Natsume, *Sanshirō*, 67; *SZ* 5:365.

92 Natsume, *Sanshirō*, 102; *SZ* 5:421.

93 On anti-Oedipus in Sōseki (referring in this case not to Deleuze and Guattari but rather to the original Greek myth), see Shimizu, *Sōseki* .

94 Natsume, *Sanshirō*, 146; *SZ* 5:486.

95 Natsume, *Sanshirō*, 148–49; *SZ* 5:489.

96 Natsume, *Sanshirō*, 149; *SZ* 5:490.

97 Sakai, *Voices of the Past*, 266–67, italics in the original.

98 Deleuze and Guattari, *Kafka*, 24.

99 See, for example, *SZ* 14:38.

100 Washburn, *Translating Mount Fuji*, 71–106.

101 Natsume, *Sanshirō*, 114–17; *SZ* 5:439–43.

102 Sakai, *Translation and Subjectivity*, 55.

103 Sakai, *Translation and Subjectivity*, 56.

104 Sōseki probably knew the phrase from the closing line of Robert Browning's poem, "The Statue and the Bust."

105 Natsume, *Sanshirō*, 201; *SZ* 5:567. "De te fabula" has a counterpart, "hydriotaphia," another word that Sanshirō associates with Professor Hirota. When Sanshirō asks the latter what it means, he is told, "I don't know myself. I suppose it's Greek" (Natsume, *Sanshirō*, 204; *SZ* 5:572).

106 Many previous critics have explored the implications of "stray sheep" and translation in the novel, including Washburn, *Translating Mount Fuji*, 101–5; and Kumasaka, "*Sanshirō* to Eikoku gaka."

107 Natsume, *Sanshirō*, 99, translation modified; *SZ* 5:417–18.

108 Natsume, *Sanshirō*, 102; *SZ* 5:420–21.

109 Natsume, *Sanshirō*, 106; *SZ* 5:426.

110 Natsume, *Sanshirō*, 223; *SZ* 5:602.

111 Nihei, "Nanji no me no mae ni totte."

112 Natume, *Sanshirō*, 228; *SZ* 5:608.

113 Deleuze and Guattari, *Kafka*, 24.

114 Jameson, "Sōseki and Western Modernism," 124.

115 Jameson, "Sōseki and Western Modernism," 138.

116 Deleuze and Guattari, *Kafka*, 6.

117 Karatani, "Sōseki's Diversity."

118 Lippit, *Electric Animals*, 165–66.

119 Sakai, *Translation and Subjectivity*, 53, 67.

120 Sakai, *Translation and Subjectivity*, 13.

121 Gandhi, *Affective Communities*, 10.

122 Hardt and Negri, *Commonwealth*, ix.

123 Gandhi, *Affective Communities*, 145.

124 Gandhi, *Affective Communities*, 184.

125 "Sōseki to janru," in Karatani, *Sōseki-ron shūsei*, 197–232.

126 Stewart, "Notes on Distressed Genres," 15. Stewart refers here to the classic work on the fable genre, Perry, "Fable."

127 On, for example, *Wagahai mitaru Amerika* [The Amerika that I saw, 1914], a sequel to Sōseki's work published in the US by Hosaka Kiichi, see Hibi, *Japaniizu Amerika*, 151–71.

128 Stewart, "Notes on Distressed Genres," 23.

129 Perry, "Fable," 18.

130 Anderton, "Dogdom."

131 Anderton, "Dogdom," 272.

An earlier version of the first half of this chapter appeared in Japanese as "Kage no shita no ie: Natsume Sōseki *Mon* to ishiki no nagare," *RILAS Journal* 3 (2015), 11–19.

1   The significance of mental illness, especially the neurasthenia from which both Sōseki and a number of his fictional characters suffered, has been widely discussed. See, for example, Ichiyanagi, "Tokkenka sareru 'shinkei'"; and Miyamoto and Seki, *Natsume Sōseki*, 69–99.

2   Natsume, *Theory of Literature and Other Critical Writings*, 49, Bourdaghs translation. For the original Japanese, see *SZ* 13:14–15. Sōseki refers here to his first three published books of fiction: the novel *I Am a Cat* (*Wagahai wa neko de aru*, 1905–6), and the short-story collections *Drifting in Space* (*Yōkyoshū*, 1906) and *Quail Cage* (*Uzurakago*, 1907).

3   *Gubijinsō*, *SZ* 4:366–67, Bourdaghs translation.

4   On this scene, see Komori, *Sōseki ron*, 89–96. On Sōseki's view of Itō, see Shibata, *Sōseki no naka no "teikoku,"* 126–28. The assassination must have touched close to home for Sōseki, who had concluded his own tour of Manchuria less than two months before Itō's death. Standing next to Itō when An Jung-geun shot him was Nakamura Yoshikoto (1867–1927, also known as Nakamura Zeko), chairman of the South Manchurian Railroad Company—a school friend of Sōseki's and his host during the novelist's own tour of Korea and Manchuria. By coincidence, Itō had in the 1860s lived in the same boardinghouse (76 Gower Street, near the University of London) as an overseas student that Sōseki would temporarily reside in upon arriving in London in 1900.

5   Natsume, *The Gate*, trans. William Sibley, 20–21; *SZ* 6:368–69. There are two published English translations of *The Gate*: in addition to Sibley, there is Sōseki, *Mon*, trans. Francis Mathy. I quote from both below.

6   Natsume, *The Gate*, 23; *SZ* 6:372.

7   See the essay by Maeda, "In the Recesses of the High City," 329–50.

8   Natsume, *Mon*, 7; *SZ* 6:350.

9   Natsume, *The Gate*, 5; *SZ* 6:350.

10   Natsume, *Mon*, 34; *SZ* 6:384.

11   Natsume, *Mon*, 168; *SZ* 6:553.

12   Natsume, *The Gate*, 166; *SZ* 6:553.

13   On the X-ray as—together with psychoanalysis and the cinema—a source of new modern shadows of visibility and invisibility, see Lippit, *Atomic Light*.

14   On the introduction of Bain in Japan, see Satō and Mizoguchi, *Tsūshi*, 24–32. On Tsubouchi and Bain, see Kamei, "The Embodied Self," 43–71. See also Kamei, *"Shōsetsu" ron*, esp. 18–34.

15   On Motora, see McVeigh, *The History of Japanese Psychology*, esp. 71–88; Satō and Mizoguchi, *Tsūshi*, esp. 74–90; Sato and Sato, "The Early 20th Century"; and Sato, Nakatsuma, and Matsubara, "Influence of G. Stanley Hall on Yuzero Motora." Motora carried out interesting laboratory experiments trying to locate patterns of pros-

ody and poetic rhythm in neurological structure. See Mehl, "The Concept of Expression in Modern Japanese Poetics," esp. 53–63 and 227–32.

16 Karatani, *Origins of Modern Japanese Literature*. Karatani, it should be noted, situates Sōseki as an outsider to this new modern literature and its interior self. Masumitsu Keiko makes a similar argument, distinguishing Sōseki's understanding of consciousness from the dominant confessional mode of Japanese Naturalism. See Masumitsu, *Natsume Sōseki ron*, 3–24.

17 See, for example, Dunlap, "Discussion."

18 Scripture, *The New Psychology*, 7. Scripture does not, however, completely dismiss introspection as a method, and he accepts the distinction between brain and mind that was crucial to advocates of introspection as a scientific methodology.

19 "At present, what can be considered advancement in psychology attempts to separate psychology from the category of philosophy and to regard it as a distinct domain of scholarship. Philosophy largely relies on introspection. Accordingly, the techniques proper to psychology involve leaving introspection behind and learning instead through observation and experimentation." Motora Yūjirō, "Beikoku shinrigaku no kinkyō," *Rikugō zasshi* 93 (September 1888), 1–8; reprinted in *Motora Yūjirō chosakushū*, 1:95–103. This passage appears on 98.

20 Lamarre, "Expanded Empiricism."

21 On Matsumoto's careers, see McVeigh, *History of Japanese Psychology*, esp. 88–96; Sato and Sato, "The Early 20th Century"; and Satō and Mizoguchi, *Tsūshi*, esp. 75–99. In 1906 Matsumoto would move to Kyoto Imperial University to open the new psychology laboratory there; in 1913 he would return to Tokyo Imperial University to replace Motora following the latter's death. (Incidentally, Matsumoto was then replaced on the Kyoto Imperial University faculty by philosopher Nishida Kitarō.) Sōseki reminisces about the young Matsumoto in his 1913 preface to *Densetsu no jidai* (Nogami Yaeko's Japanese translation of Thomas Bulfinch's *The Age of Fables, or Stories of Gods and Heroes*), SZ 16:544–47.

22 Debaene, *Far Afield*, 12. Philosophy responded in corresponding fashion to try to carve out its own disciplinary space, distinct from the sciences, a space that sometimes included and sometimes excluded psychology. See Bordogna, *William James at the Boundaries*, esp. 21–58.

23 Burt, "Frances Galton and His Contributions to Psychology," 41. See also Thomson, *The Pelican History of Psychology*, 115–16. Burt would himself later be accused of quackery and charlatanry: since the 1970s, allegations have been made (some subsequently rebutted) that he fabricated data in his experiments. For a summary of "the Burt affair," see Wooldridge, *Measuring the Mind*, 340–58; see also Gould, *The Mismeasure of Man*, esp. 303–26. Sōseki himself encountered (and underlined and wrote multiple marginal comments on) a critique of Galton's early theories of innate racial intelligence in his copy of Kidd, *Social Evolution*, 273–76.

24 Satō and Mizoguchi, *Tsūshi*, 15–40.

25 Danziger, *Constructing the Subject*, 18–19. Danziger (23–24) also notes that nineteenth-century advocates of introspection as a method are often linked to "a philosophy of

liberal individualism," with its presumption of the existence of a "private world of inner experience," closely linked to the doctrine of possessive individualism.

26 Lyons, *The Disappearance of Introspection*. For a recounting of the controversies over introspection that takes a more sympathetic stance toward the method, see Hatfield, "Introspective Evidence in Psychology," 259–86.

27 Wundt, *Principles of Physiological Psychology*, 2.

28 Danziger, *Constructing the Subject*, esp. 34–48. See also Thomson, *The Pelican History of Psychology*, 87–91. By coincidence, both Wundt's and Sōseki's personal libraries would end up archived in the same institution: the Tōhoku University Library in Sendai, Japan. Sōseki's library was moved from Tokyo to Sendai for safekeeping during World War II due to the efforts of Komiya Toyotaka (1884–1966), one of the novelist's disciples and a professor at the university. For the history of how Wundt's library was acquired in 1922, see Satō and Mizoguchi, *Tsūshi*, 219–20.

29 Danziger, *Constructing the Subject*, 41–45; Lyons, *The Disappearance of Introspection*, 16–25.

30 Stout, *Analytic Psychology*, 1:1 and 18–19.

31 Stout, *Analytic Psychology*, 1:3.

32 Stout, *Analytic Psychology*, 1:6.

33 Stout, *Analytic Psychology*, 1:45.

34 Kittler, *The Truth of the Technological World*, 61.

35 Wundt, *Principles of Physiological Psychology*, 1.

36 Wundt, *Outlines of Psychology*, 2. For an explication of Wundt's position on this point, see Hatfield, "Introspective Evidence in Psychology," 274–75.

37 Natsume, "Philosophical Foundations of the Literary Arts," 164–65; *SZ* 16:71.

38 My reading here borrows much from Komori, *Sōseki o yominaosu*, 88–107. For an account of Sōseki's evolving understanding of the notion of consciousness (*ishiki*), see also Masumitsu, *Natsume Sōseki ron*, 3–24. On the complexity of Sōseki's theorization of the continuousness of consciousness, see Lamarre, "Expanded Empiricism."

39 Natsume, "Philosophical Foundations," 165; *SZ* 16:71–72.

40 Natsume, "Philosophical Foundations," 166–67; *SZ* 16:74–75.

41 See, for example, Miyamoto and Seki, *Natsume Sōseki*; Ogura, *Natsume Sōseki*; and Ōkubo, *Sōseki to sono shisō*. In English, see Lamarre, "Expanded Empiricism"; and Summersgill, "The Influence of William James and Henri Bergson." Sōseki was also familiar with the work of William James's brother, Henry, and owned copies of *The Golden Bowl*, *Partial Portraits*, *French Poets and Novelists*, and *Notes on Novelists*. See Schultz and Yamamoto, "Egos vs. Relationships in James's *The Golden Bowl* and Soseki's *Light and Darkness*." See also Nathan, "Introduction." On James's impact on another early twentieth-century Japanese writer, the modernist poet Hagiwara Sakutarō, see Mehl, "Appropriations and Inventions."

42 Miyamoto and Seki, *Natsume Sōseki*, 10–15, 19. See, for example, Motora's not entirely positive review of *Principles of Psychology*: "Zeemusu-shi shinrigaku o yomu," originally published in *Rikigō zasshi* 131 (1891), 476–78, reprinted in *Motora Yūjirō chosakushū* 2:327–30. In 1904, Motora would finally meet James in person. Motora reports that when he asked James about his most recent work in psychology, James

chuckled and responded that he was no longer actively pursuing psychological research. See Motora Yūjirō, "Ōbei rekiyū jikkendan," originally published in *Tetsugaku zasshi* 225 (1905), 289–308, reprinted in *Motora Yūjirō chosakushū* 10:414–27.

43 While Sōseki's copy of volume 1 of *Principles* contains considerable underlining, volume 2 contains none, though Sōseki does quote from it in *Theory of Literature*.

44 Ogura, *Natsume Sōseki*, 30–32.

45 *SZ* 12:364.

46 For a survey of the direct and indirect references to James in Sōseki's works, see Shigematsu, "Sōseki to Uiriamu Jeimuzu." See also Shigematsu, "*Bungakuron* kara 'Bungei no tetsugakuteki kiso' 'Sōsakuka no taido' e."

47 Mumford, *The Golden Day*, esp. 188–92. See Livingston, *Pragmatism and the Political Economy of Cultural Revolution*, 200.

48 Michaels, *The Gold Standard and the Logic of Naturalism*, e.g., 7–9 and 154–58.

49 This was a problem that also bedeviled John Locke, the first to define the identity of the self in terms of consciousness linked to memory and the key figure in the rise of possessive individualism as a philosopheme. As Balibar argues, Locke solved the problem through linguistic creativity, creating a rhetorical identity between two subtly different English words: *self* and *own* (both in the sense of "to possess" and of "my own self" or "on my own"). Balibar, *Citizen Subject*, 74–91.

50 James, *Principles of Psychology*, 1:337, hereafter abbreviated as *Principles*.

51 James, *Principles*, 1:338–39, italics in original.

52 James, *Principles*, 1:339–40. In Sōseki's own copy of the work, there are several vertical lines written in the margins next to passages in this section of the text explaining the "Thought" and its ownership of past selves (e.g., on pp. 334, 336 [two], and 340), indicating that he read it with some interest, although none of these lines mark the specific passages I quote here.

53 Lyons, *Disappearance of Introspection*, 6–16.

54 James, *Principles*, 1:680. Sōseki would cite James's theory of the selective nature of consciousness in "The Attitude of a Creative Author" ("Sōsakuka no taido," 1908); see *SZ* 16:162.

55 James, *Principles*, 1:334–35.

56 James, *Principles*, 1:337.

57 James, *Principles*, 1:291, italics in original.

58 James, *Principles*, 1:326, bracketed insertion in original.

59 James, *Principles*, 1:327.

60 James, *Principles*, 1:333.

61 James, *Principles*, 1:293. This implicit connection between personhood and property is in contemporary societies increasingly recognized in legal codes and court decisions, which tend to provide greater degrees of protection for property that is more closely entangled with personhood. See Radin, "Property and Personhood."

62 Macpherson, *The Political Theory of Possessive Individualism*.

63 "Individuality, as noted above, is constituted through the self-recognition of one's memory of past and present thoughts. . . . The proper subject is not only he who actually owns property or is able to freely alienate his labor but is, fundamentally, he who

has the capacity to engage in the conscious reflections that marks out or defines the internal stage." Bhandar, *Colonial Lives of Property*, 167.

64 Hence, for Locke, "The Indian is a subject without a past. . . . The property logic of Indian identity is entirely different from that of the self-possessed, proprietorial subject—its temporality is static, rather than dynamic and of a cognizable duration." Bhandar, *Colonial Lives of Property*, 170. On the notion of "imperfect sovereign" in American property law, see Purdy, *The Meaning of Property*, 67–86.

65 Natsume, *Theory of Literature*, 52, Murphy translation; *sz* 14:27.

66 Natsume, *Theory of Literature*, 55, Murphy translation; *sz* 14:31.

67 See, for example, James's explication of "the field of consciousness" as being composed of a distinct center, less distinct margins, and a subconscious realm, in *Varieties*, 231–35; there are numerous underlines and marginal comments jotted down on these pages in Sōseki's copy of the work.

68 On $(F+f)$ in relation to denotation and connotation, see Shinoda, *Shōsetsu wa ika ni kakareta ka*, 35–36.

69 On the role of association in Sōseki, see Sasaki, "'Anshi' jikken toshite no Sōseki tanpen."

70 On the role of f in securing the continuousness of consciousness, see Lamarre, "Expanded Empiricism." On Sōseki's concept of temporality, see Noami, *Natsume Sōseki no jikan no sōshutsu*.

71 Natsume, *Theory of Literature*, 54–55, Murphy translation; *sz* 14:30.

72 On *The Gate*, see Komori, *Sōseki o yominaosu*, 217–23; and Ogura, *Natsume Sōseki*, 22–40. On "The Tower of London," see Murphy, *Metaphorical Circuit*, 30 and 32.

73 Natsume, *The Gate*, 10; *sz* 6:356.

74 For an account of the urban landscape as a kind of nervous stimulation in Sōseki's *Sanshirō*, see Freedman, *Tokyo in Transit*, 68–115.

75 Natsume, *The Gate*, 11–12; *sz* 6:358.

76 Natsume, *The Gate*, 12; *sz* 6:359.

77 Bourdaghs translation: both Sibley and Mathy omit this *kage* from their translations. *sz* 6:360.

78 Natsume, *The Gate*, 14; *sz* 6:361.

79 Natsume, *The Gate*, 55; *sz* 6:414.

80 Natsume, *The Gate*, 56–57; *sz* 6:415–16.

81 Shibata reads both *And Then* (*Sore kara*) and *The Gate* in terms of interrupted streams of consciousness, which he connects to the problem of Japanese imperialism and the 1910 annexation of Korea. See Shibata, *Sōseki no naka no "teikoku,"* 102–29 and 134–64.

82 Natsume, *Theory of Literature*, 145, J. Keith Vincent translation; *sz* 14:449.

83 Kishimoto, *Sōseki no hyōgen*, 85–98.

84 Natsume, *Mon*, 136; *sz* 6:515.

85 Natsume, *The Gate*, 135–36; *sz* 6:516.

86 Natsume, *Mon*, 139; *sz* 6:517–18.

87 Natsume, *Mon*, 134–35; *sz* 6:511–12.

88 Minkowski, "Findings in a Case of Schizophrenic Depression," 133. See also Kern, *The Culture of Time and Space*, 281–83.

89 Natsume, *Mon*, 161–62; *SZ* 6:544–5.

90 Natsume, *Mon*, 145; *SZ* 6:525.

91 Natsume, *Mon*, 148–49; *SZ* 6:528–29.

92 James, *Principles*, 1:255. See also Bordogna, *William James at the Boundaries*, 200–201.

93 Sasaki, "'Anshi' jikken toshite no Sōseki tanpen," 36.

94 Natsume, *The Gate*, 117–18; *SZ* 6:492–93.

95 Maeda, "In the Recesses of the High City."

96 Natsume, *The Gate*, 128; *SZ* 6:507.

97 Natsume, *Mon*, 132; *SZ* 6:509.

98 Natsume, *Mon*, 136; *SZ* 6:514.

99 Natsume, *The Gate*, 42; *SZ* 6:398.

100 Natsume, *The Gate*, 65; *SZ* 6:426.

101 Natsume, *The Gate*, 68; *SZ* 6:431.

102 Natsume, *The Gate*, 97–98; *SZ* 6:467–69.

103 Ishihara, *Sōseki no kigōgaku*, 77.

104 On this debate, see Matsuo, *Natsume Sōseki "jiishiki" no wana*, 191–92.

105 Natsume, *The Gate*, 169; *SZ* 6:558.

106 Natsume, *The Gate*, 178; *SZ* 6:569.

107 Natsume, *The Gate*, 182; *SZ* 6:574–75.

108 Natsume, *The Gate*, 183; *SZ* 6:576.

109 Natsume, *The Gate*, 185; *SZ* 6:578–79.

110 Natsume, *Mon*, 192; *SZ* 6:584.

111 Natsume, *The Gate*, 200–201; *SZ* 6:596.

112 Natsume, *The Gate*, 202–3; *SZ* 6:598–99. Sibley's "shadow" here (there is no *kage* in the original Japanese) is the darkness brought on by the setting sun.

113 Natsume, *The Gate*, 205; *SZ* 6:600.

114 Natsume, *The Gate*, 211; *SZ* 6:607.

115 Natsume, *The Gate*, 213; *SZ* 6:609.

116 Natsume, *Mon*, 213; *SZ* 6:610.

117 Kuwada, "Minzoku shinrigaku no igi to ninmu," 119.

118 See also Kuwada, *Vunto no minzokushinrigaku*; and Kuwada, "Vunto no shūkyō no genzai oyobi shōrai ni kansuru kenkai." On the late Wundt's interest in *Völkerpsychologie* (folk psychology), see Thomson, *The Pelican History of Psychology*, 67–74.

119 Motora, "Conflict of Religion and Science"; and Motora, *An Essay on Eastern Philosophy* (also known as *Idea of Ego in Eastern Philosophy*).

120 Kuwada, "Shūkyō shinri ni okeru Zēmusu to Vunto."

121 West, *The American Evasion of Philosophy*, 67.

122 Coon, "'One Moment in the World's Salvation.'"

123 Shigematsu discusses the change in James's position and sees a similar transformation in Sōseki's thought around the years 1907–8. Ogura, on the other hand, argues for a stronger continuity between the James of *Principles* and *Varieties* (noting, for

example, hints at the existence of a subconscious fringe to consciousness even in the earlier work) and argues that the shift in Sōseki's position represents not so much a move from *Principles* to *Varieties* as it does a change in Sōseki's understanding of the model of consciousness presented in *Principles*.

124 Coon, "'One Moment in the World's Salvation.'"

125 Bordogna, *William James at the Boundaries*, 192.

126 James, *Principles*, 1:121.

127 James, *Principles*, 1:653–55.

128 James, *Principles*, 1:113.

129 James, *Principles*, 1:122, italics in the original.

130 James, *Principles*, 1:125, italics in the original.

131 James, *Principles*, 1:126–27, italics in the original.

132 On habit in James, see Bordogna, *William James at the Boundaries*, 259–68.

133 James, *Varieties*, 256–57.

134 James, *Varieties*, 258–59. Other than this and similar brief mentions elsewhere, Sōseki does not seem to have directly encountered the work of Freud. But by coincidence, when Freud emigrated from Vienna to London in 1938, he ended up living a short walk away from one of the boardinghouses where Sōseki had resided, in a neighborhood supposedly known at the time as JJ Town: Jews and Japanese Town. See Itō, "Natsume Soseki und die Zwecklosigkeit des Lebens," esp. 106–7.

135 James, *Varieties*, 267.

136 Sōseki discusses Fechner, Myers, and James in relation to his own fascination with spiritualism in *Omoidasu no koto nado* (*SZ* 12:406–9), and the characters in *I Am a Cat* also discuss James's speculations that the subconscious might be populated by the spirits of the dead (*SZ* 1:70, 74). For James's views on Fechner, see *Pluralistic*, 133–77; on Myers, see *Varieties*, 555–56, and *Pluralistic*, 298–300. On the James/Myers relation, see Gandhi, *Affective Communities*, 131–41; and Bordogna, *William James at the Boundaries*, esp. 91–135.

137 James, *Principles*, 1:121.

138 James, *Varieties*, 8.

139 James, *Varieties*, 6.

140 James, *Varieties*, 269.

141 James, *Varieties*, 235.

142 Quoted in James, *Varieties*, 246.

143 James, *Varieties*, 253.

144 James, *Varieties*, 350.

145 James, *Varieties*, 393.

146 James, *Varieties*, 402–3. There is a vertical line written in the margin next to this last passage in Sōseki's copy of the work, as well as numerous other underlinings throughout this section on asceticism and poverty worship.

147 James, *Pluralistic*, 305.

148 James, *Pluralistic*, 315–16.

149 James, *Pluralistic*, 170–73.

150 James, *Pluralistic*, 254.

151 Gandhi, *Affective Communities*, 133.

152 For example, in trying to explain the mystical experience that leads to a sudden conversion, James writes, "Most of us can remember the strangely moving power of passages in certain poems read when we were young, irrational doorways as they were through which the mystery of fact, the wildness and the pang of life, stole into our hearts and thrilled them. The words have now perhaps become mere polished surfaces for us; but lyric poetry and music are alive and significant only in proportion as they fetch these vague vistas of a life continuous with our own, beckoning and inviting, yet ever eluding our pursuit" (*Varieties*, 417).

153 "For the capitalist circuit of accumulation to operate, the worker must be placed in a position in which he or she is compelled to sell this labor power as a commodity for the reason that he or she is unable, has been unable, to produce any sort of use value through it. Through a series of external conditions, through the operation of expropriation and capture, this inoperativity is installed in displacement at the heart of this cycle—the most basic and fundamental 'possession' of the worker, that is, his or her pure potentiality to produce a use value, is captured as something unusable in private life and is made into a commodity: this point of origin is the repeating loop of capitalist accumulation itself." Walker, *The Sublime Perversion of Capital*, 115.

154 See Nathan, *Sōseki*, 148–51. For the passage from *The Poppy*, see *SZ* 4:553–56. For a notebook passage comparing tragedy and comedy, see *SZ* 19:355–57.

155 Bergson, *Laughter*, 21.

156 Berlant, "Humorlessness," 328, 339, italics in the original.

157 See Lamarre, *Shadows on the Screen*; Miyao, *The Aesthetics of Shadow*; and Lippit, *Atomic Light*. By 1912, there were already forty-four movie houses in Tokyo; Gerow, *Visions of Japanese Modernity*, 52.

158 See Lippit, *Atomic Light*, 67–68; and Fusco, "Squashing the Bookworm."

159 See O'Neill, "Tragedy, Masochism, and Other Worldly Pleasures."

160 Natsume, *Theory of Literature*, 209. Bourdaghs translation. *SZ* 16:131.

161 Fusco, "Squashing the Bookworm."

162 Nancy, *The Pleasure in Drawing*, 41–42.

163 James, *Essays in Radical Empiricism*, 133.

164 Bordogna, *William James at the Boundaries*, 212–23.

CHAPTER THREE: PROPERTY AND SOCIOLOGICAL KNOWLEDGE

Earlier versions of this chapter (minus the postscript) were published as "Property and Sociological Knowledge: Natsume Sōseki and the Gift of Narrative," *Japan Forum* 20, no. 1 (2008): 79–101; and (in Japanese) as "Kiyo toshite no sutekki: Natsume Sōseki *Higan Sugi Made* no shakaigaku," *Nihon bungei ronsō* 15 (2002): 45–59.

1 "Regarding *Higan sugi made*" (Higan sugi made ni tsuite), Sōseki's statement announcing the serialization, is reprinted in *SZ* 16:487–90; this passage appears on 489. Translations of all quotations from Japanese-language materials are mine, except where noted.

2   Natsume, *Theory of Literature*, 44, Bourdaghs translation; *SZ* 14:9.
3   Murphy, *Metaphorical Circuit*, 6–12.
4   Guillory, *Cultural Capital*, 255.
5   Guillory, *Cultural Capital*, 260.
6   Guillory, *Cultural Capital*, xiv.
7   See Karatani, *Origins of Modern Japanese Literature*, 11–22; and Suzuki, *Nihon no "bungaku" gainen*.
8   Natsume, *Theory of Literature*, 43; *SZ* 14:7–8.
9   Komori, *Kōzō to shite no katari*, 31–32.
10 Ishihara, *Sōseki no kigōgaku*, 76.
11 Kamei, *Transformations of Sensibility*, 255–62. See also Bhandar, *Colonial Lives of Property*.
12 Even during the Edo period, however, attempts were made—especially by thinkers associated with the merchant and artisan classes—to reconceptualize commerce as an inherently moral activity. See, for example, Najita, *Visions of Virtue in Tokugawa Japan*.
13 Kawamura, *Sociology and Society of Japan*, 40–77.
14 Levine, *Visions of the Sociological Tradition*, 121–51.
15 MacPherson, *The Political Theory of Possessive Individualism*, 3.
16 Balibar, "'Possessive Individualism' Reversed." Balibar argues that this distinction, however, fails to hold, that the discourse of possessive individualism is built around a double bind that insists the self is both alienable and inalienable.
17 Giddings, *The Elements of Sociology*, 246.
18 Letourneau, *Property*, xi.
19 Letourneau, *Property*, 18–19.
20 Dower, *War without Mercy*, 204.
21 Letourneau, *Property*, 170.
22 Letourneau, *The Evolution of Marriage and of the Family*, 157.
23 Crozier, *History of Intellectual Development*, 119.
24 Le Bon, *The Psychology of Socialism*, 230.
25 Weber, *The Protestant Ethic and the Spirit of Capitalism*, 170.
26 Simmel, *The Philosophy of Money*, 303–7.
27 Durkheim, *Professional Ethics and Civic Morals*.
28 Mauss, *The Gift*, 76.
29 Kawamura, *Sociology and Society of Japan*. On the history of Japanese sociology, see also Barshay, *The Social Sciences in Modern Japan*.
30 For example, see Natsume, *Theory of Literature*, 56–59; *SZ* 14:32–34. See also Shibata, *Sōseki no naka no "teikoku,"* 6–35.
31 Komori, *Sōseki o yominaosu*, 75–86.
32 Satō, *Sōseki no seorii*, 8.
33 Natsume, *Theory of Literature*, 125, J. Keith Vincent translation; *SZ* 14:422.
34 *SZ* 14:261.
35 Natsume, *Theory of Literature*, 145; *SZ* 14:449.
36 Natsume, *Theory of Literature*, 147–49; *SZ* 14:452–53.
37 James, *Principles of Psychology*, 1:238–39.

38 James, *Principles of Psychology*, 1:337–39.
39 Yamada, "*Higan sugi made*," 131–38.
40 Komori, *Kōzō to shite no katari*, 66.
41 Ogura, *Natsume Sōseki*, 178–94.
42 *SZ* 7:20–22. There is a fine English translation by Kingo Ochiagi and Sanford Goldstein (Natsume, *To the Spring Equinox and Beyond*), but in order to highlight aspects of the text around which my argument revolves, I provide my own translations of quotations from the novel here.
43 *SZ* 7:344–45.
44 Komori, *Kōzō to shite no katari*, 30–32.
45 Natsume, *Kokoro*, 123–34; *SZ* 9:156–58.
46 *SZ* 7:309 and 311.
47 *SZ* 7:319.
48 This quality of the narrative voice is noted in Yamada, "*Higan sugi made*"; and Etō, "Hen'yō suru kikite."
49 See Shigematsu, "'Shukō' toshite no Sunaga Ichizō," 8:255–72; and Shimizu, "*Higan sugi made* no kōzō," 218–39.
50 For example, Ara, "*Higan sugi made* ron"; Etō, "Hen'yō suru kikite"; and Nakazawa, *Sōseki no sutekki*.
51 Satō, *Sōseki katazukanai kindai*, 188–90.
52 *SZ* 7:183.
53 *SZ* 7:160–61.
54 *SZ* 7:179.
55 *SZ* 7:183–84.
56 *SZ* 7:209.
57 *SZ* 7:251–52.
58 See the discussion of triangular relationships in chapter 1. See also Satō, *Sōseki katazukanai kindai*, 197–98.
59 *SZ* 7:234–35.
60 *SZ* 7:237.
61 Mauss, *The Gift*, 45.
62 Summersgill, "The Influence of William James and Henri Bergson on Natsume Sōseki's *Higan Sugi Made*," 13.
63 Bakhtin, *Speech Genres and Other Late Essays*, 121, emphasis added.
64 Mauss, *The Gift*, 46, italics in original.
65 Mauss, *The Gift*, 12–13.
66 *SZ* 7:51–52.
67 *SZ* 7:98.
68 *SZ* 7:100.
69 *SZ* 7:119.
70 *SZ* 7:132.
71 *SZ* 7:137–38.
72 *SZ* 7:345.
73 *SZ* 7:346.

74 *SZ* 7:346–47.

75 Derrida, *Given Time*, 24.

76 Lévi-Strauss, *Introduction to the Work of Marcel Mauss*, 24–44.

77 Derrida, *Given Time*, 12 and 7.

78 Hyde, *The Gift*, 11–24.

79 Derrida, *Given Time*, 11.

80 Derrida, *Given Time*, 80.

81 Bourdieu, *Field of Cultural Production*, 148, 201, and 207.

82 Derrida, *Given Time*, 146–47.

83 *SZ* 7:280.

84 Karatani, *Sōseki-ron shūsei*, 254–55.

85 Bourdieu, *Field of Cultural Production*, 158.

86 Derrida, *Given Time*, 156.

87 Natsume, *Theory of Literature*, 128–36; *SZ* 14:427–35.

88 Since the above was published as a journal article, another scholar has argued for the relevance of Mauss's notion of the gift economy in Sōseki's fiction, primarily *The Gate* (*Mon*). See Van Compernolle, *Struggling Upward*, 94–127.

89 Motora, "Exchange Considered."

90 Motora, *Exchange Considered*, 191.

91 Motora, *Exchange Considered*, 131.

92 Motora, *Exchange Considered*, 133–34.

93 Motora, *Exchange Considered*, 67.

94 Motora, *Exchange Considered*, 180.

95 Motora, *Exchange Considered*, 181.

96 Motora, *Exchange Considered*, 183.

97 Karatani, *The Structure of World History*, 8–9.

98 Karatani, *The Structure of World History*, 233.

99 Karatani, *The Structure of World History*, e.g., 111. Karatani cites Durkheim's above-mentioned theory of the religious origins of property rights; *Structure of World History*, 317–18n3.

100 Karatani, *The Structure of World History*, 215.

101 Karatani, "An Introduction to Modes of Exchange," 22n17.

102 Karatani, *Isonomia and the Origins of Philosophy*.

103 Karatani, *The Structure of World History*, 20.

104 Karatani, *The Structure of World History*, 22.

105 Motora, *Exchange Considered*, 100–101.

106 "Fine art, poetry, religion and all other knowledges or feelings, and their enjoyment, are not social movements proper. They influence and are influenced, to a great extent, by the social movement proper. But the important point to remember is this; that they do not directly influence society, but first influence the subjective side of man, and consequently modify the action of the formal cause, or final cause." Motora, *Exchange Considered*, 182.

107 Miner, "The Collective and the Individual," 21. On the synthetic impulse of the collection genre in early classical Japanese poetry, see Lamarre, *Uncovering Heian Japan*, esp. 13–76.

108 Zeitlin, *Historian of the Strange*, 2.

109 Kern, *The Culture of Time and Space*, 291. See also Fussell, *The Great War and Modern Memory*.

110 On Debussy, see Aucoin, "Music without Destination." For a reading of Stein's *Three Lives* in tandem with Sōseki's early experimental story "One Night" ("Ichiya," 1905), see Bourdaghs, "Sekai bungaku toshite no mittsu no seimei."

CHAPTER FOUR: THE TRAGEDY OF THE MARKET

1 Kidd, *Social Evolution*, 51. In Sōseki's marginal comment, "natural selection" and "racial prejudice" are written in English. Eta is a discriminatory name for Japan's traditional outcast status group, the *hisabetsu burakumin*. This and the following marginal comments from Kidd's *Social Evolution* are also reproduced in *SZ* 27:168–69.

2 Kidd, *Social Evolution*, 52–53.

3 Letourneau, *Property*, 90–91. For other underlining and/or marginal comments on passages in this work discussing slavery, see pages 12, 14, 66–67, 83, 87, 94, 95, 98 (here we find in addition to underlining an English marginal comment, "Slaves"), 112, 133, 146, 152, 238, 239, 244, 262, 271, 277, 285, 302, 303, 365, 370, 377. Sōseki's copy is held in the Sōseki Bunkō collection at Tōhoku University Research Library.

4 On the scandal of slavery for the modern "republic of property," see Hardt and Negri, *Commonwealth*, 71–77. See also Dayan, *The Law Is a White Dog*, esp. 39–70, for a discussion of how legal fictions and rhetoric invented to justify chattel slavery continued to haunt modern property and criminal law, undermining its claims to be rational and civilized.

5 Even Adam Smith, an advocate of free labor as a core concept of his moral economy of the market, saw slavery as one possible dystopian outcome for the ownership regime he advocated. See Purdy, *The Meaning of Property*, 14–15 and 98.

6 Harris, "Whiteness as Property," 1718. See also Dayan, *The Law Is a White Dog*, 138–76.

7 Best, *The Fugitive's Properties*.

8 On the history of slavery in Japan, see Nelson, "Slavery in Medieval Japan." Probably the best-known modern literary work to deal with historical slavery in Japan is Mori Ōgai's 1915 short story, "Sanshō the Bailiff" ("Sanshō Dayū"), the source for Mizoguchi Kenji's celebrated 1954 film adaptation of the same title.

9 Sebald, *The Civil Code of Japan*.

10 Nunokawa, *The Afterlife of Property*, 6.

11 On the unspoken gaps in *Kokoro*, see Sakaki, *Recontextualizing Texts*, 31–53. Sōseki liked to build plots around an inability to speak: think, for example, of Sōsuke's inability to speak with either his uncle or aunt about the fate of the family inheritance or with his wife about their past indiscretion in *The Gate*, or the cat's frustration at his inability to communicate with his human peers in *I Am a Cat*. For a discussion of the inability to speak about male-male eroticism in Sōseki's 1907 novella, *Nowaki*, see Reichert, *In the Company of Men*, 167–98.

12 Fujii, "Writing Out Asia," 200, 202, 208, and 213.

13 On the debates over the status of the voice as a novel form of intellectual property, on "the perception of the acoustic as property, as an element of market exchange and transfer, as a locus of value," see Best, *The Fugitive's Properties*, 59. On the history of copyright for recorded sound in Japan, see Yasar, *Electrified Voices*, 96–109. Sōseki's voice was mechanically recorded, but the sole wax cylinder recording was replayed excessively, rendering it unplayable, despite the best efforts of several teams of scientists to recover the audio. See Suzuki et al., "Rōkan ni kiroku sareta Natsume Sōseki no onsei saisei no kokoromi."

14 Ishihara Chiaki argues that the Meiji Civil Code and its revision of family law defines the difference between Sōseki's domestic novels of the early twentieth century and the 1890s genre of *katei shōsetsu* (household novels). See Ishihara, *Sōseki to Nihon no kindai*, 1:25–27 and 43–46.

15 See the chapter "Crystals and Mud in Property Law," in Rose, *Property and Persuasion*, 199–225.

16 Ito, "Writing Time in Sōseki's *Kokoro*," 18.

17 Clissold, "Heredity and Disinheritance in Joyce's *Portrait*."

18 The explicit or implicit last wills in the novel: (1) from Sensei's father to Sensei, (2) from Sensei's mother to Sensei (her last words as reported by Sensei's uncle, which Sensei later comes to doubt), (3) from K's parents to K (K is disowned), (4) from Sensei to his wife Shizu (the broken promise, described below), (5) from Sensei to the student narrator (i.e., the last half of the novel), (6) from the parents of the student's nameless friend (who accompanies him to Kamakura in the opening chapter) to that friend, (7) from the student's father to the student (who is presumably disowned), and (8) from Shizu's mother to Shizu. Only the last of these is carried out smoothly, without deceit or deviation.

19 "As literary schools change, it is not sons who inherit from their fathers, but nephews who inherit from their uncles." Shklovsky, "Literature beyond 'Plot,'" 97.

20 Lefebvre, *The Production of Space*, 25.

21 Sōseki found himself unexpectedly tangled up in this new reality: on August 12, 1914 (the day after the final installment of *Kokoro* appeared), he published "Kēberu sensei no kokubetsu" (Prof. Koeber's farewell), announcing that Prof. Raphael von Koeber (1848–1923), Sōseki's former teacher, was ending his longtime residence in Japan and leaving that day on a boat bound for Europe (*sz* 12:511–13). The next day, Sōseki had to publish a retraction. Under the title "Sensō kara kita ikichigai" (A misunderstanding brought about by the war), he announced to his readers that Prof. Koeber had in fact not departed as scheduled: the newly declared war resulted in the cancellation of his ship's departure. Prof. Koeber's "inability to leave Japan [as promised] seems entirely due to the current war. Accordingly, it was also the war that has forced me to write this correction. In other words, I am forced to conclude, the war has turned two honest men into liars" (*sz* 12:515).

22 See, for example, Kern, *The Culture of Time and Space*; and Fussell, *The Great War in Modern Memory*.

23 In his 1915 essay, "Thoughts on War and Death," Freud argues that claims of Europe's racial and civilizational superiority were revealed to be frauds by the war: "We had

expected that the great world-domination nations of white race upon whom the leadership of the human species has fallen, who were known to have world-wide interests as their concern, to whose creative powers were due not only our technical advances towards the control of nature but the artistic and scientific standards of civilization—we had expected these peoples to succeed in discovering another way of settling misunderstandings and conflicts of interest" (276).

24 Sent out not once but twice for adoption by his birth family, young Natsume Kinnosuke (his real name) was brought back to his birth family in his teens when two of his older brothers died and the family realized it might need a spare heir on hand, in case something happened to his remaining older brother. See Komori, *Sōseki o yominaosu*, 20–33.

25 On the "traffic in men" in Sōseki's *Gubijinsō* (*The Poppy*) and other works from the era, see Ito, *An Age of Melodrama*, esp. 188–236.

26 Natsume, *Grass on the Wayside*, 67. For the original Japanese, *SZ* 10:124.

27 Natsume, *Kokoro*, 56; *SZ* 9:73.

28 Natsume, *Kokoro*, 59; *SZ* 9:77.

29 Nishikawa, *Shakuya to mochiie no bungakushi*, 28. On the difference between first, second, and third sons as distinct semiotic codes in early twentieth-century Japanese fiction, see also Ishihara, *Sōseki no kigōgaku*, 45–120.

30 See Ishihara, *Sōseki to Nihon no kindai*, 1:46–50.

31 Natsume, *Kokoro*, 138; *SZ* 9:176.

32 Lefebvre, *The Production of Space*, 336–37.

33 Brown, *Cultivating Commons*, 190.

34 Tanaka, *New Times in Modern Japan*, 148.

35 Gragert, *Landownership under Colonial Rule*, 114.

36 On the relationship between enclosure and British literature, see Williams, *The Country and the City*, esp. 96–107; and Rosenberg and Yang, "Introduction."

37 Natsume, *Kokoro*, 93 and 91; *SZ* 9:124 and 121.

38 Natsume, *Kokoro*, 107 and 109; *SZ* 9:141 and 145.

39 Natsume, *Kokoro*, 110–11; *SZ* 9:146.

40 Natsume, *Kokoro*, 116–17; *SZ* 9:153.

41 Pateman, *The Sexual Contract*, 60; quoted in Dickenson, *Property, Women and Politics*, 76.

42 Letourneau, *The Evolution of Marriage and of the Family*, 158–59.

43 The classic study of the familial traffic in women is Rubin, "The Traffic in Women."

44 Nunokawa, *Afterlife of Properties*, esp. 10–39. These quotations appear on 10, 29, and 98. Silvia Federici likewise argues that under the sexual division of labor introduced with the rise of capitalism, women become a kind of nonmarket compensation for lands taken away from the proletariat through enclosure. "For in pre-capitalist Europe women's subordination to men had been tempered by the fact that they had access to the commons and other communal assets, while in the new capitalist regime *women themselves became the commons*, as their work was defined as a natural resource, laying [*sic*] outside the sphere of market relations." Federici, *Caliban and the Witch*, 97.

45 Rubin, "The Traffic in Women," 171–75. Rubin argues that the sex/gender system of modern societies is in many ways a property system: "If the sexual property system

were reorganized in such a way that men did not have overriding rights in women (if there was no exchange of women) and if there were no gender, the entire Oedipal drama would be a relic. In short, feminism must call for a revolution in kinship" (199).

46 On Mineko's property in *Sanshirō*, see Komori, *Sōseki o yominaosu*, 146–52.

47 Natsume, *Kokoro*, 210–11; *SZ* 9:268–69.

48 Natsume, *Kokoro*, 73–74; *SZ* 9:99–100.

49 See Komori Yōichi, "'Kokoro' o sesei suru haato," originally published in *Seijō Kokubungaku* in March 1985, revised and reprinted in Komori, *Buntai toshite no monogatari*, 293–317; and Ishihara, "Manazashi toshite no tasha: *Kokoro*," originally published in *Tōkō Kokubungaku* in March 1985, and reprinted in Ishihara, *Hanten suru Sōseki*, 155–80.

50 Oshino, "'Shizu' ni koe wa aru no ka." It seems significant that the major occasion in the novel when Shizu speaks independently of Sensei occurs in the scene when the student comes to stay at Sensei's house during the master's absence because of a fear of burglary. The possibility of her speaking, in other words, is associated with a violation of property norms.

51 Ishihara, "Manazashi toshite no tasha."

52 Natsume, *Kokoro*, 123–24; *SZ* 9:156–58.

53 James, *Principles of Psychology*, 1:238–39.

54 Natsume, *Kokoro*, 234; *SZ* 9:300.

55 Natsume, *Kokoro*, 224; *SZ* 9:287.

56 Shibata Shōji, however, reads the novel allegorically as a figuration of Japanese imperialism, with the betrayals between characters symbolizing the 1895 Tripartite Intervention in which Japan was deprived of its territorial gains from the Sino-Japanese War and with K, in particular, standing in for Korea. See Shibata, *Sōseki no naka no "teikoku,"* 196–229.

57 Satō, *Sōseki Katazukanai kindai*, esp. 183–86. On colonial imagination in *Higan*, see also Oshino, "'Roman shumi' no chihei."

58 This lineage includes the work of Pak Yuha, who cites Sōseki's use of racist expressions and imperialist ideologies of hygiene in his depiction of Chinese and Koreans and his invoking of the civilizational ideology of improvement in his travelogue *Mankan tokorodokoro* (1909). See Pak, *Nashonaru aidentiti to jendā*, 129–56. For readings that situate Sōseki as more critical of the contradictions inherent in Japanese imperialism, see Komori, *Sōseki-ron*, 78–106; and Shibata, *Sōseki no naka no "teikoku."*

59 Fujii, "Writing Out Asia." The travelogue is available in English translation in Brody and Tsunematsu, *Rediscovering Natsume Soseki*.

60 Natsume, *Kokoro*, 38; *SZ* 9:52.

61 Bhandar, *Colonial Lives of Property.*

62 Suzuki, *Re-inventing Japan*, 27. Eiko Asato notes that "in Okinawa, private land ownership was legalized in 1903 following a Japanese government land survey. Before then, all land was collectively owned, managed, and used by village communities. This system was called *jiwarisei*. A piece of land was cultivated by a certain person (generally a household head) for two to thirty years, and then, because the quality of

land differs from place to place, the land was rotated to another person to maintain equality." Asato, "Okinawan Identity and Resistance to Militarization and Maldevelopment," 239. On Hokkaido, see Komori, "Rule in the Name of Protection."

63 Eckert et al., *Korea Old and New*, 265.

64 Bhandar, *Colonial Lives of Property*, esp. 33–74.

65 Eckert, et al., *Korea Old and New*, 266.

66 Murai, *Nantō ideorogii no hassei*, esp. 21–39.

67 Gragert, *Landownership under Colonial Rule*.

68 Gragert, *Landownership under Colonial Rule*, 32.

69 Gragert, *Landownership under Colonial Rule*, 121.

70 Bhandar, *Colonial Lives of Property*, 18.

71 "In the minds of the Japanese government and public, Korea as a policy issue ended with its annexation in 1910, and the Japanese turned their focus to other parts of the Asian continent. Other than the 1919 March First Movement, Korea rarely appeared in the Japanese media during this period. Rather, it was the growing presence of Koreans in Japan that was of more interest and concern." Gragert, *Landownership under Colonial Rule*, 115–16.

72 "Senmin matamata bōdō," *Asahi Shinbun* (Tokyo), April 30, 1914, 4; and "Chōsen bōto okoru," *Asahi Shinbun* (Tokyo), May 18, 1914, 4. The riots were widely reported elsewhere in the Japanese press, as well. See, for example, "Riot by Koreans (Pusan)" ["Chōsenjin no bōdō (Pusan)"], *Nichi-Nichi* (Tokyo), April 28, 1914, 2. A week later the same newspaper reported indignantly that a Korean newspaper from Hawaii was publishing anti-Japan stories that insulted the Japanese emperor: "Chōsen shinbun no hai-Nichi," *Nichi-Nichi* (Tokyo), May 6, 1914, 2.

73 "Tochi chōsa shūryō," *Asahi Shinbun* (Tokyo), May 11, 1914, 4.

74 Natsume, *Kokoro*, 232; *SZ* 9:297.

75 Natsume, *Kokoro*, 225; *SZ* 9:288–89.

76 Shibata likewise reads Sensei's guilt and his monthly visits to K's grave as a figuration for repentance and apology for Japan's colonization of Korea. See Shibata, *Sōseki no naka no "teikoku,"* 220.

77 Murai Osamu notes that the new term *heigō* that was coined as the official name for the act of annexation was chosen because it seemed to resemble a voluntary act of union, like a marriage between two consenting partners. Murai, *Nantō ideorogii no hassei*, 39–43.

78 See Bourdaghs, "Introduction," 1–17.

79 Hepburn, "Introduction," 5.

80 Hardin, "The Tragedy of the Commons."

81 Rose, *Property and Persuasion*, 105–50.

82 Rose, *Property and Persuasion*, 132–50.

83 Natsume, *Kokoro*, 135; *SZ* 9:171.

84 Natsume, *Kokoro*, 138; *SZ* 9:175–76.

85 Bhandar, *Colonial Lives of Property*, 85.

86 Bhandar, *Colonial Lives of Property*, 95.

1 See Harris, "Whiteness as Property"; and Reardon and Tall Bear, "'Your DNA Is *Our* History.'"

2 Best, *The Fugitive's Properties*, 14. Best is describing the situation in the United States.

3 Eri Oka, "Sōseki isan no daihan wa 'kabu,'" *Asahi Shinbun*, May 18, 2016, 37. On Sōseki's personal finances and their relation to his literary and theoretical work, see Yamamoto, *Sōseki no kakeibo.*

4 Yamamoto, *Sōseki no kakeibo*, esp. 71–75.

5 Natsume, *I Am a Cat*, 2:53–54; *SZ* 1:169–70.

6 Natsume, *I Am a Cat*, 2:65–66; *SZ* 1:178.

7 See Uyehara, *The Political Development of Japan*, 255–61; and Mitchell, *Political Bribery in Japan*, 22–26.

8 Natsume, *Grass on the Wayside*, 75–76; *SZ* 10:140–42.

9 Natsume, *Grass on the Wayside*, 28; *SZ* 10:49.

10 Natsume, *Grass on the Wayside*, 156; *SZ* 10:294.

11 *SZ* 10:163–64, Bourdaghs translation. McClellan's much-abbreviated translation of this passage appears in Natsume, *Grass on the Wayside*, 140–41.

12 This is according to the endnotes found in Natsume, *Michikusa*, 326n.

13 Earlier versions of some of the material in this and the following section were previously published as Michael Bourdaghs, "Owning Up to Sōseki: The Theory of Literature vs. the Theory of Copyright," *Proceedings of the Association for Japanese Literary Studies*, 9 (2008): 15–29.

14 "Somehow I managed to get into Preparatory School, but I liked nothing better than to laze around and hardly studied. Mizuno Rentarō, the current president of the Academy of Art, Masaki Naohiko, and Haga Yaichi were all in my class, but they were serious students, unlike the lazybones I hung out with, and given this difference we had little contact and went our separate ways. I suppose they looked down on us lazybones as good-for-nothings, while we saw little reason to consort with fellows who seemed interested only in their exam scores, and so, taking pride in our merrymaking, we avoided all work." From "Rakudai," a transcript of Sōseki's reminiscences about his school days first published in the June 20, 1906, issue of *Chūgaku bungei*, reprinted in *SZ* 25:161–66. This passage appears on 163. Translation of this and passages from all Japanese-language works below are by Bourdaghs, except where otherwise noted.

15 *SZ* 14:708.

16 Natsume, *Theory of Literature and Other Critical Writings*, 47; *SZ* 14:11–12.

17 Komori, *"Yuragi" no Nihon bungaku*, 62–69; and Komori, *Sōseki o yominaosu*, 110–32.

18 Nakayama, "Shōsetsu no shihon ron."

19 On the rise of the newly industrialized publishing industry in Meiji Japan, see Mack, *Manufacturing Modern Japanese Literature*, esp. 17–49.

20 *SZ* 14:11. On the historical development of the concepts of literature and pure literature in Japan, see Suzuki, *Nihon no "Bungaku" Gainen.*

21 On Kawakami's suicide and its portrayal in the media, including lengthy quotations from a June 17, 1907, Tokyo *Asahi* newspaper article, see Igari, "Kawakami Bizan no shi."

22 Asaoka, "Meijiki shuppansha to chosha no derikeeto baransu." I thank Ted Mack for bringing Asaoka's work to my attention.

23 Nakayama, "Shōsetsu no shihon ron," 70.

24 Asaoka, "Meijiki shuppansha to chosha no derikeeto baransu," 51–52.

25 Senuma, *Shimazaki Tōson*, 57. On Tōson's finances, see Bourdaghs, *The Dawn That Never Comes*, 80.

26 Shimazaki, "Chosaku to shuppan," 76.

27 On Tokugawa-era copyright practices and their collapse and replacement by the new modern regime in the Meiji period, see Maeda, *Kindai dokusha no seiritsu*; Yasar, *Electrified Voices*, 93–96; and Wang, *Pirates and Publishers*, 21–61.

28 Quoted in Kurata, *Chosakuken shiwa*, 10.

29 Sakaki, "*Kajin no kigū.*"

30 Asaoka, "Meijiki shuppansha to chosha no derikeeto baransu," 54.

31 Mizuno, *Chosakuken hō.*

32 Mizuno, *Chosakuken hō*, 24.

33 Mizuno, *Chosakuken hō*, 9.

34 Mizuno, *Chosakuken hō*, 27.

35 Mizuno, *Chosakuken hō*, 34–37.

36 Mizuno, *Chosakuken hō*, 45–47.

37 Mizuno, *Chosakuken hō*, 66–69.

38 Mizuno, *Chosakuken hō*, 76–77.

39 See, for example, Murphy, *Metaphorical Circuit*, 24–54.

40 On Sōseki's conception of the author in his *Theory of Literature*, see Iida, "Dokusha toshite no Sōseki."

41 *SZ* 14:147.

42 Natsume, *Theory of Literature*, 57, Murphy translation; *SZ* 14:33.

43 *SZ* 14:261.

44 *SZ* 16:175.

45 Sakaki, "*Kajin no kigū*," 103.

46 Natsume, "Philosophical Foundations of the Literary Arts," 208–9; *SZ* 16:130–31.

47 I should note here that I am clumsily pirating ideas from Lamarre, "Expanded Empiricism."

48 De Certeau, *The Practice of Everyday Life*, xxi.

49 De Certeau, *The Practice of Everyday Life*, 173.

50 Cooper, "Expressive Genericity," 413–14.

51 Cooper, "Expressive Genericity," 402–3.

52 Coombe, *The Cultural Life of Intellectual Properties*, 71.

53 Coombe, *The Cultural Life of Intellectual Properties*, 69.

54 Lury, *Cultural Rights*, 35. See also Coombe, *The Cultural Life of Intellectual Properties*, 283.

55 For the details of this legal dispute, see Bourdaghs, "Owning Up to Sōseki."

56 Rose, *Property and Persuasion*, esp. 199–232.

57 "Hanmoto ni 'fukkoku-ken': Sōseki shohanbon sawagi, wakai," *Asahi Shinbun*, September 1, 1979, 22.

58 Woodmansee, *The Author, Art, and the Market*, esp. 25–31.

59 Massumi, *Parables for the Virtual*, 19–21; and Lamarre, "Expanded Empiricism."

60 De Certeau, *The Practice of Everyday Life*, xx.

61 Butler, "Who Owns Kafka?"

62 Apter, *Against World Literature*, 15.

63 *SZ* 16:284.

64 See, for example, Bourdaghs, "Natsume Sōseki no 'sekai bungaku.'"

65 Said, *Culture and Imperialism*, 48.

66 Said, *Culture and Imperialism*, 89.

67 Natsume, *Theory of Literature*, 43; *SZ* 14:8.

68 Natsume, *Theory of Literature*, 44; *SZ* 14:8.

69 Damrosch, *What Is World Literature?*

70 He does, however, translate some quotations from nonliterary English-language works that he cites.

71 Bourdaghs, "Natsume Sōseki no 'sekai bungaku.'"

72 *SZ* 22:518–20.

73 Letter to Yamada Kōsaburō, August 9, 1916, *SZ* 24:550.

74 Quoted in Yu, *Natsume Sōseki*, 8. For the original Japanese, see *SZ* 24:544.

75 Mufti, *Forget English!*, 10, italics in original.

76 Ueda, "*Bungakuron* and 'Literature' in the Making."

77 See, for example, Casanova, *The World Republic of Letters*; and Moretti, *Distant Reading*.

78 *SZ* 14:389.

79 Saitō, "*Bungakuron* no shatei."

80 See, for example, Moretti, *Graphs, Maps, Trees*.

81 Casanova, *The World Republic of Letters*, 5.

82 Natsume, *Theory of Literature*, 146 and 148, J. Keith Vincent translation; *SZ* 14:451–53.

83 *SZ* 16:167.

84 Natsume, *Theory of Literature*, 250, Jay Rubin translation; *SZ* 16:594.

85 Williams, *Marxism and Literature*, 54.

86 "Language, for example, like affects and gestures, is for the most part common, and indeed if language were made either private or public—that is, if large portions of our words, phrases, or parts of speech were subject to private ownership or public authority—then language would lose its powers of expression, creativity, and communication." Hardt and Negri, *Commonwealth*, ix.

87 Berlant, "The Commons," 395.

88 Natsume, *Theory of Literature*, 43; *SZ* 14:8.

89 See Berlant, "The Commons," 413. Gavin Walker likewise argues that the commons "should never be associated with that which merely exists as a plentitude within the order of being, because it is first and foremost a project, not a fait accompli." Walker, *The Sublime Perversion of Capital*, 138.

BIBLIOGRAPHY

Anderton, Joseph. "Dogdom: Nonhuman Others and the Othered Self in Kafka, Beckett, and Auster." *Twentieth-Century Literature* 62, no. 3 (2016): 271–88.

Andō Fumihito. "Wagahai wa 'We' de aru: Neko ni okeru katarite to dokusha." *Hikaku Bungaku Nenshi* 29 (1999): 22–43.

Apter, Emily. *Against World Literature: On the Politics of Untranslatability*. London: Verso, 2013.

Ara Masahito. "*Higan sugi made* ron: 'Myō na sutteki.'" In *Sōseki sakuhinron shūsei*, edited by Tamai Takayuki and Tsubouchi Toshinori, 8:147–56. Tokyo: Ōfūsha, 1991.

Asaoka Kunio. "Meijiki shuppansha to chosha no derikeeto baransu." *Kokubungaku* 49, no. 6 (May 2004): 50–59.

Asato, Eiko. "Okinawan Identity and Resistance to Militarization and Maldevelopment." In *Islands of Discontent: Okinawan Responses to Japanese and American Power*, edited by Laura Hein and Mark Selden, 228–42. Lanham, MD: Rowman and Littlefield, 2003.

Aucoin, Matthew. "Music without Destination." *New York Review of Books* 65, no. 19 (December 6, 2018): 8–12.

Bakhtin, Mikhail. *Speech Genres and Other Late Essays*. Translated by Vern W. McGee. Austin: University of Texas Press, 1986.

Balibar, Etienne. *Citizen Subject: Foundations for Philosophical Anthropology*. Translated by Steven Miller. New York: Fordham University Press, 2017.

Balibar, Etienne. "'Possessive Individualism' Reversed: From Locke to Derrida." *Constellations* 9, no. 3 (2002): 299–317.

Barshay, Andrew. *The Social Sciences in Modern Japan: The Marxian and Modernist Traditions*. Berkeley: University of California Press, 2007.

Benveniste, Emile. *Problems in General Linguistics*. Miami: University of Miami Press, 1971.

Berger, John. "Why Look at Animals?" In *About Looking*, 3–31. New York: Vintage, 1991.

Bergson, Henri. *Laughter: An Essay on the Meaning of the Comic*. Translated by Cloudesley Brereton and Fred Rothwell. London: Macmillan, 1911.

Berlant, Lauren. "The Commons: Infrastructures for Troubling Times." *Environment and Planning D: Society and Space* 34, no. 3 (2016): 393–419.

Berlant, Lauren. "Humorlessness (Three Monologues)." *Critical Inquiry* 43 (2017): 305–40.

Best, Stephen Michael. *The Fugitive's Properties: Law and the Poetics of Possession*. Chicago: University of Chicago Press, 2004.

Bhandar, Brenna. *Colonial Lives of Property: Law, Land, and Racial Regimes of Owner-ship*. Durham, NC: Duke University Press, 2018.

Bond, Michael. *Paddington Helps Out*. London: Collins, 1960.

Bordogna, Francesca. *William James at the Boundaries: Philosophy, Science, and the Geography of Knowledge*. Chicago: University of Chicago Press, 2008.

Borges, Jorge Luis. "Kafka and His Precursors." In *Labyrinths: Selected Stories and Other Writings*, 199–201. New York: New Directions, 1962.

Bourdaghs, Michael K. *The Dawn That Never Comes: Shimazaki Tōson and Japanese Nationalism*. New York: Columbia University Press, 2004.

Bourdaghs, Michael K. "Introduction: Overthrowing the Emperor in Japanese Literary Studies." In *The Linguistic Turn in Contemporary Japanese Literary Studies: Textuality, Language, Politics*, edited by Michael Bourdaghs, 1–17. Ann Arbor: University of Michigan, Center for Japanese Studies, 2010.

Bourdaghs, Michael K. "Natsume Sōseki no 'sekai bungaku': Eigoken kara *Bungakuron* o yominaosu." *Bungaku* 13, no. 3 (2012): 2–16.

Bourdaghs, Michael K. "Owning Up to Sōseki: The Theory of Literature vs. the Theory of Copyright." *Proceedings of the Association for Japanese Literary Studies* 9 (2008): 15–29.

Bourdaghs, Michael K. "Sekai bungaku toshite no mittsu no seimei: Sōseki, Sutain, Jeemuzu." In *Sekai bungaku to Nihon kindai bungaku*, edited by Noami Mariko, 213–30. Tokyo: University of Tokyo Press, 2019.

Bourdieu, Pierre. *The Field of Cultural Production*. New York: Columbia University Press, 1993.

Brody, Inger Sigrun, and Sammy I. Tsunematsu. *Rediscovering Natsume Soseki: With the First English Translation of "Travels in Manchuria and Korea."* Folkstone, UK: Global Oriental, 2000.

Brown, Philip C. *Cultivating Commons: Joint Ownership of Arable Land in Early Modern Japan*. Honolulu: University of Hawaiʻi Press, 2011.

Burt, Cyril. "Frances Galton and His Contributions to Psychology." *British Journal of Statistical Psychology* 15, no. 1 (1962): 1–49.

Butler, Judith. "Who Owns Kafka?" *London Review of Books* 33, no. 5 (March 3, 2011): 3–8.

Casanova, Pascale. *The World Republic of Letters*. Translated by M. B. DeBevoise. Cambridge, MA: Harvard University Press, 2004.

Ching, Leo T. S. *Becoming "Japanese": Colonial Taiwan and the Politics of Identity Formation*. Berkeley: University of California Press, 2001.

Clissold, Bradley D. "Heredity and Disinheritance in Joyce's Portrait." In *Troubled Legacies: Narrative and Inheritance*, edited by Allan Hepburn, 191–218. Toronto: University of Toronto Press, 2007.

Coombe, Rosemary J. *The Cultural Life of Intellectual Properties: Authorship, Appropriation, and the Law*. Durham, NC: Duke University Press, 1998.

Coon, Deborah J. "'One Moment in the World's Salvation': Anarchism and the Radicalization of William James." *Journal of American History* 83, no. 1 (1996): 70–99.

Cooper, Rochelle. "Expressive Genericity: Trademarks as Language in the Pepsi Generation." *Notre Dame Law Review* 65 (1990): 397–424.

Crozier, John Beattie. *History of Intellectual Development: On the Lines of Modern Evolution*, vol. 1. London: Longmans, Green, 1897.

Damrosch, David. *What Is World Literature?* Princeton, NJ: Princeton University Press, 2003.

Danziger, Kurt. *Constructing the Subject: Historical Origins of Psychological Research.* Cambridge: Cambridge University Press, 1990.

Dayan, Colin. *The Law Is a White Dog: How Legal Rituals Make and Unmake Persons.* Princeton, NJ: Princeton University Press, 2011.

Debaene, Vincent. *Far Afield: French Anthropology between Science and Literature.* Translated by Justin Izzo. Chicago: University of Chicago Press, 2014.

de Certeau, Michel. *The Practice of Everyday Life.* Translated by Steven Rendall. Berkeley: University of California Press, 1984.

Deleuze, Gilles, and Félix Guattari. *Anti-Oedipus: Capitalism and Schizophrenia.* Translated by Robert Hurley, Mark Seem, and Helen R. Lane. Minneapolis: University of Minnesota Press, 1983.

Deleuze, Gilles, and Félix Guattari. *Kafka: Toward a Minor Literature.* Translated by Dana Polan. Minneapolis: University of Minnesota Press, 1986.

Derrida, Jacques. *Given Time: I. Counterfeit Money.* Translated by Peggy Kamuf. Chicago: University of Chicago Press, 1992.

Derrida, Jacques. *Specters of Marx: The State of the Debt, the Work of Mourning, and the New International.* Translated by Peggy Kamuf. New York: Routledge, 1994.

Dickenson, Donna. *Property, Women and Politics: Subjects or Objects?* New Brunswick, NJ: Rutgers University Press, 1997.

Dodd, Stephen. "The Significance of Bodies in Sōseki's *Kokoro.*" *Monumenta Nipponica* 53, no. 4 (1998): 473–98.

Dower, John. *War without Mercy: Race and Power in the Pacific War.* New York: Pantheon, 1986.

Dunlap, Knight. "Discussion: The Case against Introspection." *Psychological Review* 19, no. 5 (1912): 404–13.

Dunn, Malcolm H. "The Property Rights Paradigm and the Meiji Restoration in Japan." *Jahrbücher für Nationalökonomie und Statistik* 207, no. 3 (1990): 271–85.

Durkheim, Emile. *Professional Ethics and Civic Morals.* Translated by Cornelia Brookfield. Westport, CT: Greenwood, 1958.

Eckert, Carter J., Ki-baik Lee, Young Ick Lew, Michael Robinson, and Edward W. Wagner. *Korea Old and New: A History.* Seoul: Ilchokak, 1990.

Etō Kyōko. "Hen'yō suru kikite: *Higan sugi made* no Keitarō." *Nihon kindai bungaku* 46 (1992): 29–42.

Favre, David. "Living Property: A New Status for Animals within the Legal System." *Marquette Law Review* 93 (2009–10): 1021–27.

Federici, Silvia. *Caliban and the Witch: Women, the Body and Primitive Accumulation*, 2nd rev. ed. Brooklyn, NY: Autonomedia, 2014.

Figal, Gerald. *Civilization and Monsters: Spirits of Modernity in Modern Japan.* Durham, NC: Duke University Press, 1999.

Fisher, Mark. *K-Punk: The Collected and Unpublished Writings of Mark Fisher*. London: Repeater, 2018.

Foster, Frances F. "Should Pets Inherit?" *Florida Law Review* 63, no. 4 (2011): 802–55.

Foster, Michael. *Pandemonium and Parade: The Japanese Culture of Yōkai*. Berkeley: University of California Press, 2009.

Freedman, Alisa. *Tokyo in Transit: Japanese Culture on the Rails and Road*. Stanford, CA: Stanford University Press, 2011.

Freud, Sigmund. "Thoughts on War and Death." In *The Standard Edition of the Complete Psychological Works of Sigmund Freud*, 14:273–308. London: Hogarth, 1971.

Fujii, James A. *Complicit Fictions: The Subject in the Modern Japanese Prose Narrative*. Berkeley: University of California Press, 1993.

Fujii, James A. "Writing Out Asia: Modernity, Canon, and Natsume Soseki's *Kokoro*." *Positions: East Asia Critique* 1, no. 1 (1993): 194–223.

Fusco, Katherine. "Squashing the Bookworm: Manly Attention and Male Reading in Silent Film." *Modernism/Modernity* 22, no. 4 (2015): 627–50.

Fussell, Paul. *The Great War and Modern Memory*. Oxford: Oxford University Press, 1975.

Gandhi, Leela. *Affective Communities: Anticolonial Thought, Fin-de-Siècle Radicalism, and the Politics of Friendship*. Durham, NC: Duke University Press, 2006.

Gerow, Aaron. *Visions of Japanese Modernity: Articulations of Cinema, Nation, and Spectatorship, 1895–1925*. Berkeley: University of California Press, 2010.

Giddings, Franklin Henry. *The Elements of Sociology: A Text-Book for Colleges and Schools*. New York: Macmillan, 1898.

Girard, René. *Deceit, Desire, and the Novel: Self and Other in Literary Structure*. Translated by Yvonne Freccero. Baltimore, MD: Johns Hopkins University Press, 1965.

Gould, Stephen Jay. *The Mismeasure of Man*. New York: Norton, 1981.

Graeber, David. *Debt: The First 5,000 Years*. Brooklyn, NY: Melville House, 2011.

Gragert, Edwin H. *Landownership under Colonial Rule: Korea's Japanese Experience, 1900–1935*. Honolulu: University of Hawai'i Press, 1994.

Guillory, John. *Cultural Capital: The Problem of Literary Canon Formation*. Chicago: University of Chicago Press, 1993.

Haraway, Donna. *Companion Species Manifesto: Dogs, People, and Significant Otherness*. Chicago: Prickly Paradigm, 2003.

Hardin, Garrett. "The Tragedy of the Commons." *Science*, n.s., 162, no. 3859 (1968): 1243–48.

Hardt, Michael, and Antonio Negri. *Commonwealth*. Cambridge, MA: Belknap.

Harris, Cheryl I. "Whiteness as Property." *Harvard Law Review* 106, no. 8 (1993): 1709–91.

Hatfield, Gary. "Introspective Evidence in Psychology." In *Scientific Evidence: Philosophical Applications and Theories*, edited by Peter Achinstein, 259–86. Baltimore, MD: Johns Hopkins University Press, 2005.

Hattori Tetsuya. *Hajimari no Sōseki: Bungakuron to shoki sōsaku no seisei*. Tokyo: Shin'yōsha, 2019.

Hegel, G. W. F. *Elements of the Philosophy of Right*. Translated by H. B. Nisbet. Cambridge: Cambridge University Press, 1991.

Hein, Carola. "Shaping Tokyo: Land Development and Planning Practice in the Early Modern Japanese Metropolis." *Journal of Urban History* 36, no. 4 (2010): 447–84.

Hepburn, Allan. "Introduction: Inheritance and Disinheritance in the Novel." In *Troubled Legacies: Narrative and Inheritance*, edited by Allan Hepburn, 3–25. Toronto: University of Toronto Press, 2007.

Hibi Yoshitaka. *Japaniizu Amerika: Imin bungaku, shuppan bunka, shūyōjo.* Tokyo: Shin'yōsha, 2014.

Hintereder-Emde, Franz. "Erkenntnis geht durch den Magen: Wirklichkeitserfahrung am Leitfaden des Essens in Sosekis *Wagahai wa neko de aru.*" *Japanstudien* 12 (2000): 65–90.

Hyde, Lewis. *The Gift: Imagination and the Erotic Life of Property.* New York: Vintage, 1979.

Ichiyanagi Hirokata. "Tokkenka sareru 'shinkei': *Sore kara* ichimen." *Sōseki kenkyū* 10 (1998): 34–44.

Igari Akira. "Kawakami Bizan no shi; Meiji bunshi no keizai seikatsu." *Nihon kindai bungaku* 12 (1970): 89–101.

Iida, Yuko. "Dokusha toshite no Sōseki (Sōseki as Reader)." *PAJLS (Proceedings of the Association for Japanese Literary Studies)* 9 (2008): 51–63.

Ishihara Chiaki. *Hanten suru Sōseki.* Tokyo: Seidosha, 1997.

Ishihara Chiaki. *Sōseki no kigōgaku.* Tokyo: Kōdansha, 1999.

Ishihara Chiaki. *Sōseki to Nihon no kindai.* 2 vols. Tokyo: Shinchōsha, 2017.

Itahana Junji. "*Wagahai wa neko de aru* ron: Sono tagen sekai o meguri." *Nihon bungaku* 31, no. 11 (1982): 1–12.

Ito, Ken K. *An Age of Melodrama: Family, Gender, and Social Hierarchy in the Turn-of-the-Century Japanese Novel.* Stanford, CA: Stanford University Press, 2008.

Ito, Ken K. "Writing Time in Sōseki's *Kokoro.*" In *Studies in Modern Japanese Literature: Essays and Translations in Honor of Edwin McClellan*, edited by Dennis Washburn and Alan Tansman, 3–21. Ann Arbor: University of Michigan, Center for Japanese Studies, 1997.

Itō Tōru. "Natsume Soseki und die Zwecklosigkeit des Lebens als das Wesen der Modernisierung." *Asiatische Studien: Zeitschrift der Schweizerischen Asiengesellschaft* 66, no. 1 (2012): 103–28.

Jacobowitz, Seth. *Writing Technology in Meiji Japan: A Media History of Modern Japanese Literature and Visual Culture.* Cambridge, MA: Harvard University Asia Center, 2015.

James, William. *Essays in Psychical Research.* Cambridge, MA: Harvard University Press, 1986.

James, William. *Essays in Radical Empiricism.* London: Longmans, Green, 1912.

James, William. *A Pluralistic Universe.* Lincoln: University of Nebraska Press, 1996.

James, William. *Principles of Psychology.* 2 vols. New York: Henry Holt, 1890.

James, William. *The Varieties of Religious Experience.* London: Longmans, Green, 1902.

Jameson, Frederic. *Marxism and Form.* Princeton, NJ: Princeton University Press, 1971.

Jameson, Frederic. "Sōseki and Western Modernism." *Boundary 2* 18, no. 3 (1991): 123–41.

Kafka, Franz. "Investigations of a Dog." In *Investigations of a Dog and Other Creatures*, translated by Michael Hoffman, 146–89. New York: New Directions, 2017.

Kamei Hideo. "The Embodied Self." Translated by Jennifer M. Lee. In *The Linguistic Turn in Contemporary Japanese Literature Studies: Politics, Language, Textuality*, edited by Michael K. Bourdaghs, 43–71. Ann Arbor: University of Michigan, Center for Japanese Studies, 2010.

Kamei Hideo. *"Shōsetsu" ron: Shōsetsu shinzui to kindai*. Tokyo: Iwanami Shoten, 1999.

Kamei Hideo. *Transformations of Sensibility: The Phenomenology of Meiji Literature*. Translation edited by Michael Bourdaghs. Ann Arbor: University of Michigan, Center for Japanese Studies, 2002.

Kanda Shōko. "'Kagaku' to iu shinkō: Natsume Sōseki 'Koto no sorane' o shiza toshite." *Tōkyō Daigaku Kokubungaku Ronshū* 5 (2010): 159–73.

Karatani, Kōjin. "An Introduction to Modes of Exchange." Translated by Michael K. Bourdaghs. Kojin Karatani, 2017. http://www.kojinkaratani.com/en/pdf/An _Introduction_to_Modes_of_Exchange.pdf.

Karatani, Kōjin. *Isonomia and the Origins of Philosophy*. Translated by Joseph A. Murphy. Durham, NC: Duke University Press, 2017.

Karatani, Kōjin. *Origins of Modern Japanese Literature*. Translation edited by Brett de Bary. Durham, NC: Duke University Press, 1993.

Karatani, Kōjin. *Sōseki-ron shūsei*. Tokyo: Daisan Bunmei Sha, 1992.

Karatani, Kōjin. "Sōseki's Diversity: On Kokoro." Translated by Richard Calichman. In *Contemporary Japanese Thought*, edited by Richard Calichman, 119–29. New York: Columbia University Press, 2005.

Karatani, Kōjin. *The Structure of World History: From Modes of Production to Modes of Exchange*. Translated by Michael K. Bourdaghs. Durham, NC: Duke University Press, 2014.

Kawamura, Nozomu. *Sociology and Society of Japan*. London: Kegan Paul, 1994.

Kern, Stephen. *The Culture of Time and Space: 1880–1918*. Cambridge, MA: Harvard University Press, 1983.

Kidd, Benjamin. *Social Evolution*. New York: Macmillan, 1898.

Kimata Satoshi. *"Wagahai wa neko de aru*: Richi to konton." *Kokubungaku: kaishaku to kyōzai* 39, no. 2 (1994): 12–18.

Kishimoto Tsugiko. *Sōseki no hyōgen: Sono gikō ga dokusha ni genwaku o umu*. Osaka: Waizumi Shoten, 2014.

Kittler, Friedrich A. *The Truth of the Technological World: Essays on the Genealogy of Presence*. Translated by Eric Butler. Stanford, CA: Stanford University Press, 2013.

Komori Yōichi. *Buntai toshite no monogatari*. Tokyo: Chikuma Shobō, 1988.

Komori Yōichi. *Kōzō to shite no katari*. Tokyo: Shinyōsha, 1988.

Komori Yōichi. "Rule in the Name of Protection: The Japanese State, the Ainu and the Vocabulary of Colonialism." Translated by Michele M. Mason. *Asia-Pacific Journal: Japan Focus* 11, no. 8–2 (February 25, 2013). https://apjjf.org/2013/11/8/Komori -Yoichi/3903/article.html.

Komori Yōichi. *Sōseki o yominaosu*. Tokyo: Chikuma Shobō, 1995.

Komori Yōichi. *Sōseki ron: 21-seiki o ikinuku tame ni*. Tokyo: Iwanami Shoten, 2010.

Komori Yōichi. *"Yuragi" no Nihon bungaku*. Tokyo: NHK Books, 1998.

Kumasaka Atsuko. "*Sanshirō* to Eikoku gaka." *Nihon Joshi Daigaku Kiyō: Bungaku bu* 34 (1984): 11–23.

Kurata Yoshihiro. *Chosakuken shiwa.* Tokyo: Senninsha, 1980.

Kuwada Yoshizō. "Minzoku shinrigaku no igi to ninmu." *Shinri Kenkyū* 3, no. 13 (1913): 119–28.

Kuwada Yoshizō. "Shūkyō shinri ni okeru Zēmusu to Vunto." *Tetsugaku zasshi* 318 (1913): 807–40.

Kuwada Yoshizō. *Vunto no minzokushinrigaku.* Tokyo: Bunmei Shoin, 1918.

Kuwada Yoshizō. "Vunto no shūkyō no genzai oyobi shōrai ni kansuru kenkai." *Tetsugaku zasshi* 278 (1910): 63–68.

Kwon, Grace. *State Formation, Property Relations, and the Development of the Tokugawa Economy (1600–1868).* New York: Routledge, 2002.

Lamarre, Thomas. "Expanded Empiricism: Natsume Sōseki with William James." *Japan Forum* 20, no. 1 (2008): 47–77.

Lamarre, Thomas. *Shadows on the Screen: Tanizaki Jun'ichirō on Cinema and "Oriental" Aesthetics.* Ann Arbor: University of Michigan, Center for Japanese Studies, 2005.

Lamarre, Thomas. *Uncovering Heian Japan: An Archaeology of Sensation and Inscription.* Durham, NC: Duke University Press, 2000.

Layoun, Mary N. *Travels of a Genre: The Modern Novel and Ideology.* Princeton, NJ: Princeton University Press, 1990.

Le Bon, Gustave. *The Psychology of Socialism.* London: T. Fisher Unwin, 1899.

Lefebvre, Henri. *The Production of Space.* Translated by Donald Nicholson-Smith. Oxford: Blackwell, 1991.

Letourneau, Charles. *The Evolution of Marriage and of the Family.* London: Walter Scott, 1891.

Letourneau, Charles. *Property: Its Origin and Development.* London: Walter Scott, 1892.

Levine, Donald N. *Visions of the Sociological Tradition.* Chicago: University of Chicago Press, 1995.

Lévi-Strauss, Claude. *Introduction to the Work of Marcel Mauss.* Translated by Felicity Baker. London: Routledge and Kegan Paul, 1987.

Lippit, Akira. *Atomic Light (Shadow Optics).* Minneapolis: University of Minnesota Press, 2005.

Lippit, Akira. *Electric Animal: Toward a Rhetoric of Wildlife.* Minneapolis: University of Minnesota Press, 2000.

Livingston, James. *Pragmatism and the Political Economy of Cultural Revolution, 1850–1940.* Chapel Hill: University of North Carolina Press, 1994.

Lury, Celia. *Cultural Rights: Technology, Legality and Personality.* London: Routledge, 1993.

Lyons, William. *The Disappearance of Introspection.* Cambridge, MA: MIT Press, 1986.

Mack, Edward. *Manufacturing Modern Japanese Literature: Publishing, Prizes, and the Ascription of Literary Value.* Durham, NC: Duke University Press, 2010.

Macpherson, C. B. *The Political Theory of Possessive Individualism.* Oxford: Oxford University Press, 1962.

Maeda, Ai. "In the Recesses of the High City: On Sōseki's *Gate*." Translated by William Sibley. In *Text and the City: Essays on Japanese Modernity*, edited by James A. Fujii, 329–50. Durham, NC: Duke University Press, 2004.

Maeda, Ai. *Kindai dokusha no seiritsu*. Tokyo: Chikuma Shobō, 1989.

Maeda, Ai. "Neko no kotoba, neko no ronri." In *Kindai Nihon no Bungaku Kūkan: Rekishi kotoba jōkyō*, 337–58. Tokyo: Shinchōsha, 1983.

Massumi, Brian. *Parables for the Virtual: Movement, Affect, Sensation*. Durham, NC: Duke University Press, 2002.

Masumitsu Keiko. *Natsume Sōseki ron: Sōseki bungaku ni okeru "ishiki."* Osaka: Izumi Shoin, 2004.

Matsui, Sakuko. *Natsume Sōseki as a Critic of English Literature*. Tokyo: Centre for East Asian Cultural Studies, 1975.

Matsumoto, Matataro. "Researches on Acoustic Space." *Studies from the Yale Psychological Laboratory* 5 (1897): 1–75.

Matsuo Naoaki. *Natsume Sōseki "jiishiki" no wana: Kōki sakuhin no sekai*. Osaka: Waizumi Shoin, 2008.

Matsuyama Megumi and Itō Hirohisa. "Meiji-ki ni okeru Yotsuya Samegahashi no toshi kūkan kōzō." *Kenkyū Hōkokushū* 69 (1999): 561–64.

Mauss, Marcel. *The Gift: The Form and Reason for Exchange in Archaic Societies*. Translated by W. D. Halls. New York: Norton, 1990.

McVeigh, Brian J. *The History of Japanese Psychology: Global Perspectives, 1875–1950*. London: Bloomsbury Academic, 2017.

Mehl, Scott. "Appropriations and Inventions: Hagiwara's Divided Poetics and James's Stream of Consciousness." *Japanese Language and Literature* 49, no. 2 (2015): 259–95.

Mehl, Scott. "The Concept of Expression in Modern Japanese Poetics: Thought, Consciousness, Language." PhD diss., University of Chicago, 2013.

Metzler, Mark. *Lever of Empire: The International Gold Standard and the Crisis of Liberalism in Prewar Japan*. Berkeley: University of California Press, 2006.

Michaels, Walter Benn. *The Gold Standard and the Logic of Naturalism*. Berkeley: University of California Press, 1987.

Miner, Earl. "The Collective and the Individual: Literary Practice and Its Social Implications." In *Principles of Japanese Literature*, edited by Earl Miner, 17–62. Princeton, NJ: Princeton University Press, 1985.

Minkowski, Eugène. "Findings in a Case of Schizophrenic Depression." Translated by Barbara Bliss. In *Existence: A New Dimension in Psychiatry and Psychology*, edited by Rollo May, 127–38. New York: Basic Books, 1958.

Mitchell, Richard H. *Political Bribery in Japan*. Honolulu: University of Hawai'i Press, 1996.

Miyamoto Moritarō and Seki Shizuo. *Natsume Sōseki: Shisō no hikaku to michi no tankyū*. Kyoto: Minerva Shobō, 2000.

Miyao, Daisuke. *The Aesthetics of Shadow: Lighting and Japanese Cinema*. Durham, NC: Duke University Press, 2013.

Mizuno Rentarō. *Chosakuken hō*. Tokyo: Mizuno Rentarō Chosakuken Ronbun Kankō Kai, 1974.

Moretti, Franco. *Distant Reading.* London: Verso, 2013.

Moretti, Franco. *Graphs, Maps, Trees: Abstract Models for Literary History.* London: Verso, 2005.

Motora, Yūjirō. "Conflict of Religion and Science: From a Japanese Point of View." *The Monist* 15, no. 3 (1905): 398–408.

Motora, Yūjirō. *An Essay on Eastern Philosophy.* Leipzig: R. Voigtlinder's Verlag, 1905.

Motora, Yūjirō. *Motora Yūjirō chosakushū.* 16 vols. Tokyo: Kuresu Shuppan, 2013–15.

Motora, Yuzero [Yūjirō]. "Exchange Considered as the Principle of Social Life." PhD diss., Johns Hopkins University, 1888. In Motora Yūjirō, *Motora Yūjirō chosakushū,* 1:23–200. Tokyo: Kuresu Shuppan, 2013.

Mufti, Aamir R. *Forget English! Orientalisms and World Literatures.* Cambridge, MA: Harvard University Press, 2016.

Mumford, Lewis. *The Golden Day.* New York: Horace Liveright, 1926.

Murai Osamu. *Nantō ideorogii no hassei.* Rev. ed. Tokyo: Ōta Shuppan, 1995.

Murphy, Joseph A. *Metaphorical Circuit: Negotiations between Literature and Science in 20th Century Japan.* Ithaca, NY: Cornell University East Asia Series, 2004.

Najita, Tetsuo. *Visions of Virtue in Tokugawa Japan: The Kaitokudō Merchant Academy of Osaka.* Honolulu: University of Hawai'i Press, 1987.

Nakamura, Miri. *Monstrous Bodies: The Rise of the Uncanny in Modern Japan.* Cambridge, MA: Harvard University East Asia Center, 2014.

Nakayama Hiroaki. "Shōsetsu no shihon ron." *Bungei to hihyō* 7, no. 10 (1994): 67–80.

Nakazawa Kōki. *Sōseki no sutekki.* Tokyo: Daiichi Shobō, 1996.

Nancy, Jean-Luc. *The Pleasure in Drawing.* Translated by Philip Armstrong. New York: Fordham University Press, 2013.

Nathan, John. "Introduction." In Natsume Sōseki, *Light and Dark: A Novel,* translated by John Nathan, 1–18. New York: Columbia University Press, 2014.

Nathan, John. *Sōseki: Modern Japan's Greatest Novelist.* New York: Columbia University Press, 2018.

Natsume, Sōseki. *The Gate.* Translated by William Sibley. New York: New York Review of Books, 2013.

Natsume, Sōseki. *Grass on the Wayside.* Translated by Edwin McClellan. Tokyo: Tuttle, 1971.

Natsume, Sōseki. *I Am a Cat.* Translated by Aiko Itō and Graeme Wilson. 3 vols. Rutland, VT: Charles E. Tuttle, 1972.

Natsume, Sōseki. *Kokoro.* Translated by Meredith McKinney. New York: Penguin, 2010.

Natsume, Sōseki. *Kusamakura.* Translated by Meredith McKinney. London: Penguin, 2008.

Natsume, Sōseki. *Light and Dark: A Novel.* Translated by John Nathan. New York: Columbia University Press, 2014.

Natsume, Sōseki. *The Miner.* Translated by Jay Rubin. London: Aardvark Bureau, 2015.

Natsume, Sōseki. *Michikusa.* Tokyo: Shinchō Bunko, 1951.

Natsume, Sōseki. *Mon.* Translated by Francis Mathy. Tokyo: Tuttle, 1972.

Natsume, Sōseki. "Philosophical Foundations of the Literary Arts." Translated by Michael K. Bourdaghs. In *Theory of Literature and Other Critical Writings,* edited by Michael K. Bourdaghs, Atsuko Ueda, and Joseph A. Murphy, 159–213. New York: Columbia University Press, 2009.

Natsume, Sōseki. *Recollections*. Translated by Maria Flutsch. London: Sōseki Museum in London, 1997.

Natsume, Sōseki. *Sanshirō*. Translated by Jay Rubin. London: Penguin, 2009.

Natsume, Sōseki. *Sōseki zenshū*. 29 vols. Tokyo: Iwanami Shoten, 1993–99.

Natsume, Sōseki. *Ten Nights of Dreams, Hearing Things, The Heredity of Taste*. Translated by Aiko Itō and Graeme Wilson. Rutland, VT: Charles E. Tuttle, 1974.

Natsume, Sōseki. *Theory of Literature and Other Critical Writings*. Edited by Michael K. Bourdaghs, Atsuko Ueda, and Joseph A. Murphy. New York: Columbia University Press, 2009.

Natsume, Sōseki. *The Three-Cornered World*. Translated by Alan Turney. Tokyo: Charles E. Tuttle, 1968.

Natsume, Sōseki. *To the Spring Equinox and Beyond*. Translated by Kingo Ochiagi and Sanford Goldstein. Rutland, VT: Tuttle, 1985.

Nelson, Thomas. "Slavery in Medieval Japan." *Monumenta Nipponica* 59, no. 4 (2004): 463–92.

Nihei Michiaki. "Nanji no me no mae ni totte: Sanshirō no kōzu." *Kokubungaku* 46, no. 1 (2001): 78–84.

Nishikawa Yūko. *Shakuya to mochiie no bungakushi*. Tokyo: Sanseidō, 1998.

Noami Mariko. *Natsume Sōseki no jikan no sōshutsu*. Tokyo: Tōkyō Daigaku Shuppankai, 2012.

Nunokawa, Jeff. *The Afterlife of Property: Domestic Security and the Victorian Novel*. Princeton, NJ: Princeton University Press, 1994.

Ogura Shūzō. *Natsume Sōseki: Uiriamu Jēmuzu juyō no shūhen*. Tokyo: Yūseidō, 1989.

Ōkubo Junichirō. *Sōseki to sono shisō*. Tokyo: Aratake Shuppan, 1974.

O'Neill, D. Cuong. "Tragedy, Masochism, and Other Worldly Pleasures: Reading Natsume Sōseki's *Bungakuron*." *Discourse* 28, no. 2–3 (2006): 78–97.

Oshino Takeshi. "*Kokoro* ronsō no yukue." In *Sōryoku tōron: Sōseki no* Kokoro, edited by Komori Yōichi and Miyagawa Takeo, 12–27. Tokyo: Kanrin Shobō, 1994.

Oshino Takeshi. "'Roman shumi' no chihei: *Higan no sugi made* no kyōdōsei." *Sōseki Kenkyū* 11 (1998): 62–76.

Oshino Takeshi. "'Shizu' ni koe wa aru no ka: *Kokoro* ni okeru yokuatsu no kōzō." *Bungaku* 3, no. 4 (1992): 41–49.

Pak Yuha [Park Yuha]. *Nashonaru aidentiti to jendā: Sōseki, bungaku, kindai*. Tokyo: Kurein, 2007.

Pateman, Carole. *The Sexual Contract*. Cambridge: Polity, 1988.

Pels, Dick. *Property and Power in Social Theory: A Study in Intellectual Rivalry*. London: Routledge, 1998.

Perry, B. E. "Fable." *Studium Generale* 20 (1959): 17–37.

Poovey, Mary. *Genres of the Credit Economy: Mediating Value in Eighteenth- and Nineteenth-Century Britain*. Chicago: University of Chicago Press, 2008.

Purdy, Jedediah. *The Meaning of Property: Freedom, Community, and the Legal Imagination*. New Haven, CT: Yale University Press, 2010.

Putz, Otto. "Nachwort." In Sōseki Natsume, *Ich der Kater*, translated by Otto Putz, 647–57. Frankfurt am Main: Insel Verlag, 1996.

Radin, Margaret Jane. "Property and Personhood." *Stanford Law Review* 34 (1982): 957–1015.

Reardon, Jenny, and Kim Tall Bear. "'Your DNA Is *Our* History': Genomics, Anthropology, and the Construction of Whiteness as Property." *Current Anthropology* 53, suppl. 5 (2012): S233–45.

Reichert, James. *In the Company of Men: Representations of Male-Male Sexuality in Meiji Literature*. Stanford, CA: Stanford University Press, 2006.

Rin Shūmei. *Shōwa ideorogii: Shisō toshite no bungaku*. Tokyo: Heibonsha, 2005.

Rose, Carol M. *Property and Persuasion: Essays on the History, Theory, and Rhetoric of Ownership*. Boulder, CO: Westview Press, 1994.

Rosenberg, Jordana, and Chi-ming Yang. "Introduction: The Dispossessed Eighteenth Century." *Eighteenth Century* 55, no. 2–3 (2014): 137–52.

Rubin, Gayle. "The Traffic in Women: Notes on the 'Political Economy' of Sex." In *Toward an Anthropology of Women*, edited by Rayna R. Reiter, 157–210. New York: Monthly Review Press, 1975.

Said, Edward. *Culture and Imperialism*. New York: Knopf, 1993.

Saitō Mareshi. "*Bungakuron* no shatei: Disukūru no kagaku." *Bungaku* 13, no. 3 (2012): 44–55.

Sakai, Naoki. *Translation and Subjectivity: On "Japan" and Cultural Nationalism*. Minneapolis: University of Minnesota Press, 1997.

Sakai, Naoki. *Voices of the Past: The Status of Language in Eighteenth-Century Japanese Discourse*. Ithaca, NY: Cornell University Press, 1991.

Sakaki, Atsuko. "*Kajin no kigū*: The Meiji Political Novel and the Boundaries of Literature." *Monumenta Nipponica* 55, no. 1 (2000): 83–108.

Sakaki, Atsuko. *Recontextualizing Texts: Narrative Performance in Modern Japanese Fiction*. Cambridge, MA: Harvard University Asia Center, 1999.

Sasaki Hideaki. "'Anshi' jikken toshite no Sōseki tanpen: 'Ichiya' 'Kyō ni tsukeru yūbe' Eijitsu shōhin no shinsō." *Nihon kindai bungaku* 76 (2007): 32–45.

Sato, Hajime. "The Emergence of 'Modern' Ownership Rights Rather Than Property Rights." *Journal of Economic Issues* 52, no. 3 (2018): 676–93.

Satō Izumi. *Sōseki katazukanai kindai*. Tokyo: NHK Raiburarī, 2002.

Satō Tatsuya and Mizoguchi Hajime. *Tsūshi: Nihon shinrigaku*. Kyoto: Kitaoji Shobō, 1997.

Sato, Tatsuya, and Takao Sato. "The Early 20th Century: Shaping the Discipline of Psychology in Japan." *Japanese Psychological Research* 47, no. 2 (2005): 52–62.

Sato, Tatsuya, Takuya Nakatsuma, and Norika Matsubara. "Influence of G. Stanley Hall on Yuzero Motora, the First Psychology Professor in Japan." *American Journal of Psychology* 125, no. 4 (2012): 395–407.

Satō Yūko. *Sōseki no seorii: Bungakuron kaidoku*. Tokyo: Ōfūsha, 2005.

Schultz, Elizabeth, and Fumiko Yamamoto. "Egos vs. Relationships in James's *The Golden Bowl* and Soseki's *Light and Darkness*." *Comparative Literature Studies* 20, no. 1 (1983): 48–65.

Scripture, E. W. *The New Psychology*. London: Walter Scott, 1898.

Sebald, W. G., trans. *The Civil Code of Japan*. London: Butterworth, 1934.

Sedgwick, Eve Kosofsky. "Paranoid Reading and Reparative Reading, Or, You're So Paranoid, You Probably Think This Essay Is About You." In *Touching Feeling*, 123–52. Durham, NC: Duke University Press, 2003.

Senuma Shigeki. *Shimazaki Tōson: Sono shōgai to sakuhin*. Tokyo: Hanawa Shobō, 1953.

Shibata Shōji. *Sōseki no naka no "teikoku": "Kokumin sakka" to kindai Nihon*. Tokyo: Kanrin Shobō, 2006.

Shigematsu Yasuo. "*Bungakuron* kara 'Bungei no tetsugakuteki kiso' 'Sōsakuka no taido' e: Uiriamu Jeimuzu to no kanren ni oite." In *Sakuhinron Natsume Sōseki*, edited by Uchida Michio and Kubota Yoshitarō, 361–82. Tokyo: Sōbunsha, 1976.

Shigematsu Yasuo. "'Shukō' toshite no Sunaga Ichizō: Higan sugi made kanken." In *Sōseki sakuhinron shūsei*, edited by Tamai Takayuki and Tsubouchi Toshinori, 8:255–72. Tokyo: Ōfūsha, 1991.

Shigematsu Yasuo. "Sōseki to Uiriamu Jeimuzu." *Kokubungaku* 16, no. 12 (1971): 128–34.

Shimazaki Tōson. "Chosaku to shuppan." In *Tōson zenshū*, 13:70–77. Tokyo: Chikuma Shobō, 1971.

Shimizu Takayoshi. "*Higan sugi made* no kōzō: Unmei no aironii to sono chōetsu." In *Sakuhinron Natsume Sōseki*, edited by Uchida Michio and Kubota Yoshitarō, 218–39. Tokyo: Sōbunsha, 1976.

Shimizu Takayoshi. *Sōseki: Sono han-Oidipusu-teki sekai*. Tokyo: Kanrin Shobō, 1993.

Shinoda Kōichirō. *Shōsetsu wa ika ni kakareta ka: Hakai kara Shirei made*. Tokyo: Iwanami Shoten, 1982.

Shklovsky, Viktor. *Viktor Shklovsky: A Reader*. Edited and translated by Alexandra Berlina. New York: Bloomsbury, 2017.

Simmel, Georg. *The Philosophy of Money*. Translated by Tom Bottomore and David Frisby. London: Routledge, 1990.

Smits, Gregory, and Bettina Gramlich-Oka, eds. *Economic Thought in Early Modern Japan*. Leiden: Brill, 2010.

Stewart, Susan. "Notes on Distressed Genres." *Journal of American Folklore* 104, no. 411 (1991): 5–31.

Summersgill, Harue. "The Influence of William James and Henri Bergson on Natsume Sōseki's *Higan Sugi Made*." *Kyūshu American Literature* 22 (1981): 5–17.

Stout, G. F. *Analytic Psychology*. 2 vols. London: Swan Sonnenschein, 1896.

Suzuki Hideo, Yamazaki Osamu, Miida Junrō, Hiratsuka Ken'ichi, and Kido Ken'ichi. "Rōkan ni kiroku sareta Natsume Sōseki no onsei saisei no kokoromi [An attempt to reproduce Soseki Natsume's voice from a wax cylinder recording]." Hideo Suzuki's World of Acoustics, 2002. http://suzukihideo.cool.coocan.jp/suzuki_image /2003_Natsume_souseki.pdf.

Suzuki Sadami. *Nihon no "bungaku" gainen*. Tokyo: Sakuhinsha, 1998.

Suzuki, Tessa Morris. *Re-inventing Japan: Time Space Nation*. Armonk, NY: M.E. Sharpe, 1998.

Takayoshi, Matsuo. "A Note on the Political Thought of Natsume Sōseki in His Later Years." In *Japan in Crisis: Taishō Democracy*, edited by Bernard S. Silberman and H. D. Harootunian, 67–85. Princeton, NJ: Princeton University Press, 1974.

Tanaka, Stefan. *New Times in Modern Japan*. Princeton, NJ: Princeton University Press, 2004.

Tateiwa Shin'ya. *Shiteki shoyūron*. Tokyo: Keisō Shobō, 1997.

Tawada Yōko. *Yuki no renshūsei*. Tokyo: Shinchōsha, 2011.

Terada, T. "Acoustical Investigation of the Japanese Bamboo Pipe, Syakuhati." *Journal of the College of Science, Imperial University Tōkyō, Japan* 21, no. 10 (1907): 1–34.

Thomson, Robert. *The Pelican History of Psychology*. Middlesex, UK: Penguin, 1968.

Ueda, Atsuko. "*Bungakuron* and 'Literature' in the Making." *Japan Forum* 20, no. 1 (2008): 25–46.

Uyehara, George Etsujiro. *The Political Development of Japan, 1867–1909*. New York: E.P. Dutton, 1910.

Van Compernolle, Timothy J. *Struggling Upward: Worldly Success and the Japanese Novel*. Cambridge, MA: Harvard University Asia Center, 2016.

Vincent, J. Keith. *Two-Timing Modernity: Homosocial Narrative in Modern Japanese Fiction*. Cambridge, MA: Harvard University Asia Center, 2012.

Walker, Gavin. *The Sublime Perversion of Capital: Marxist Theory and the Politics of History in Modern Japan*. Durham, NC: Duke University Press, 2016.

Wang, Fei-Hsien. *Pirates and Publishers: A Social History of Copyright in Modern China*. Princeton, NJ: Princeton University Press, 2019.

Washburn, Dennis. *Translating Mount Fuji: Modern Japanese Fiction and the Ethics of Identity*. New York: Columbia University Press, 2007.

Weber, Max. *The Protestant Ethic and the Spirit of Capitalism*. Translated by Talcott Parsons. New York: Scribner's, 1958.

West, Cornel. *The American Evasion of Philosophy: A Genealogy of Pragmatism*. Madison: University of Wisconsin Press, 1989.

Williams, Raymond. *The Country and the City*. New York: Oxford University Press, 1973.

Williams, Raymond. *Culture and Society: 1780–1950*. New York: Columbia University Press, 1983.

Williams, Raymond. *Marxism and Literature*. Oxford: Oxford University Press, 1977.

Woodmansee, Martha. *The Author, Art, and the Market: Rereading the History of Aesthetics*. New York: Columbia University Press, 1994.

Wooldridge, Adrian. *Measuring the Mind: Education and Psychology in England, c. 1860–1990*. Cambridge: Cambridge University Press, 1994.

Wundt, Wilhelm. *Outlines of Psychology*. Translated by Charles Hubbard Judd. Leipzig: Wilhelm Engelmann, 1902.

Wundt, Wilhelm. *Principles of Physiological Psychology*. Translated by Edward Bradford Titchener. London: Swan Sonnenschein, 1904.

Yamada Yūsaku. "*Higan sugi made*: Keitarō wo megutte." In *Natsume Sōseki hikkei II*, edited by Takemori Ten'yu, 131–38. Tokyo: Gakutōsha, 1982.

Yamamoto Yoshiaki. *Sōseki no kakeibo: Okane de yomitoku seikatsu to sakuhin*. Tokyo: Kyōiku Hyōron Sha, 2018.

Yasar, Kerim. *Electrified Voices: How the Telephone, Phonograph, and Radio Shaped Modern Japan, 1868–1945*. New York: Columbia University Press, 2018.

Yoda, Tomiko. "First-Person Narration and Citizen-Subject: The Modernity of Ōgai's 'The Dancing Girl.'" *Journal of Asian Studies* 65, no. 2 (2006): 277–306.

Yu, Beongcheon. *Natsume Sōseki*. New York: Twayne, 1969.

Zeitlin, Judith T. *Historian of the Strange: Pu Songling and the Chinese Classical Tale*. Stanford, CA: Stanford University Press, 1993.

INDEX

Stout, G. F., 58

stream of consciousness. *See* consciousness

Tagore, Rabindranath, 169–70

Taiwan, 4, 149s

Takahama Kyoshi, 170

taxation, 3, 130, 139, 156

temporality, 21, 66, 80–81, 102, 114

"Ten Nights of Dreams" (Natsume), 61

Terada Torahiko, 32

territoriality, 17

Tetsugaku zasshi (magazine), 60

theft, 2, 17, 18, 20–21, 32, 53, 71, 77, 96, 125, 128, 138, 142, 165, 181n24

Theory of Literature (Natsume), 10–11, 26–27, 144, 148, 152–54, 156, 158–62, 164–69, 171–75; collective *F* in, 69, 100, 173; language in, 42–43; "Preface" to, 51, 92; psychology in, 56–67; sociology in, 100–101; tragedy in, 87–88

Three-Cornered World, The (Natsume). See *Kusamakura*

Titchener, Edward B., 58

Tōkai Sanshi, 155

Tokyo Imperial University, 25, 32, 56, 61, 81, 95, 152, 187n21

Tolstoy, Leo, 15, 23, 179n6

To the Spring Equinox and Beyond (Natsume), 37, 61, 90–94, 102–15, 119–120, 137

"Tower of London" (Natsume), 67

Toyama Masakazu, 95

tragedy, 11, 86–88, 144–45

translation, 15, 36, 42–44, 46–48, 169–71, 173

triangular desire, 37–41, 45, 106–7, 133, 134

truth, 27–28, 66, 100, 158, 159

Tsubouchi, Shōyō, 55

Uchida Masao, 6–7, 94

Unequal Treaties, 3, 123, 156

university system, 5, 57

Wagahai wa neko de aru (Natsume). See *I Am a Cat*

Walker, Gavin, 20

"Watakushi no kojinshugi" (Natsume). *See* "My Individualism"

Wayfarer, The (Natsume), 37

Weber, Max, 98–99, 100

will, 83–85

Williams, Raymond, 9

wives, 77, 125, 132–34

women, 30, 38, 40, 124, 132–36, 199n44

world literature, 148–49, 165–74

World War I, 126–27

Wundt, Wilhelm, 56, 57–58, 59, 81, 115, 171

Yano Ryūkei, 6, 94

"Yume jūya" (Natsume). *See* "Ten Nights of Dreams"

Zeitlin, Judith, 120

CPSIA information can be obtained
at www.ICGtesting.com
Printed in the USA
LVHW080744241221
707058LV00013B/1462